Modern Epic

Modern Epic

The World–System from Goethe to García Márquez

———◆———

FRANCO MORETTI

Translated by
Quintin Hoare

VERSO

London • New York

First published by Verso 1996
This edition © Verso 1996
Translation © Quintin Hoare 1996
First published as *Opere Mondo: saggio sulla forma epica dal*
Faust *a* Cent'anni di solitudine
© Giulio Einaudi editore spa, Turin, 1994
All rights reserved

Verso
UK: 6 Meard Street, London W1V 3HR
USA: 180 Varick Street, New York NY 10014–4606

Verso is the imprint of New Left Books

ISBN 1–85984–934–2
ISBN 1–85984–069–8 (pbk)

British Library Cataloguing in Publication Data
A catalogue record for this book is available from the British Library

Library of Congress Cataloging-in-Publication Data
Moretti, Franco, 1950–.
   [Opere mondo. English]
   Modern epic: the world-system from Goethe to García Márquez /
Franco Moretti; translated by Quintin Hoare.
      p.   cm.
   Includes bibliographical references (p.   ) and index.
   ISBN 1–85984–934–2
   1. Epic literature—History and criticism.   2. Fiction—19th
century—History and criticism.   3. Fiction—20th century—History
and criticism.   4. Goethe, Johann Wolfgang von, 1749–1832. Faust.
5. Joyce, James, 1882–1941. Ulysses.   I. Title.
   PN56.E65M6713   1994   95–43983
   809—dc20   CIP

Typeset by M Rules
Printed and bound in Great Britain by Biddles Ltd, Guildford and King's Lynn

For Teri

CONTENTS

Acknowledgements   *xi*
Introduction   *1*

PART I: *Faust* **and the Nineteenth Century**

Chapter 1   *11*
  'I want a hero . . .'
  'In the beginning was the Deed'
  Literary evolution. I
  Rhetoric of innocence. I
  'He sees visions of giant undertakings . . .'

Chapter 2   *35*
  An inherited form
  Non-contemporaneity. I
  'So many little independent worlds'
  World texts. I

Chapter 3   *56*
  'An incredible musical pandemonium'
  Polyphony in America. I
  Polyphony in America. II
  'With all the certainty of a mechanical process'
  Literary evolution. II

Chapter 4   77
  Allegory and modernity. I
  'You, I think, should know us all'
  The sign run amok
  Allegory and modernity. II
  'But infinite forms do not exist . . .'

TRANSITION: **The Nibelung's Ring**

Chapter 5   *101*
  'Drink first, hero, so that distant things don't escape you'
  Monumental dilettantism
  Twofold myth
  Art of transition
  Complexity. I

PART II: **Ulysses and the Twentieth Century**

Chapter 6   *123*
  The Ladies' Paradise
  Stream of consciousness
  Sociology of absentmindedness
  The great Perhaps
  Epiphany, madeleine, Leitmotiv
  World texts. II
  Free association

Excursus: Stream of consciousness – evolution of a technique   *168*
  'Why, it's I!'
  Lost opportunities
  Why Joyce

Chapter 7   *182*
  The other Ulysses
  Literary evolution. III
  Liberation of the device
  Joyce/Kafka
  Soul and precision

Contents

Chapter 8   *213*
  Complexity. II
  Countermodernism
  Compromise

EPILOGUE: ***One Hundred Years of Solitude***

Chapter 9   *233*
  Magical realism
  From Lübeck to Macondo
  Non-contemporaneity. II
  Rhetoric of innocence. II

Index   *251*

ACKNOWLEDGEMENTS

The present work took shape slowly, between the universities of Verona, Los Angeles, San Diego and finally Columbia. I presented parts of it to the Gauss Seminars at Princeton, in the autumn of 1991; the often quite heated ensuing discussion gave me copious food for reflection. From Enrica Villari and Franco Fiorentino, I received criticism and encouragement when I had need of both; from Teri Reynolds, a wealth of intelligent ideas, imagination – and logic. Finally, I am indebted to Vittorio Marchetta for everything I know about musical language, and to Quintin Hoare for a beautiful translation.

The following editions have been used for translated material quoted in the text but not otherwise referenced. Johann Wolfgang von Goethe, *Faust*, Parts One and Two, translated by David Luke, Oxford University Press, Oxford and New York 1987 and 1994. Boris Pasternak, *Doctor Zhivago*, translated by Max Hayward and Manya Harari, HarperCollins, London 1988. Henrik Ibsen, *Peer Gynt*, translated by R. Farquharson Sharp, J.M. Dent, London 1950. Robert Musil, *The Man Without Qualities*, volumes 1, 2 and 3, translated by Eithne Wilkins and Ernst Kaiser, Secker and Warburg, London 1953, 1954 and 1960. Gustave Flaubert, *Bouvard and Pécuchet*, translated by A.J. Krailsheimer, Penguin Books, Harmondsworth 1976. *Richard Wagner's Ring of the Nibelung*, translated by Stewart Spencer, Thames and Hudson, London 1993. Émile Zola, *The Ladies' Paradise*, translated (1886) under the supervision of

Henry Vizetelly, University of California Press, Berkeley – Los Angeles – Oxford 1992 (cited here for reference only). Louis Aragon, *The Nightwalker* [*Le Paysan de Paris*], translated by Frederick Brown, Prentice-Hall, Englewood Cliffs NJ 1970. André Breton, *Nadja*, translated by Richard Howard, Grove Press, New York 1960. Rainer Maria Rilke, *The Notebooks of Malte Laurids Brigge*, translated by John Linton, Oxford University Press, Oxford and New York 1984. Marcel Proust, *Remembrance of Things Past*, translated by C.K. Scott Moncrieff and Terence Kilmartin, Penguin Books, Harmondsworth 1983. Jules Verne, *Around the World in Eighty Days*, translated by Jacqueline Rogers, Penguin Books, Harmondsworth 1994. Leo Tolstoy, *Anna Karenin*, translated by Rosemary Edmonds, Penguin Books, Harmondsworth 1978. Thomas Mann, *Lotte in Weimar*, translated by Helen Lowe-Porter, Penguin Books, Harmondsworth 1968. Thomas Mann, *The Magic Mountain*, translated by Helen Lowe-Porter, Penguin Books, Harmondsworth 1960. Franz Kafka, *The Trial*, translated by Douglas Scott and Chris Waller, Pan Books, London 1977. Homer, *The Iliad*, translated by Robert Fitzgerald, Oxford University Press, Oxford 1984. Alejo Carpentier, *The Kingdom of This World*, translated by Harriet de Onis, André Deutsch, London 1990. Gabriel García Márquez, *One Hundred Years of Solitude*, translated by Gregory Rabassa, Jonathan Cape, London 1970. Joseph Roth, *The Radetzky March*, translated by Eva Tucker and Geoffrey Dunlop, Allen Lane, London 1974.

References to James Joyce's *Ulysses* are to the edition edited by Hans Walter Gabler, Bodley Head, London 1986, which numbers the text by line.

> Enter freely, and of your own will
> *Dracula*

Take *Faust*, what is it? A 'tragedy', as its author states? A great philosophical tale? A collection of lyrical insights? Who can say. How about *Moby-Dick*? Encyclopaedia, novel or romance? Or even a 'singular medley', as one anonymous 1851 review put it? How about *The Nibelung's Ring*, with its millenarian notion of being a 'total art-work': drama, opera or myth? Ezra Pound described *Bouvard and Pécuchet* in 1922 as 'no longer a novel'; 'it is no longer a novel' T.S. Eliot repeated of *Ulysses* a few months later. But if not novels, then what are they? And *The Cantos*, or *The Waste Land*? Is *The Last Days of Mankind* a theatrical work? How about *The Man Without Qualities*: novel or essay? And those splendid stories arriving from Latin America and India? 'Magical realism'? As if we did not know that contradictions in terms are quite meaningless . . .

Faust, Moby-Dick, The Nibelung's Ring, Ulysses, The Cantos, The Waste Land, The Man Without Qualities, One Hundred Years of Solitude. These are not just any old books. They are monuments. Sacred texts that the modern West has subjected to a lengthy scrutiny, searching in them for its own secret. Literary history, though, is puzzled about what to do with them. It does not know how to classify them; it treats them instead as isolated phenomena: one-off cases, oddities, anomalies. Which, of course, is quite possible. But possible once or twice, not in every case. With so many and such prominent anomalies, it is far likelier there is something wrong with the initial taxonomy. So, rather than recording one exception after another, it would be better to change perspective, and postulate a different rule.

The idea behind this book, therefore, is that the works just mentioned – along with others we shall encounter along the way – all belong to a single field that I shall term 'modern epic'. 'Epic', because of the many structural similarities binding it to a distant past (something to which I shall naturally return, when the time comes for analysis). But 'modern' epic, because there are certainly quite a few discontinuities: important enough, indeed, in one case – the supranational dimension of the represented space – to dictate the cognitive metaphor of the 'world text' (which, in what is not just a verbal calque, recalls the 'world-economy' of Braudel and Wallerstein).

The category of epic is not, of course, without its defects. But it has fewer than others, as well as having some additional advantages. So let it be taken for what it is: a hypothesis designed to introduce a little order into a question too important to remain so confused. A working hypothesis, which I have tried to formulate as clearly as possible so that it may more easily be put to the test – and if necessary refuted. 'People who write obscurely', Peter Medawar has said, 'are either unskilled in writing or up to some mischief.' Quite true. Better a clearly visible error than a thousand confused half truths.

Initially, to be honest, my project was entirely different. I was thinking about modernism – a theme on which I had already written on more than one occasion, and which I had been studying for years. During all that time, however, Perry Anderson had been trying to convince me that so heterogeneous a category (Mayakovksy and George, Kafka and Proust, perhaps even Lawrence and Tzara) could be of little use: it was too contradictory, or too vague, to have real explanatory value. For a long while I thought Anderson was mistaken. Then I came to the conclusion that he was half right (and modernism should precisely be described as a field of contradictions). Finally, at a certain point, I decided that it was I who was mistaken. Weary of trying to square the circle, I resolved to abandon modernism and broke off my original project.

During more or less the same period (in 1987 or '88), I chanced to read a long typescript by Fredric Jameson ('The existence of Italy', later

2

published in *Signatures of the Visible*[1]), in which the expression 'sacred text' was used on more than one occasion for such classics of modernism as *The Cantos* or *The Waste Land*. In my state of uncertainty, this label – which I discussed at length with Jameson – acted as a catalyst. Within the space of a few months, almost without my realizing it, modernism had effectively vanished, and been replaced by the epic. To be more accurate, the epic had halved modernism, and prolonged it in time. Suddenly many works written around the First World War struck me as being part of a much more extensive history (from, say, 1800 to 2000), of which they constituted merely one moment. A moment of great inventiveness and complexity, to be sure – the high point of the whole process, if you like – but no longer an autonomous, coherent reality demanding a specific category.

So I began to read *Ulysses* thinking of *Faust*, rather than *Le Cimetière marin* or *Mrs Dalloway*; to read Eliot against a background of Wagner and Whitman, instead of Mallarmé and Hofmannsthal. And I found that these 'modernist' works could be understood much better, in fact, if you forgot modernism. Initially, I must admit, certain omissions (Kafka, the symbolist current, the 'historical avant gardes') struck me as serious. But after a bit I decided that, if the notion of epic did not cover the whole of modernism, this was not a defect of the new classification but precisely its *raison d'être*. Modernism had become unusable because it contained *too many things*: the solution, therefore, lay in learning to omit – to restrict the field. The ambition of the historiographical hypothesis here coincided with its modesty. *Weniger ist mehr*, as Mies van der Rohe used to say: less is more.

Less is more. Very well. But was I not exaggerating a bit? Is it not odd that, in two centuries of history, a form of such importance should notch up only about half a dozen really achieved specimens? This objection, raised by P. Adams Sitney at Princeton when the structure of the work was already complete, made me think long and hard. I could, of course, without too many scruples draft in everything bearing any resemblance to the epic: but that would have been to repeat the error of modernism. Or

---

[1] F. Jameson, *Signatures of the Visible*, Routledge, New York and London 1990, pp. 155–229.

I could abandon my project on the epic, as I had the one on modernism – but that idea did not attract me at all. Then an article by Edward Mendelson put me on the right track.

> Each major national culture in the west, as it becomes aware of itself as a separate entity, produces an encyclopedic author, one whose work attends to the whole social and linguistic range of his nation, who makes use of all the literary styles and conventions known to his countrymen [. . .] and who becomes the focus of a large and persistent exegetic and textual industry comparable to the industry founded upon the Bible.[2]

Well, I shall not call them encyclopaedias, and I shall propose a different geographical distribution. But on one point I entirely agree with Mendelson: the rarity of world texts is a constitutive aspect of this symbolic form. A work can be the 'sacred text' of a culture *if it is unique*: thirty Bibles do not enlarge the sphere of the sacred, but pulverize it. The same is true indeed of literary genres as of animal species: not all reproduce at the same rate. Some, like the novel, rely on numbers and breed like wildfire. Others concentrate their hopes on a few specimens, of fairly long and arduous gestation – and the works with which we shall be concerned behave precisely like this.

Only a few works, fine. But that was not the worst of it. Whenever anybody asked me to explain in a few words the characteristics of a world text, I found myself replying with growing irritation: 'That's easy – it's very long, and very boring.' How many people read *Faust* Part Two or *Ulysses* unless forced to do so at school? Note, moreover, that I am confining myself here to Goethe and Joyce; pointless even to mention Madach or Dos Passos, *The Cantos* or *The Death of Virgil* . . .

This is another odd feature of the modern epic: it is an almost supercanonical form, yet one that is virtually unread. Obligatory for any educated person (in our century you *have to* have read *Ulysses*, just like

---

[2] E. Mendelson, 'Encyclopedic Normatives: From Dante to Pynchon', in *Modern Language Notes* 91 (1976), p. 1268. 'Encyclopedia' is the term used by N. Frye in *Anatomy of Criticism*, Princeton University Press, Princeton 1957; I have preferred 'epic' because of its narrative connotations.

Faust in the last century), yet not at all agreeable. The fact that world texts depend so closely upon scholastic institutions, moreover, is a sure sign that something is amiss: that they are not self-sufficient. And they are not self-sufficient because they do not really work all that well. They are masterpieces, of course; but often, as people used to say of *Faust*, *flawed* masterpieces. And sometimes, to be candid, they are semi-failures.

I hope to be able to demonstrate this thesis in the chapters that follow. Here, I shall merely repeat that it was by no means my starting hypothesis. I thought I should be studying *achieved* masterpieces, and approached them with all the humility of the neophyte. When I began to have my first suspicions, I tried to stifle these and square the circle anyway. But in the long run I realized that the 'flaws' I kept coming up against could not be concealed. Better highlight them without further ado – indeed, view them as a characteristic feature of the modern epic. They reveal a kind of antagonism between the noun and the adjective: a discrepancy between the totalizing will of the epic and the subdivided reality of the modern world. The imperfection of world texts is the sure sign that they live in history.

I then realized I was predisposed to accept the constructional flaws of world texts by my sympathies for Darwinism, which sees precisely in morphological imperfection proof of the evolutionary path. The idea that evolutionary theory can be a model for literary history is, of course, a questionable hypothesis – the theoretical justifications for which I have set out elsewhere and to which I shall return at length on another occasion.[3] Here, meanwhile, I shall seek to prove the fruitfulness of the Darwinian paradigm, showing how it allows us to explain in a new – and better – way numerous questions that literary history has never succeeded in resolving satisfactorily.

Explain in a better way . . . In the present critical atmosphere, drawing inspiration from the natural sciences is a programme with scant chance of success. But no matter. A materialist history of literary forms is too splendid a challenge to intelligence to be let slip. To see clearly – and understand – how they function, those complicated things that

---

[3] See 'On Literary Evolution', in *Signs Taken for Wonders*, 2nd enlarged edn, Verso, London 1987.

human beings enjoy reading: in all honesty I know of nothing better, for anyone concerned with literature. But it is an irrational pleasure, which I shall not try in any way to justify.

Another couple of words, however, on a technical matter. Notoriously, one of the main differences between the evolutionary theories of Lamarck and Darwin lies in the fact that, for Lamarck, variations are always functional to evolutionary requirements, while for Darwin they are not. In Darwin, in other words, history is the interweaving of *two* wholly independent paths: random variations, and necessary selection. In our case: *rhetorical innovations*, which are the result of chance; and a *social selection*, which by contrast is the daughter of necessity. The literary history that will emerge from this book is one split in two: less imposing than the habitual one, but perhaps more interesting; uncertain; discontinuous; full of oddities and question marks. To do it justice, a centaur critic would be required: half formalist, to deal with the 'how'; half sociologist, to deal with the 'why'. *Nota bene*: half and half. Not some reasonable compromise, but Jekyll and Hyde. To bring it off, I would have drunk any potion.

But will they agree, the formalist and the sociologist? Yes, if the sociologist accepts the idea that the social aspect of literature resides *in its form*, and that the form develops according to its own laws; and if the formalist, for his part, accepts the idea that literature *follows* great social changes – that it always 'comes after'. To come after, however, does not mean to repeat ('reflect') what already exists, but the exact opposite: to *resolve* the problems set by history. For every transformation carries with it a quantity of ethical impediments, perceptual confusions, ideological contradictions. It involves, in short, a *symbolic overload* that risks rendering social cohesion precarious, and individual existence wearisome. Well, literature helps reduce this tension. It has a problem-solving vocation: to make existence more comprehensible, and more acceptable. And, as we shall see, to make power relations more acceptable too – even their violence.

One final word here on this incredible chess game between life and form, history and rhetoric. I have attempted to account for both, and also for the inequality – the imperfection, again – that does still persist. In order to highlight the discontinuity of spheres, I have been lavish with

6

direct quotations: partly out of respect for specialisms, partly because direct quotations are clear and candid. They come straight to the point. They remind me of Emma Castelnuovo, the mathematician who all those years ago taught me – along with a host of other things – a never subsequently blunted impatience with superfluous passages.

On, then, to the real work. With just one warning. This study is a unitary whole. The first part is a bit more theoretical, the second a bit more analytical: but they are two phases of a single argument. The same goes for each individual chapter. Ideally, the pages that follow should be read straight through.

Faust and the Nineteenth Century

C H A P T E R

1

'I want a hero . . .'[1]

The Hegelian conception of the epic form rests on three foundations. The first has to do with the story:

> The epic [. . .] acquires as its object the occurrence of an action which must achieve expression in the whole breadth of its circumstances and relations . . .

This action, Hegel goes on, must enable a totality to emerge:

> in the whole breadth of its circumstances and relations, [. . .] as a rich event connected with the total world of a nation and epoch.

Finally, the epic totality has the following characteristic:

> Everything that later becomes firm religious dogma or civil and moral law still remains a living attitude of mind, not separated from the single individual as such.[2]

---

[1] 'I want a hero, an uncommon want' is the first line of Byron's *Don Juan*. 'I want a hero', of course, may mean either 'I wish for' a hero, or 'I lack' a hero.

[2] G. Hegel, *Aesthetics*, translated by T.M. Knox, Oxford University Press, Oxford 1975, vol. 2, pp. 1044–5 (translation modified).

11

A totality that is 'living' and inseparable from individuality: a world that takes form thanks to a hero, and recognizes itself in him. This is the third element of the Hegelian epic – and also the most vulnerable, since historical evolution very soon puts an end to the age of heroes. For once 'State life' becomes established, the unity of universal and individual dissolves: 'the ethical and the right' cease to 'depend exclusively upon individuals' and become objectified in laws and the state apparatus:

> The universal as such rules in its universality, in which the vitality of the individual appears as transcended, or as incidental and unimportant.[3]

With the coming of the State, in short, individuality must no longer give totality a form, but confine itself to obeying it: master its own energies, and keep to what is prescribed. It is enough, Hegel adds shortly after this – combining politics with literature – to think of 'monarchs in our day', who:

> unlike the heroes of the mythical ages, are no longer the *concrete* heads of the whole, but a more or less abstract centre of institutions already independently developed and established by law and the constitution.[4]

More than in its analytical content (not so very different from that of neo-classicism), the great novelty of the Hegelian conception lies precisely in its merciless historicization of epic poetry. For if epic conventions have a real foundation only in the pre-State era – and this is a historiographic judgement that will not henceforth be questioned – then between epic and modernity an inversely proportional relation obtains. Where there is the one, the other cannot be – and vice versa. The nearer we come to the present, the more epic loses any meaning. In a world of 'trousers, machinery, and policemen', writes the Hegelian Bradley at the start of the twentieth century:

> we have Law: and Law [. . .] is a vast achievement and priceless possession; but it is not favourable to striking events or individual actions on the grand scale.[5]

---

[3] Ibid., vol. 1, p. 184 (translation modified).
[4] Ibid., vol. 1, p. 193.
[5] A.C. Bradley, 'The Long Poem in the Age of Wordsworth', in *Oxford Lectures on Poetry* (1909), Macmillan, New York 1955, p. 191.

And this is what the young Joyce writes at around the same time:

> Life indeed nowadays is often a sad bore [. . .] Epic savagery is rendered impossible by vigilant policing.[6]

Epic savagery. . . a phrase that describes perfectly the problem of the modern epic: the 'individual vitality' of the *Aesthetics* is now experienced as something savage. *Faust* and *Moby-Dick* will be dubbed 'barbaric', Wagner and much of modernism 'primitive'. We might even add: 'reactionary'. Reactionary in the proper meaning of the term: an attempt to turn history back, abolishing the excessive complexity of modern societies and restoring the unchallenged dominion of an individual. This is a temptation we shall often encounter in the pages that follow: in Faust, in Ahab, in Wagner. But that is precisely what it is: a *temptation*, rather than a reality. This is shown by one of Ibsen's early works, *Emperor and Galilean*, which recounts at length the life of Emperor Julian: the one who sought to abrogate Christian law and react against the fragmentation of power. But the course of history can no longer be halted: Julian's epic sacrilege comes to naught, and Ibsen turns to writing bourgeois plays. The Hegelian verdict does indeed seem confirmed.

Yet, in the same years in which Hegel was holding his courses on aesthetics, and pointing to the deliberate modesty of *Hermann and Dorothea* as the only path still open for the epic imagination, the author of that idyll was completing a work of very different ambitions. One in which the hero ranges freely across the 'grand world', loudly proclaiming his desire to be at one with all humanity:

> I tell you, the mere pleasure's not the point!
> To dizzying, painful joy I dedicate
> Myself, to refreshing frustration, loving hate!
> I've purged the lust for knowledge from my soul;
> Now the full range of suffering it shall face,

---

[6] The passage is taken from the paper 'Drama and Life', delivered in Dublin in January 1900. It is included in E. Mason and R. Ellmann, eds, *The Critical Writings of James Joyce*, Viking Press, New York 1959, p. 45.

13

And in my inner self I will embrace
The experience allotted to the whole
Race of mankind, my mind shall grasp the heights
And depths, my heart know all their sorrows and delights.
Thus I'll expand myself, and their self I shall be,
And perish in the end, like all humanity.

Faust, 1765–75

So who was right, then: Hegel, who declared the modern epic impossible, or Goethe, who was just writing one?

'In the beginning was the Deed'

Action is the clearest revelation of the individual, of his temperament as well as his aims: what a man is at bottom and in his inmost being comes into actuality only by his action.[7]

Hegel's words. More recently and rather more turgidly, Maurice Blanchot has taken up the same theme:

Heroism is revelation, the marvellous brilliance of deed that joins essence and appearance. Heroism is the act's luminous sovereignty. Only the act is heroic, and the hero is nothing if he does not act . . .[8]

Without action, in short, no hero. Hence, no epic. This is the right background against which to read one of the great monologues in *Faust*:

'In the beginning was the Word'; why, now
I'm stuck already! I must change that; how?

---

[7] Hegel, *Aesthetics*, vol. 1, p. 219.

[8] M. Blanchot, 'The End of the Hero', in *The Infinite Conversation*, University of Minnesota Press, Minneapolis 1993, p. 370. The term hero, here, is not male by chance or mere habit. The original interweaving of epic and war did indeed relegate female figures to a marginal role, which has persisted to our own day. Joyce's Penelope is fortunate enough to have a tremendous monologue – but she is restricted to the book's last chapter. It is because of this symbolic imbalance, I think, that European women writers have always preferred novels to epic storytelling.

14

Is then 'the word' so great and high a thing?
There is some other rendering,
Which with the spirit's guidance I must find.
We read: 'In the beginning was the Mind.'
Before you write this first phrase, think again;
Good sense eludes the overhasty pen.
Does 'mind' set worlds on their creative course?
It means: 'In the beginning was the Force'.
So it should be – but as I write this too,
Some instinct warns me that it will not do.
The spirit speaks! I see how it must read,
And boldly write: 'In the beginning was the Deed!'

1224–37

'Im Anfang war die Tat': this is undoubtedly the idea defended by Faust in the 'Study' scene that follows shortly afterwards and that Goethe, in the plan he drafted in about 1800, made the basis for the entire poem. But the principle so proudly proclaimed never finds much correspondence in the actual work. Before the first part of *Faust* was even finished, Schiller was already communicating his own doubts to Goethe in this respect: 'In my opinion', he wrote on 26 June 1797, 'Faust should be led into active life. . .' With the publication of Part Two, the disappointment increased. Heine criticized Goethe's 'indifference' to action, while Vischer hoped for a Faust caught up in the Peasants' War.[9] Finally, at a juncture decisive for the destiny of the 'grand world' – 1938 – this is what Thomas Mann wrote:

> Goethe did not do much to represent poetically those 'depths of sweet and sensual sin' [*Faust*, 1751], or that life of action alternating between success and chagrin, to which he would have liked his hero to sacrifice himself [. . .] A long time had to go by before Faust, after so many bizarre magical adventures, turned to undertakings that might truly be termed tests of indefatigable human activity.[10]

---

[9] Among the many Fausts contemporary with that of Goethe, at least two – Klinger's in 1791, and von Soden's in 1797 – had taken part in politico-patriotic activities. (See, on this, E.M. Butler, *The Fortunes of Faust*, Cambridge University Press, Cambridge 1952.)

[10] Thomas Mann, 'Über Goethes *Faust*' (1938), in *Adel des Geistes*, Bermann – Fischer Verlag, Stockholm 1948, p. 682.

15

Well, then: Goethe wants an active hero, he gives him marvellous and fitting words to pronounce, he lends him the aid of the infernal powers, and yet – nothing. For scene after scene – the long promenade in 'Outside the Walls'; the silence in 'Auerbach's Tavern' and 'A Witch's Kitchen'; the sleep and dreams scattered almost everywhere; the mere walk-on part in the two 'Walpurgis Night' scenes and in the civil war – Faust remains ever more enmired in a kind of idle contemplation. Here, the contrast with the ancient epic is really very strong. In Homer, even the hero's *inactivity* – Achilles in his tent – produces practical consequences of great importance: it is, in its own way, action. In *Faust*, on the contrary, the hero's presence seems always to leave things as they were, in a kind of gigantic spectacle. In the words of Mephistopheles:

> You soon will *see* what I can do.
> No man has ever known a *spectacle* so rare.
> 1673–4

We were seeking a hero, and have found a spectator. What is to be done?

Perhaps, to begin with, we can reverse the argument and see in Faust's inertia the only chance for the modern epic totality. If Hegel is actually right, and in the modern world 'the vitality of the individual appears as transcended', then nothing is left but to seek 'the universal individual of mankind'[11] *in passivity*. In this new scenario, the grand world of the epic no longer takes shape in transformative action, but in imagination, in dream, in magic. It is a shift clearly perceptible in the passage from Marlowe to Goethe. This is how Faust speaks in the last years of the sixteenth century:

> Having thee ever to attend on me,
> To give me whatsoever I shall ask,
> To tell me whatsoever I demand
> *Doctor Faustus*, I, 3, 93–5

---

[11] The definition is taken from C.F. Göschel, *Über Goethes Faust und dessen Fortsetzung*, 1824; according to H. Schwerte, *Faust und das Faustische. Ein Kapitel deutscher Ideologie*, Klett, Stuttgart 1962, p. 58, it is here that Faust is first described in world-historical terms.

Here, everything still depends upon Faustus's will. The first person pronoun grips the passage, appearing twice in each line, as origin and aim of every action ('To give *me* whatsoever *I* shall ask'); as for Mephistopheles, he is a mere executor, devoid of creativity or autonomy. But since everything depends on Faust, the hero's subjectivity is also the *limit* of the work: whatever is not 'inside' him does not belong in his world – which consequently cannot amount to much. Ultimately, Faustus sells his soul in exchange for a few fairground tricks, while the high ambitions of those 'whatsoevers' (apart from the vision of Helen) remain a dead letter. If the strong-willed hero does make Faust's *tragedy* extraordinarily vivid, the legend's *epic* potential, on the other hand, is totally thwarted by him.

Very well. And here is Goethe's Faust:

> And *in my inner self* I will embrace
> The experience allotted to the whole
> Race of mankind; *my mind* shall grasp the heights
> And depths . . .
>
> 1770–73

Here, the dramatic will has almost turned back upon itself. Basically, Faust wills not to will: to share the destiny of his species, rather than intervene in it. With respect to Marlowe, the situation is reversed: the tragic potential of the plot is weaker, and its epic potential more powerful. For Faust's words allude precisely to what was of no interest to Marlowe's hero: the genuinely epic immensity – the experience allotted to the whole of mankind – of a universe to be 'embraced in one's inner self'. We are speaking, of course, of a totality cut in half, unidimensional, where passivity threatens to transform the hero into his exact opposite. But it is nevertheless a totality rediscovered – and at a moment, as we shall see, in which Europe has a great need for breadth of vision. Moreover, this passive hero has a great virtue: remaining extraneous to action, he also remains extraneous *to guilt*. A brief parenthesis, and I shall have more to say about this.

Literary evolution. I

An epic with no hero. A *Faust* without Faust, or at any rate with a non-Faustian Faust. But if that were the case, why the compact with the

17

Devil? Is it not precisely Faust's will to act that makes it necessary? And does Mephistopheles not make his appearance at the very moment in which Faust translates St John's '*logos*' by the word 'Deed'?

All true. But the genesis of a figure does not always coincide with its effective function, and there is nothing to prevent us surmising that Mephistopheles – albeit initially created to be Faust's servant, as in Marlowe – actually performs a very different role. Some confirmation of this already comes, in fact, from the first great episode in which Mephistopheles is involved: the seduction of Margareta. Here, when Faust is quite clear about what he wants, no assistance is of any use to him: if he just had a little time, he exclaims soon after meeting the girl,

> Two weeks! That child! Why, I'll be bound,
> If I had even half a day
> I'd not need the Devil to get my way
> 2642–44

When Faust is ready to act, in other words, Mephistopheles is very little use. To be sure, he collects a few jewels and helps Faust to fence: but it is not he who drives the action forward, and Part One could easily do without him. Part One: the 'tragic' part. But not Part Two – the 'epic' part – in which Mephistopheles moves decidedly to the foreground: he invents paper money, sets the Empire on fire, brings the legends of antiquity back to life, fights a civil war, constructs Holland, flies from one witches' sabbath to another . . .

So let us linger for a moment on this discontinuity between genesis and function. Mephistopheles, as I have just said, was devised for the initial tragic nucleus of *Faust*, but there serves practically no purpose. On the other hand, he fulfils a decisive function in the poem's epic expansion, which did not form part of Goethe's initial plans: the 'Prologue in Heaven', 'Walpurgis Night' and gradually all the great phantasmagorias of Part Two. Without Mephistopheles, there would be nothing of all this. In other words, there would be no *Faust* Part Two, and perhaps not the modern epic either. At all events, not *this* modern epic, which started off from *Faust*. So, an entire literary genre became possible (became, finally, imaginable) because Goethe found the character capable of supporting its construction. Yet, *that character had not been created to fulfil that function at all*. What is more, Goethe had him there, ready and available, from the first scenes of the Margareta tragedy. Yet, *it took him a quarter of a century to realize what he could do with him.*

Faust Part Two as the result of chance, in other words. And a delayed-action chance, what is more. Strange? Yes. Indeed absurd, if you think that literature is the product of a conscious project. But the strangeness disappears if you look at things with a touch of irreverence, and apply to Goethe the antithesis formulated in his day by Lévi-Strauss in *The Savage Mind*. Despite all his plans of work and well-ordered days, the author of *Faust* was not an engineer but a *bricoleur*. Rather than planning an epic poem and rationally preparing the means to achieve it, he chanced to find in his hands – right in the middle of a tragedy – a character with a strong epic potential. And so, after decades of hesitation, he eventually put together an epic poem. With respect to the dominant historiographical models, the relationship between means and ends is precisely reversed: the tools, the concrete technical possibilities, are everything; the project, the ideology, the poetics – nothing.[12] And this, let it be clear, is not a defect. Quite the contrary. Because plans and poetics function (perhaps) when inside a stable formal paradigm: in times of 'normal' literature, so to speak. But if paradigms are shifting they are a waste of time, because change is not planned: it is the fruit of the most irresponsible and free – the blindest – rhetorical experimentation. Poetics plod along behind this, often far behind. They certainly do not guide it, and usually do not even really understand it. The most famous invention of the twentieth century – the stream of consciousness – will provide us with a splendid example.

Bricolage as the motor of literary evolution. Mephistopheles as the key to epic *bricolage*. Yet Mephistopheles is there by chance, since Goethe

---

[12] Not just the 1800 outline, but even the working plan for *Faust* Part Two that Goethe dictated in 1816 for the fourth volume of *Dichtung und Wahrheit* ('Poetry and Truth', translated into English as *The Autobiography of Goethe*), basically bears no relation to the completed work. The same will be true of the outlines for *Ulysses*, which will regularly be belied by the final product. Joyce's method of work, incidentally – collecting every possible detail concerning Dublin, because, you never know, anything might come in useful – is precisely that of the *bricoleur*.

decides without any real dramatic necessity to abandon the familiar wicked counsellor of seduction tragedies (the Marinelli of *Emilia Galotti*, the Wurms of *Love and Intrigue*) and replaces him with the Devil. For years and years, the difference between the two figures seems negligible. Then, all of a sudden, it emerges. Unlike the counsellor, Mephistopheles can do more than one thing: in other words, he is capable of *changing function*. And this is a decisive quality. For literary evolution does not normally proceed by inventing new themes or new methods out of the blue, but precisely by discovering *a new function for those that already exist*. This is an idea that is at the centre of Darwin's theory,[13] and that returns in the 'refunctionalization' of the Russian formalists. One example (among many), from Viktor Shklovsky:

> The device does not in every individual case preserve the same [. . .] function it had at the moment of its creation [. . .] It may even happen that, like the colours on a cheap print, the device overruns its outline, or when applied takes an opposite direction.[14]

It may happen that the device overruns its outline . . . 'How did dissonances ever come to be used?' Schönberg wonders in his *Theory of Harmony*, obviously raising a decisive issue for the work of his own maturity. And he replies by describing point by point the mechanism of refunctionalization:

> I believe that dissonance appeared first in passing from one tone to another through intervening tones and that such passing stemmed from the portamento, from the desire to soften leaps, to connect disjunct tones melodically, in this case by scale step. That this desire coincides with another, with the desire to make use also of the more

---

[13] See S.J. Gould and E. Vrba, 'Exaptation: a missing term in the science of form', in *Paleobiology* 1, 1982.

[14] V. Shklovsky, *Material i stil v romane L.N. Tolstogo 'Vojna i mir'* (Moscow 1928). On the relations between evolutionary theory and Russian formalism, see Franco Moretti, 'On Literary Evolution', in *Signs Taken for Wonders*, 2nd enlarged edn, Verso, London 1987.

distant overtones, is perhaps only a fortunate coincidence, such as historical evolution indeed often produces.[15]

Bricolage, then. And refunctionalization. The former is a *macro*-structural concept: it describes how a text functions as a whole. The latter is a *micro*-structural concept: it describes what happens to the elementary components of a work. Yet, in this case, there is a profound need for agreement between micro and macro. Refunctionalization can occur only in an elastic structure, able to absorb novelty without disintegrating. *Bricolage*, for its part, requires versatile 'bits', able to add a new function to the original one. It is a circle, in which the parts and the whole presuppose one another and mutually support one another. At times, moreover, it is a genuinely virtuous circle: Mephistopheles and the growth of *Faust*; the historical material and the development of *War and Peace*; dissonance and serial music; the stream of consciousness, as we shall see, and the metamorphosis of *Ulysses*. All fortunate, successful encounters. But never *wholly* successful – as is, in any case, logical. For when one element develops a new function, what happens to the old one?

What sometimes happens is that it withdraws discreetly. But what far more often occurs is that the old function remains in circulation, and may easily turn into a genuine structural encumbrance. The wealth of historical material enormously enriches *War and Peace*; but it imposes on Tolstoy the novel's notorious second epilogue. Mephistopheles begins as a tragic devil, then becomes transformed into an epic demiurge; yet something of the devil remains, and Goethe finds himself constrained to a theological finale that has never convinced anybody. In *The Nibelung's Ring* we shall find an analogous problem at the intersection of music and drama; and again in the complexity of *Ulysses*. And this imperfection, I repeat, is

---

[15] Anton Schönberg, *Theory of Harmony* (1922), translated by Roy Carter, University of California Press, Berkeley 1978, p. 47. As Schönberg wrote in another essay ('New Music, Outmoded Music, Style and Idea', in *Style and Idea*, translated by Dika Newlin, Williams and Norgate, London 1951, p. 48): 'Adversaries have called me a constructor, an engineer, an architect, even a mathematician – not to flatter me – because of my method of composing with twelve tones.' But even he, although at first sight he really does remind one more of an engineer than of a *bricoleur*, calmly recognizes the role of 'fortunate coincidence' in technical evolution.

entirely logical: for between *bricolage* and refunctionalization there may well be an admirable agreement – but certainly, by definition, no preordained harmony. If then, as I hope, these two concepts will make literary history more comprehensible and more interesting, they will nevertheless introduce into it also the very concrete possibility of *failure*. Which again makes it more comprehensible, and far more interesting.[16]

Rhetoric of innocence. I

Let us return to Faust. And to his first victim: Margareta. Seduced; driven to poison her mother and drown her son; then herself slain, as her

---

[16] Polemic against anyone who extols the 'perfection' of natural evolution is one of the arguments dearest to Stephen Jay Gould, who has counterposed the 'Panda principle' of the inevitable imperfection of every product of evolution: '[Perfection] is a lousy argument for evolution, for it mimics the postulated action of an omnipotent creator. Odd arrangements and funny solutions are the proof of evolution – paths that a sensible God would never tread, but that a natural process, constrained by history, follows perforce.' ('The Panda's Thumb', in S.J. Gould, *The Panda's Thumb*, Penguin, London 1983, p. 20. On this, see also F. Jacob, 'Evolution and Tinkering', in *Science*, vol. 196, June 1977; and N. Eldredge, *Time Frames*, Princeton University Press, Princeton NJ 1985, pp. 147–9.)

As for literary criticism, it is divided equitably between creationist faith (the text is a complete and perfect world, and the author is the watchmaker who foresees everything) and deconstructionist gnosis (at the slightest contradiction, the text collapses into total chaos). Once again, Russian formalism – and especially Shklovsky – had sketched the solution: to accept the 'imperfect bond' between the various parts of the text as an absolutely normal fact, to be neither hidden nor exaggerated. Identical the stance of Erwin Panofsky, who presents the evolution of artistic technique as a very concrete process of cut and thrust: made up of chance opportunities and 'perplexities', structural problems and 'acrobatic solutions' – or even ones that are 'courageous, though not quite honest'. I take these expressions from *Perspective as Symbolic Form* (1927), translated by Christopher Wood, Zone Books, New York and Cambridge Mass. 1992; and, especially, *Gothic Architecture and Scholasticism*, Archabbey Press, Latrobe Pa. 1951, pp. 70 ff., with its marvellous discussion of the 'problem of the rose window in the West facade' and the difficulties this created for French Gothic.

brother had already been. Object of an extreme affective ambivalence, wherein love conflicts with impatience at the narrow world's fetters (so that Faust introduces himself to her under the name 'Heinrich', which will also – in a stroke of intuitive genius – be her very last word). So there would be nothing strange if Margareta were the 'phantasm' par excellence of the Faust story, and returned to haunt him – as, for example, in Lenau's gloomy *Faust*.[17] But although Margareta does indeed return, she does so in the guise of an angel ('Una Poenitentium, once known as Gretchen') and in order to intercede for Faust's salvation. And more generally, although *Faust* is a work literally invaded by phantasms and ghosts,[18] the uncanny, sinister element plays almost no role in it. This is a singular feature, and deserves further examination.

Among the many peculiarities of the composition of *Faust*, there is one that leaps to the eye. The tragedy of Margareta is written straight off, indeed is already complete in 1775. It could and should be the end of the work. But no, the thing seems to condemn Goethe to forced labour – additions, plans, rewritings, alterations – for over half a century, until the very last months of his life. Why on earth such tenacity? Is it perhaps because that very early *Faust* has not been much of a success?

On the contrary. It has turned out only too well, and Goethe wishes precisely to exculpate his hero from the burden of that bygone sin. This is the 'de-tragicization of Faust's tragedy': an operation that Hans Schwerte considers fundamental to the 'Faustian ideology', and that – judging by the popular commentaries so important in the formation of

---

[17] 'At night, hyena-like, dreams enjoy/Disinterring my dead ones from their graves', N. Lenau, *Faust*, 1836. And again: 'Dreams, restive beasts, still drag/Even the wretched corpses of madness'. See also the entire scenes: 'The farrier's workshop', 'The lake' and 'The dream'.

[18] 'This is creepy; don't you feel/Spells being woven? It's not real –/Something's whirring round my head. . .' (5486–8). 'I think no magic words are needed here', Mephistopheles reflects, 'Now of their own accord the spirits will appear' (6375–6). And then again: Classical Walpurgis Night, Helen, the phantom army of Act Four, and so on to the lines chosen by Freud as the epigraph to *The Psychopathology of Everyday Life*: 'The air is swarming now/With ghosts we would avoid if we knew how' (11410–11).

general culture – really does succeed to perfection.[19] It is a process that begins as early as the 'Prologue in Heaven' added in 1799, where Faust's name echoes for the first time when the Lord challenges Mephistopheles to lead him astray: as if to demonstrate that Faust is not master of his own existence, since higher powers contend over – and even bet upon – it. And when we get to the evocation of Mephistopheles, likewise composed in 1799 . . . evocation? – not at all! Faust is piously translating the sacred words of the Gospel 'Into the German tongue I hold so dear' (1223), when he finds the Devil in his room – and eventually accepts his company only after two very heated scenes, in which Mephistopheles resorts to wheedling, promises, dazzling quips, professions of humility . . .

In short: Faust makes his compact with the Devil because he is seduced by him. Like Margareta, before Margareta – and actually more than Margareta, since it is the Lord himself who has incited Mephistopheles to tempt him. And can he who has been seduced ever be guilty of seduction?

But that's not all there is, in those two scenes entitled 'Faust's Study' in which the compact is sealed. To start with, there is another oddity of com-

---

[19] It is surprising how often such commentaries pass over the tragedy of Margareta, either not referring to it at all – see, for example, J.A. Hartung, 'Beiträge zur populäre Erklärung des Faust', in *Jahresbericht des Königlichen Preussischen Gymnasium zu Schleusingen*, 1844; F. von Sallet, *Zur Erläuterung des zweiten Theiles vom Goethe'schen Faust. Für Frauen geschrieben*, August Schultz, Breslau 1844; J.C.E. Loesch, *Das böse Prinzip in Goethes Faust und Chamissos Schlemihl. Eine Parallele*, 1835 [?] – or declaring that the Faust of Part Two 'casts a veil over what has occurred', and thus produces some kind of 'reconcilement' (C.H. Weisse, *Kritik und Erläuterung des Goethe'schen Faust*, Reichenbach, Leipzig 1837, p. 51).

Postscript 1995. On 23 May, *Il Manifesto* (Rome) published an article from Bonn by Guido Ambrosino, explaining that 'Hans Schwerte' is actually Hans Ernst Schneider, former SS captain, and possibly a collaborator with war criminal Klaus Barbie. After the war, Schneider/Schwerte remarried his 'widow' Annemarie, 'adopted' his daughter, and proceeded to a brilliant intellectual career, which included a sympathy for the 1968 student movement, and personal friendship with Social-Democrat leaders. That his most significant study should focus on the 'de-tragicization of tragedy' (or, as I put it, on a 'rhetoric of innocence') makes a lot of sense.

position. In the many variants of the Faust legend, one fact always remains constant: the compact with the Devil is the main thing, so it precedes everything else. The first scene with Mephistopheles to be written by Goethe, however, is the one entitled 'A Gloomy Day. Open Country' (probably dating from 1772–3), in which Faust curses his companion, blames him for Margareta's fate, and swears to be rid of him: almost as though Goethe wanted first and foremost to emphasize in his own mind the *hostility* between Faust and Mephistopheles, rather than their agreement. The latter is indeed for him the hardest moment in the entire poem: he will succeed in tackling it only after *thirty years* of hesitation, thus finally filling the 'great lacuna' of which he writes to Schiller on 6 April 1801. And it takes some doing, even then: for hundreds and hundreds of lines, as Emil Staiger has shown, the moment of the compact is curiously delayed by false starts, digressions, postponements and duplications.[20]

Compact? Not even that, but a wager – half agreement, half challenge. Hence, impossible to decide whether Mephistopheles is Faust's ally or his worst adversary: a constitutive duplicity of the work, which allows Faust to unload ultimate responsibility for his own actions on to his wicked companion. This is what Mephistopheles is needed for in *Faust* Part One. Not to help Faust seduce Margareta, but for the opposite reason: because Faust could actually do everything on his own – and Goethe wants to *avoid* that. Just as he parries Valentino's blows in the nocturnal duel, Mephistopheles shields Faust from the violence of the seduction and, in effect, from all violence.[21] Thanks to him, a strategy is born that will be fundamental for the modern epos, indeed for the whole of Western culture: a strategy of denial and disavowal – a projection of violence outside oneself. Goethe's brilliant and terrible discovery: the rhetoric of innocence.

The mechanism of projection, activated as early as the 'Evening' scene – when Faust would like to go, but Mephistopheles makes him leave the jewels in Margareta's room – becomes intensified, of course, once the

---

[20] E. Staiger, *Goethe*, Atlantis Verlag, Zurich – Freiburg 1956, vol. 2, pp. 334 ff.

[21] The disavowal of violence is a constant of modern epic form. In the *Faust* planned by Lessing, an angel gives the devil a replica of Faust but keeps the real one safe; in *Peer Gynt*, the hero is exonerated because his (dreadful) actions are not very 'serious'.

seduction has occurred. It is the 'disgust' for Mephistopheles of 'A Forest Cavern', the hatred of 'A Gloomy Day. Open Country'. But Mephistopheles, unruffled, illuminates with well-mannered cynicism the reality of projection: 'In short, good sir, by all means do/Delude yourself if it amuses you' (3297–8). Deep down, the true compact is precisely this: not to 'say/Out loud what modest minds are filled with anyway'; to keep well separated the heaven of values and the earth of desires – unsullied ends and unscrupulous means. After the murder of Philemon and Baucis:

> And this you claim to have done for me?
> I said exchange, not robbery!
> Deaf savages! I curse this deed
>
> 11370–73

But Mephistopheles was not deaf: it is just that, in the places and times of *Faust*, 'war and trade and piracy' form an 'undivided trinity' (11187–8). *Faust* is the poem of primary accumulation, Lukács writes in *Goethe and his Age*: it tells us of 'capital running with blood'. Quite true, and Mephistopheles is there to take upon himself the curse of that blood. In the counterpoint between him and Faust, there is thus established that blend of truth and lie ('bad faith', Sartre will call it) typical of a West that is proud of its own world dominion, but prefers to overlook the violence sustaining it. In the words of Herman Melville:

> From the points which the whale's eyes had once occupied, now protruded blind bulbs, horribly pitiable to see. But pity there was none. For all his old age, and his one arm, and his blind eyes, he must die the death and be murdered, in order to light the gay bridals and other merry-makings of men, and also to illuminate the solemn churches that preach unconditional inoffensiveness by all to all.[22]

---

[22] *Moby-Dick*, 80. Among the works I shall be discussing, *Moby-Dick* is most lucid in recognizing the necessity of violence for the West's civilized life, and the necessity of its disavowal for the West's civilized consciousness. But even there, masking mechanisms are not lacking: violence is exercised not upon human beings but upon animals, indeed upon the metaphysical creature that is Moby-Dick; and the hero, as and more than in *Faust*, is split between the innocuous Ishmael and the satanic Ahab.

We have seen how Goethe exculpates Faust from the violence exercised upon Margareta. Let us now turn to the female figure at the centre of *Faust* Part Two. At the start of Act Three:

> So much admired and so much censured, Helena,
> Now from the sea come I . . .
>
> 8488–9 (translation modified)

Admired, censured: Helena is defined by the judgements of others, closed upon themselves in the form of a chiasmus. Her present reality is relegated to the second line, the first person pronoun still further – to the most distant grammatical position possible. Even her name is detached from the living person, enclosed between two commas, like something alien: and all this from Helena's own lips. This really is not a woman, but a thing – of which Faust will easily take possession. But how will he manage to justify his conquest, and transform force into right?

In the first place, thanks to a laborious preceding history ('In Front of the Palace of Menelaus in Sparta'), in which the Greek king seeks to make Helen a sacrificial victim.[23] Against this background, the arrival of Faust takes on a wholly different value. It is no longer an act of conquest, but a *liberation from barbarism*: an ideologically very effective reversal, that for good reason appears in one way or another in all the masterpieces of colonial imagination. Robinson Crusoe saves Friday from the cannibalism of the other natives; Lord Jim protects the village of Doramin from Ali's rascally attacks; Passepartout and Phileas Fogg save Aouda from the 'barbarous custom' of suttee. And it is also significant that (*Robinson Crusoe* apart) all these works contemplate a marriage between the Westerner and the Native Woman: for, in marriage, conquest becomes *consent* and is thus fully legitimized.

And there is something else as well. Here is Faust, upon the arrival of Helena:

---

[23] 'Do I come here as wife? Do I come here as queen?/Or will the king avenge on me his bitter grief/And all these long misfortunes that the Greeks have borne?/I am a prize of war, perhaps a prisoner!' (8527–30).

27

A double sight, oh queen, amazes me:
Your surely-speeding arrow, and its victim.
I see the bow that winged it on its way,
And him who felt the wound. Arrows apace
Assail me now, I sense their feathering flight
At me from all sides, here within the castle.
What has become of me? my truest followers
You turn to rebels all at once, my walls
You weaken. Will my army now obey
Me, or this conquering unconquered lady?
What choice now, but to give myself and all
My supposed wealth to you in vassalage?

> 9258–69

Here, according to the commentaries, Christian-mediaeval love and pagan-classical beauty meet. Certainly true – and similar things can indeed be said for Verne and Conrad. But the courtly love of Faust serves also to reverse, and thus mask, the real relation of power: to declare the booty of war, prisoner in the conqueror's castle, a 'conquering unconquered lady'. The mechanism of projection is now flanked by that of reversal.

So, an innocent compact. Then, innocent behaviour. Finally, an innocent *desire*. Given that concrete action is Mephistopheles's business, Faust's wishes take on a quite specific form. 'Well, tell me – I'll be governed by/Your will – what *whim* you now would satisfy', declares Mephistopheles in Act Four (10196–7). And Faust: 'My eye was drawn . . .' The passive construction at once invests his vision with something involuntary. And then:

My eye was drawn, in passing, to the high sea.
[. . .]
Landward it streams, and countless inlets fill;
Barren itself, it spreads its barren will;
It swells and swirls, its rolling waves expand
Over the dreary waste of dismal sand;
Breaker on breaker; all their power upheaved
And then withdrawn, and not a thing achieved!
I watch dismayed, almost despairingly,
This useless elemental energy!

28

And so my spirit dares new wings to span:
This I would fight, and conquer if I can
10198–221

A vast, untamable expanse, full of strange creatures and infinite riches, at the disposal of whomsoever can exploit them . . . Beyond its literal meaning, Goethe's sea cannot but remind us of the world outside Europe: its energy incapable of progress relates it to the Hegelian 'peoples without history', and justifies conquest of it as a process bestowing meaning. Yet all this still remains in the form *of a metaphor*: present in Faust's words – but also masked by them. To battle the waves, and even consign them to exile (10229 ff.), is certainly no crime. More than a concrete act of conquest, moreover, this is just a seashore reverie: once again, the activity of a 'passive' hero. And what harm can it ever do to dream?

> In scanning prospects in the spatial sense – as landscape panoramas – [the explorer's] eye knows itself to be looking at prospects in the temporal sense – as possibilities for the future, resources to be developed, landscapes to be peopled or repeopled by Europeans. [. . .] More commonly, European aspirations are introduced in the form of a reverie that overtakes the seer as he ponders the panorama before him [. . .] Such reveries abound in nineteenth-century exploration writing [. . .] the reverie convention often very specifically projects the civilizing mission onto the scene.[24]

> At a place called Sigunga, we put in for lunch. An island at the mouth of the bay suggested to our minds that this was a beautiful spot for a mission station . . . The island, capable of containing quite a large village, and perfectly defensible, might, for prudence's sake, contain the mission and its congregation; the landlocked bay would protect their fishery and trade vessels.[25]

---

[24] M.L. Pratt, 'Scratches on the Face of the Country; or, What Mr Barrow Saw in the Land of the Bushmen', in H.L. Gates Jr, ed., *'Race', Writing, and Difference*, Chicago University Press, Chicago 1984, pp. 144–5.

[25] H.M. Stanley, *How I found Livingstone* (1874), quoted by M. Torgovnick, *Going Primitive*, Chicago University Press, Chicago 1990, p. 27. The colonial idea is 'suggested' by the island, and takes form in the conditional: like Faust, Stanley is not responsible for anything.

No, to dream is no crime. It is a wholly innocent activity. Or, perhaps, it is a wholly innocent way of preparing oneself for something else, which is not innocent at all.

'He sees visions of giant undertakings . . .'

Another of Faust's visions:

> From branch to branch I planned to build
> Great platforms, to look far afield,
> From panoramic points to gaze
> At all I've done; as one surveys
> From an all-mastering elevation
> A masterpiece of man's creation.
> I'd see it all as I have planned:
> Man's gain of habitable land.
>
> 11243–50

These inspired lines give no hint of it, but within a few moments Faust will command Mephistopheles to 'clear from my path' the old couple (Philemon and Baucis) ruining the masterpiece. This is the 'splitting' characteristic of bad faith, as I said earlier: and it has been a productive splitting, in which Faust's vision has acquired an extraordinary force and intensity. 'As one surveys/From an all-mastering elevation/A masterpiece of man's creation': who would not wish to be there at his side? And again:

> I'll drain it [the swamp] too; that rotten place
> Shall be my last great project.
> [. . .]
> I see green fields, so fertile: man and beast
> At once shall settle that new pleasant earth,
> Bastioned by great embankments that will rise
> About them, by bold labour brought to birth.
> Here there shall be an inland paradise:
> [. . .]
> Yes! to this vision I am wedded still
>
> 11561–73

An inland paradise. Careful, though. This is not a seducer who has repented and whose only thought is now of work. Faust has not repented at all: he has merely shifted his field of action, transforming himself into an *economic* seducer. 'Lyrical enthusiasm', writes Werner Sombart, is precisely the 'condition' of the speculator's 'soul':

> He himself, with all the passionate intensity he is capable of, dreams the dream of the successful issue of his undertaking [. . .] Let him but have completed the work in hand and others will be added unto it, until the two hemispheres resound with the praise of his enterprises. He sees visions of giant undertakings [. . .] If he is a specially able type of speculating undertaker, he may possibly possess the poet's gift of calling up to the eyes of his audience ravishing pictures of realms of gold, in order to show [. . .] the blessings his enterprise will shower on the world, as well as on those who cooperate with him.[26]

Sombart is referring here to Zola's *L'Argent*; but the last scenes of *Faust*, with their sinister grandeur, are almost equally appropriate. As in the painting by Wright of Derby that is in all probability the first image of the modern factory, work in *Faust* is typically *night* work: a working day which does violence to the solar day, and subverts the natural rhythms themselves.[27] In the 'ravishing pictures' of the Faustian visions, however, this despotism of the first industrial revolution is rewritten precisely as a 'blessing . . . on those who cooperate with him'. Here, the wage labourers[28] are not the 'helots' described by the critics of civil society, dragging themselves exhausted through the mire of industrial cities: they are '*tätigfrei*', free and active, or more accurately, free-at-work.

To separate work from capitalism, in short: to hide the alien, violent

---

[26] W. Sombart, *The Quintessence of Capitalism* (1913), translated by M. Epstein, T. Fisher Unwin Ltd, London 1915, pp. 91–2.

[27] 'I hasten to complete my great designs:/My words alone can work my mastering will./Rise from your sleep, my servants, every man!/Give visible success to my bold plan!/Set to work now with shovel and with spade:/I have marked it all out, let it be made!' (11501–6).

[28] 'Until the edifice of this achievement stands,/One mind shall move a thousand hands' (11509–10). 'The "hands" = the "workers" of political economy', notes G. Della Volpe in *Critique of Taste*, NLB, London 1978, p. 65 (translation modified).

31

forms work is assuming, and thus save it. This is a true constant of Goethe's work, and not of his alone:

> Ishmael is never so happy as when he is finding in some dull, arduous, or onerous task an allegory of universal truth. Work takes on extra value when Ishmael can interpret it symbolically, when it assumes the pattern of some larger structure or condition of human life.[29]

True, the *Pequod* is a floating factory, and of the worst kind: yet it does not produce stupidity and disease, but intelligence and health. And this first mask of capitalism is then supplemented by the even more effective one provided by Ahab. In his person, the nineteenth-century metaphor of the 'captain of industry' splits. Industry vanishes, and the captain remains alone to dominate the scene:

> Ahab's madness, his usurpation of power, and his rigid authoritarianism all deflect criticism away from the economic system that launched the *Pequod*. Ahab is more dangerous than the ship's owners [. . .] his revolt against the system of profit diverts Ishmael's criticism away from the whaling industry itself, which in its pristine form regularly sacrificed human life to the production of capital.[30]

Ahab as lightning conductor. Something all the more interesting if one thinks that the captain of the *Pequod* is not just the most Faustian of nineteenth-century heroes, but actually more Faustian than Faust himself. 'I lack the low, enjoying power', murmurs Ahab at sunset (*Moby-Dick*, 36), echoing the 'enjoyment makes common' of *Faust*: but while Faust is thereafter in no way constrained by such words ('I have merely desired, achieved, and then/Desired some other thing': 11437–8), Ahab really is left only with the memory of 'the desolation of solitude [. . .] Guinea-coast slavery of solitary command [. . .] and how for forty years I have fed upon dry salted fare' (*Moby-Dick*, 131). It is the last evening of Faust's life when Care knocks at his door; in Melville, the 'mighty woe' (*Moby-Dick*, 28) is there from the outset, to impose that continuous renunciation, that imperious motion in a straight line, which is the exact opposite of Faust's

---

[29] P. Royster, 'Melville's Economy of Language', in S. Bercovitch and M. Jehlen, eds, *Ideology and Classic American Literature*, Cambridge University Press, Cambridge 1986, pp. 313–14.

[30] Ibid., p. 322.

free roaming.[31] Finally, Ahab does not disavow the violence of his conduct: he himself unhesitatingly gives the order that will immolate all the *Pequod*'s 'hands'. Here they are, the words that Faust should speak, but never does:

> What is it, what nameless, inscrutable, unearthly thing is it; what cozening, hidden lord and master, and cruel, remorseless emperor commands me; that against all natural lovings and longings, I so keep pushing [. . .]? Is Ahab, Ahab? Is it I, God, or who, that lifts this arm?
>
> *Moby-Dick*, 131

Unearthly cozener, inscrutable emperor . . . It is the Devil, here too: but *within* Ahab, not outside him (Melville's Mephistopheles, Fedallah, is an insignificant figure). But who, then, is the captain of the *Pequod*? Is Ahab Faust? Or is he Mephistopheles? 'What sort of double game is Melville playing with the very myth [of the compact with the Devil] which lies at the center of his world?'[32]

To Fiedler's question, one might reply: the game already played by Goethe, and then repeated by Wagner – the splitting of the hero. After all, it is a device that characterizes the epic genre from its beginnings:

> Achilles is the hero, but Agamemnon is the king of kings. This difference – writes Blanchot – will for ever continue to exist [. . .] Nephew of the emperor, paladin, and necessarily noble, the hero is close to power, and often stronger than power, but his power is excentric.[33]

Excentric? That depends. For Ahab, it is true. But not for Ishmael, not for Faust, not for Bloom. In general, indeed, one might say that the

---

[31] 'Captain Ahab stood erect, looking straight out beyond the ship's ever-pitching prow. There was an infinity of firmest fortitude, a determinate, unsurrenderable wilfulness, in the fixed and fearless, forward dedication of that glance' (*Moby-Dick*, 28). And further on: 'Swerve me? The path to my fixed purpose is laid with iron rails, whereon my soul is grooved to run' (*Moby-Dick*, 36).

[32] L. Fiedler, *Love and Death in the American Novel*, Criterion Books, New York 1960, p. 542.

[33] Blanchot, 'The End of the Hero', p. 370.

modern epic has shifted the hero from the frontier to the centre of his world. From the risk, and perhaps the guilt, of epic action to the safe enjoyment of its advantages.

The outcome – to cast a retrospective glance over this first chapter – is the very particular form assumed in these works by the notion of 'totality': a term which we had encountered in the *Aesthetics*, in Faust's monologue, and in a number of commentaries, but which I then left aside to speak of devils and phantasms, reveries and innocence. Yet I was not changing the subject. For those metaphors are the pillars, and the masks, of the modern totality: they embody its violence – and *hide* its violence. And something similar happens also to the hero. 'Universal individual of mankind', Faust has been called: true, and false. False, if this is taken to mean that his person combines within it all that is significant in modern humankind. True, if it means that Goethe put Faust in a position to desire, and obtain, the advantages of an entire world. The universal hero, in short, as a figure based upon the universal *dominion* of the West: that is the theme of the following chapters.

CHAPTER

2

An inherited form

'*Amerika, du hast es besser*' runs one of Goethe's later lyrics, entitled 'To the United States':[1]

> America, you have it better
> than our continent, the old one,
> you have no ruined castles
> and no basalts.
>
> Your inner self is not troubled,
> when it is a time for living,
> by pointless memories
> and futile strife.
>
> Use the present fortunately!
> And if your children write verses,
> may a happy fate protect them
> from tales of knights, brigands and ghosts.

Ruined castles, pointless memories, futile strife . . . We might be reading Hans Blumenberg's great study on the legitimacy of the modern age.

---

[1] Goethe, *Werke*, vol. 1, Winkler Verlag, Munich 1972, pp. 294–5.

On the one hand, the attempt to win legitimacy by making 'a radical break with [the] tradition' of Antiquity and Christianity; on the other, the fact that 'the reality of history . . . can never begin entirely anew', so the past – devalued by the new age, but not therefore abolished – continues to impinge upon it.[2] Indeed, Blumenberg goes on, the past imposes its own 'inherited problematics' upon it: the big theological questions – about the creation of the world, or its purpose – which, once formulated, can no longer be eluded, thus forcing modernity onto a terrain not its own, where it eventually loses its own specific spiritual physiognomy.

Blumenberg's argument has many other aspects, but here I shall confine myself to this one, using it to formulate a question that may already have occurred to some readers. A modern epic . . . was there really any *need* for this symbolic form, between the eighteenth and nineteenth centuries? And why was the undertaking not abandoned, once its numerous difficulties emerged? And, in any case, was the novel not sufficient? All questions that can be answered – paraphrasing Blumenberg – as follows: a modern epic came into being because it was an 'inherited form'. It was the form through which classical antiquity, Christianity and the feudal world had represented the basis of civilizations, their overall meaning, their destiny. In theory, modern literature could certainly have dispensed with that precedent, and contented itself with the far narrower space-time of the novel. But that would have been to admit its own inferiority with respect to the greatness of the past. So even though, in his *Meister*, Goethe had just convinced the European novel to 'be happy with the present', there he was – little by little, scene by scene, and for a long while without any definite plan – going back in time to challenge antiquity on its own terrain.

If Blumenberg's argument is valid, and holds also in the realm of literature, then the question I have just formulated ('was there really any need for a modern epic?') must be changed completely. Because of pressure from the past, a modern epic could not help but emerge; the proper question is *whether it could ever succeed*. The idea of an inherited form, if

---

[2] H. Blumenberg, *The Legitimacy of the Modern Age*, MIT Press, Cambridge Mass. 1985, p. 116.

you think about it, implies epic *attempts*; it does not at all guarantee their success – indeed, it suggests that ideal conditions no longer subsist.[3]

We are back to the imperfection of literary evolution – compounded, in this case, by a specific difficulty of the epic form. For the epic, from Homer on, normally functioned as a veritable encyclopaedia of a society's own culture: a storehouse of its essence and basic knowledge. But modern Europe, which has subdivided and specialized the sphere of knowledge, renders any such ambition anachronistic and almost unreal. 'Suddenly', a character in *Doctor Zhivago* says,

> [I] have understood why this stuff is so deadly, so insufferable and arti-
> ficial even when you come across it in *Faust*. The whole thing is an
> affectation, no one is genuinely interested in it. Modern man has no
> need of it. When he is vexed by the mysteries of the universe he turns
> to physics, not to Hesiod's hexameters.
>
> *Doctor Zhivago*, 'A Girl from a Different World', 10

He turns to physics and forgets Hesiod. Blumenberg, who precisely locates modernity's legitimation in 'scientific curiosity', would be in complete agreement. But the question has another aspect too. François Jacob:

> The price to be paid for this [the scientific] outlook, however, turned
> out to be high. It was, and is perhaps more than ever, renouncing a
> unified world view [. . .] Most other systems of explanation – mythic,
> magic, or religious – generally encompass everything. They apply to
> every domain. They answer any possible question [. . .] Science pro-
> ceeds differently [. . .] Actually, the beginning of modern science can
> be dated from the time when such general questions as, 'How was the
> universe created?' were replaced by such limited questions as, 'How
> does a stone fall? How does water flow in a tube?'[4]

---

[3] 'The truly amazing phenomenon during [the period from 1790 to 1825] is the proliferation of epics in England, which is unique in the history of Western literature', writes Stuart Curran. And he adds: 'a survey of [. . .] minor poems with major pretensions [. . .] does accentuate the difficulties of writing an epic poem, even in an age that thrived upon them' (*Poetic Form and British Romanticism*, Oxford University Press, Oxford 1986, pp. 158, 166).

[4] F. Jacob, 'Evolution and Tinkering', in *Science*, vol. 196, June 1977, p. 1161.

It is as if Jacob were here replying to Pasternak: physics will never replace Hesiod, *because it does not confront the same questions*. And vice versa: so long as the need is felt for 'a unitary world-view', modern science will have to yield to those 'systems which apply to everything . . . and answer all questions'. Like *Faust*, in fact, which – as one enthusiastic commentator writes – furnishes the equivalent 'of a vast quantity of books on the most diverse matters'.[5] And one thinks of *The Cantos*, and of *Ulysses*; of the fifteen hundred books that ended up in *Bouvard and Pécuchet*; or of *The Waste Land*, which according to I.A. Richards's famous dictum contains within it half a dozen volumes of the *Encyclopaedia Britannica*.

So here we are again, back at the epic's encyclopaedic ambition. And we have returned to it with an additional paradox. For Jacob and Pasternak are both right, in a sense: on the one hand, physics has eliminated neither Hesiod nor the epic; on the other, however, it has truly made them unacceptable. This is the double bind of the inherited form: it is possible neither to do without it, nor really to believe in it. So only one solution is left: to put epic universalism into practice – but without taking it seriously. *Gargantua*, *Tristram Shandy*, the 'Walpurgis Nights', *Bouvard and Pécuchet*, *Peer Gynt*, *Ulysses* . . .

'It is in satire and irony', writes Northrop Frye, 'that we should look for the continuing encyclopedic tradition'.[6] Absolutely true. But is it also true, as Frye seems to believe, that the ironic option involves a *critique* of the encyclopaedic project? In one case – *Bouvard and Pécuchet* – it is easy to answer yes. But in the other cases there is always something elusive and unclear: a persistent ambiguity, recurring in just the same way from Goethe to Pound. The encyclopaedic work is ridiculed, to be sure: *yet it is written*. The irony that renders its meaning unstable compels us for that very reason to take it terribly seriously: to read *Faust* or *Ulysses* with a voluminous commentary in our hands – in short, to *study* them.[7]

---

[5] C. Loewe, *Commentar zum zweiten Theile des Goethe'schen Faust*, Logier, Berlin 1834, p. 2.

[6] N. Frye, *Anatomy of Criticism*, Princeton University Press, Princeton NJ 1957, p. 322.

[7] In general, the modern epic is a scholastic genre, in all possible senses of the term including the worst, and Joyce's famous promise 'to keep the critics busy for three hundred years' perfectly illustrates its true nature. Were it not for Gymnasium and college, moreover, *Faust* Part Two and *Ulysses* would probably

Rather than dispatching the 'unitary world view', irony thus seems the ideal strategy for keeping it alive: it is a splendid defence mechanism, that eludes the double bind of the inherited form and allows the epic to survive in the new world. To survive: but, in all honesty, not much more. Turning the encyclopaedia into farce is a way of avoiding failure, rather than the beginning of a new form. It is a sign of great intelligence – but of an unfree intelligence, which has given itself an impossible task, and labours under the tremendous pressure of history. In this respect, the mocking epithet that has followed *Faust* and all the rest like a shadow is fully justified. Masterpieces, to be sure. But flawed masterpieces.

Non-contemporaneity. I

So many difficulties, for the sacred texts of the modern world. But let us return to the one indicated in Goethe's poem to the United States: the weight of the past. A twofold problem, on closer inspection, since the epic is not just inherited from the past, but also *dominated* by it. For Staiger, '[its] greatest vitality lies in the depths of the past';[8] for Bakhtin, the past appears here as 'absolute and immutable [. . .] lacking any relativity', thereby imposing on author and readers alike 'the reverent point of view of a descendant'.[9] And at first sight Goethe does indeed seem to

---

have almost vanished from the cultural horizon. But schools are fond of didactic works, so they have readily selected the modern epic as one of their favourite genres.

    We encounter here an example of restricted, institutional formation of the canon, very different from the spontaneous and diffuse kind typical, for example, of the nineteenth-century novel. Whether the normal way is the restricted one (as people think in America, where they believe in the omnipotence of the academy) or the diffuse one (as people think in Europe, where they believe in the omnipotence of the educated petty bourgeoisie) is a question to be resolved empirically, case by case. As a general rule, however, the press and literacy must have reinforced diffuse as against restricted canonization. In this respect too, the case of the epic is probably quite atypical.

[8] E. Staiger, *Basic Concepts of Poetics*, translated by J. Hudson and L. Frank, Pennsylvania State University Press, Philadelphia 1991, p. 100.

[9] M. Bakhtin, 'Epic and Novel', in *The Dialogic Imagination*, University of Texas Press, Austin 1981, pp. 13 ff.

submit to such supremacy. *Faust* is a kind of Europe in verse, full of ruined castles and pointless conflicts, and literally invaded by the past: characters, places, metres, stories, allegories, phantasms . . .

The present invaded by the past: but is the burden an overwhelming one? And is Goethe's attitude really the 'reverent' one of a 'descendant'? Certainly not. If anything, *Faust* is an epoch-making work for the opposite reason: because it *lightens* antiquity, and so neutralizes what might threaten the spiritual wellbeing of the modern world. Hardly an unchangeable past:

> In the Classical Walpurgis Night, all the forms of ancient history and myth are released from their traditional positions and transformed in their very essence. It is the de-functionalization of myth [. . .] the emancipation of the past from the fetters of necessity.[10]

And again:

> If the past must be allowed a form of existence in the present [. . .] then it must abandon the mode of Reality for that of Possibility.[11]

The past as 'Archive of the ages', Schlaffer goes on: 'a storehouse of poetical and historical memories' to be manipulated as you please.[12] 'I'll . . . float like a feather upon the stream/Of history;', Peer Gynt enthuses, 'and live again/As in a dream, the days of old;/See the fierce fights the heroes waged –/But from a vantage-point that's safe,/That of an onlooker . . .' (*Peer Gynt*, IV, 9). In this Universal Exhibition ambience – a place where, just as in *Faust* or in *Peer Gynt*, 'one can live a long time in a few hours, and travel across vast distances in a few steps'[13] – very little remains of the inflexible past of Bakhtin and Blumenberg. Only 'Mr Arsey-Phantarsey' – the parody Enlightenment man of 'A Walpurgis Night' – is left to suffer beneath the weight of bygone centuries and assail

---

[10] R. Wieland, *Zur Dialektik des ästhetischen Scheins*, Anton Hain, Königstein/Ts 1981, p. 144.

[11] H. Schlaffer, *Faust Zweiter Teil. Die Allegorie des 19 Jahrhunderts*, J.B. Metzler, Stuttgart 1981, p. 107.

[12] Ibid., pp. 104–5.

[13] *Revue de Paris*, 15 March 1900, quoted in R.H. Williams, *Dream Worlds. Mass Consumption in Late Nineteenth-Century France*, California University Press, Berkeley 1982, p. 77.

the 'despotism of spirits'.[14] But Faust by no means anathematizes the *altes Volk* of mediaeval illusions: instead, he takes it into his service, and makes it conquer the land where his industrial empire will arise – just as, at other moments, he uses the figures of antiquity to entertain the imperial court. Vampires in reverse, the living feed off the dead, and force the shades of the past to recite for them. Wieland again:

> The theme of the Classical Walpurgis Night is not creation *tout court*, but creation of the new from – and by means of – the past.[15]

Creation of the new from the past . . . As in *bricolage*: old materials, and new treatment. The result is an ambiguous register, halfway between Fair and archaeology; between satirical reduction and scholarly seriousness. What is more important here: the 'objective' meaning of the classical figures, fixed by tradition – or their 'subjective' reinterpretation, mediated through the modern hero? 'Are these now dreams', Faust wonders beside the Peneus, 'or memories?' (7275).

Dreams or memories? Goethe does not reply, because they are both; and the first consequence of such interweaving is a drastic devaluation of the historical sense, culminating in the notorious pastiche of the third act, when Faust, in the guise of a crusader knight, teaches Helen of Greece to speak rhymed verse. Freed from their historical positions, figures and styles from different epochs coexist here, as on the Pharsalian plain, 'outside time' (7436). As Schlaffer writes, it is the passage from the *Nacheinander* to the *Nebeneinander*: from an irreversible sequence emphasizing the 'after' to a synchronic arrangement highlighting the 'alongside'.[16] And thereby it is also an excellent example of that paradoxical state of affairs that Ernst Bloch called 'non-contemporaneity': the fact that many individuals, albeit living in the same period, from the cultural or political viewpoint belong to different epochs. 'Not all people

---

[14] 'This is outrageous! Why are you still here?/The world has been enlightened! You must disappear!/–Damned lawless sprites, they dance on, nothing daunted./We state the rules, and still that house in Tegel's haunted!/All my life long I've tried to sweep away/This superstitious junk. It's an outrage, I say!' (4158–63).

[15] Wieland, *Zur Dialektik des ästhetischen Scheins*, pp. 146–7.

[16] Schlaffer, *Faust Zweiter Teil*, pp. 106–7.

exist in the same Now . . .', runs the first sentence of Bloch's essay: 'They do so only externally, through the fact that they can be seen today. But that does not mean they are living at the same time as each other.'[17]

Bloch was writing in Germany, in 1932, so he was naturally only too conscious of the destructive potentialities of his spatial–temporal paradox. Many years later, and independently of him, Jens Kruse found in *Faust* an equally explosive situation: a present in which 'past and future participate simultaneously'; a present that is compressed – like the 'pressant' of *Finnegans Wake* or the 'strange present' of magical realism – hence always on the point of disintegrating.[18] The man of the future, Homunculus,

---

[17] This essay was written by Bloch in 1932 and published three years later in *Erbschaft dieser Zeit* (1935) (*Heritage of Our Times*, Polity Press, Oxford 1994). The idea of non-contemporaneity [*Ungleichzeitigkeit*, sometimes also rendered into English as 'non-synchronism'] had been in the air, however, since the previous century. 'The Germans are of the day before yesterday and the day after tomorrow – *they have as yet no today*', writes Nietzsche in *Beyond Good and Evil* (translated by R.J. Hollingdale, Penguin, London 1973, p. 152). And Strindberg, in the preface to *Miss Julie* (1888): 'As modern characters living in an age of transition [. . .] my people are more vacillating and disintegrating than their predecessors, a mixture of the old and the new [. . .] conglomerates of past and present cultural phases.'

In years closer to Bloch, the jarring superimposition of the modern upon the archaic is often encountered in psychoanalytical culture (culminating in the doubts of 'Analysis Terminable and Interminable' [1937] as to 'whether the dragons of primaeval ages are really extinct'), and also in early Soviet literature: in Pilnyak's *The Naked Year*, Babel's stories, or *The Master and Margarita*. Lastly, here is Hermann Broch in *The Sleepwalkers* (translated by Willa and Edwin Muir, Martin Secker, London 1932, pp. 79–80): 'To him Joachim and Ruzena seemed creatures who lived only with a small fraction of their being in the time to which they belonged, the age to which their years entitled them; and the greater part of them was somewhere else, perhaps on another star or in another century, or perhaps simply in their childhood. Bertrand was struck by the fact that the world was full of people belonging to different centuries, who had to live together, and were even contemporaries; that accounted perhaps for their instability and their difficulty in understanding one another rationally.'

[18] J. Kruse, *Der Tanz der Zeichen*, Anton Hain, Königstein/Ts 1985, especially pp. 156–66. The clearest example of this compressed present is the 'Helen' Act. Where are we here, and 'when'? In the age of the Homeric poems? – classical tragedy? – the 'migrations of peoples'? – the Crusades? – or the struggle for Greek independence?

ends by shattering against Galatea's mythical shell; the son of Helen and Faust repeats the flight of Icarus, and plunges to earth with the face of Byron. Economic crises in the first and fourth acts of Part Two; wars in the third and fourth; fires in the first, second and fifth; an earthquake during the Classical Walpurgis Night, which moreover commemorates the most celebrated civil war of Antiquity . . .

Criticism has so insisted on the 'serenity' of *Faust* Part Two that one scarcely gives it a second thought: but this is actually the poem of the 'state of exception'. And Faust, for his part, finds himself perfectly at ease in the radical crisis of every established order. Powerful, but not hampered by the weight of landed estates; always ready to move and to shift his own interests; remote, yet at the same time close to us – Faust is already the 'Stranger' of whom Wilhelmine sociology will speak. In his very person he embodies the imbalance of non-contemporaneity and exploits it ruthlessly. He always arrives with Mephistopheles from another epoch, bearing with him some brilliant invention with which he upsets the normal course of things, so that he is then needed once again to re-establish order. It is his way of penetrating every place and effectively taking control of it. To go back to the theme of the last chapter, it is a way of constituting a totality and turning it to his own advantage. And yet . . .

And yet, after first destroying then saving an empire, Faust asks for a ridiculous reward: a strip of salt water, where 'no such land exists' (11039). 'Let him be master who'll impose/Peace', the Imperial Diet proclaims (10279): and the one to make peace is Faust. But Faust renounces the empire. Why?

'So many little independent worlds'

Marlowe, *Doctor Faustus*:

> Had I as many souls as there be stars,
> I'd give them all for Mephistophilis.
> By him I'll be great emperor of the world
> And make a bridge thorough the moving air
> To pass the ocean with a band of men.
> I'll join the hills that bind the Afric shore

> And make that country continent to Spain
> And both contributory to my crown.
> The Emperor shall not live but by my leave
> Nor any potentate of Germany.
>> Act I, Sc. 3, 102–111

Here is a Faust who likes giving orders. A Tamburlaine–Faust, dazzled by the idea of territorial empire: a politico-military unit that razes enemy frontiers to the ground and makes the whole world into a single continent, with a single sovereign at its centre. But the world has changed between Marlowe and Goethe, and the dream of a planet levelled by arms no longer makes much sense. Immanuel Wallerstein:

> It is the peculiarity of the modern world-system that a world-economy has survived for 500 years and yet has not come to be transformed into a world-empire – a peculiarity that is the secret of its strength.
>
> This peculiarity is the political side of the form of economic organization called capitalism. Capitalism has been able to flourish precisely because the world-economy has had within its bounds not one but a multiplicity of political systems.
>
> [. . .] capitalism as an economic mode is based on the fact that the economic factors operate within an arena larger than that which any political entity can totally control. This gives capitalists a freedom of manoeuvre that is structurally based.[19]

Let us be clear. It is not that the advent of the capitalist world-system makes the Faustian aspiration to world dominance null and void. If anything, the opposite is true: it gives it extra sustenance and scope – and even extra wickedness. But such dominance is no longer conceivable as military conquest pure and simple, and the Marlowesque figure of the 'emperor of the world' no longer has any real meaning. That is where the new Faust comes in. One who has nothing of the warrior about him, as we saw in Chapter 1 (even if he by no means rules out others fighting on his behalf); and who, instead of laying waste the world, prefers to 'incorporate it': to insert here and there such limited but highly effective

---

[19] I. Wallerstein, *The Modern World-System*, Academic Press, New York–San Francisco–London 1974, p. 348.

devices as banknotes or a feudal castle, which will tilt the reality of things to his own advantage.[20] Just like the great hegemonic powers of the modern world, moreover, Faust is interested not in a uniform subjection, but in dominance of the sea and the sky, in order to move speedily from one end to the other of this composite system (Greek periphery in Act III, imperial semi-periphery in Act IV, 'Dutch' core in Act V).[21]

In this light, the well-known dispute about the unity of Goethe's poem may perhaps be viewed with fresh eyes. All the main scenes of *Faust*, says Eckermann on 13 February 1831,

> are so many little independent worlds, each complete in itself; and although they do impinge upon one another, they scarcely come into any contact. The poet's principal object is to represent a multiform world, and he uses the story of a famous hero merely as a sort of connecting thread upon which to string together whatsoever he pleases. – 'You are perfectly correct', Goethe replied . . .

No, perhaps not quite perfectly. The famous hero is something more than a mere thread: and *Faust*, for its part, is the story of how the independence of those 'little worlds' is lost. To be sure, the 'grand world' is by no means uniform, here. However, it is always *one*. A question of narrative technique will help clarify the matter.

'The autonomy of the parts', Schiller writes to Goethe in April 1797, 'is a fundamental characteristic of epic poetry.' This is a judgement that

---

[20] On the concept of 'incorporation', see *The Modern World-System III*, Academic Press, London 1989, pp. 127 ff. Wallerstein fixes the moment of the process's greatest intensity – when Russia, the Ottoman Empire, India and West Africa are engulfed by it – between 1750 and 1850: a century four-fifths of which overlap with Goethe's life, and whose central sixty years (1772–1832) cover the composition of *Faust*. In his *Civilisation de l'Europe des Lumières* (Paris 1971), Pierre Chaunu likewise locates around 1780 'the beginning of the erosion by Europe of other cultural-temporal spaces'.

[21] The transition from dominance of the land to that of the sea is signalled also by Melville: 'Let America add Mexico to Texas, and pile Cuba upon Canada; let the English overswarm all India, and hang out their blazing banner from the sun; two thirds of this terraqueous globe are the Nantucketer's. For the sea is his; he owns it, as Emperors own empires . . .' (*Moby-Dick*, 14).

Goethe, and later Hegel, accept almost as given (and that recurs as such in Eckermann's words). In the previous century, however, the matter had been far from obvious. In a late seventeenth-century article we find:

> One of the principal Rules in this [Epic] Poem, is Unity of Action [. . .] And therefore 'tis requisite so to connect all the *Episodes* in the principal Action, that they may necessarily depend upon one another: they must be the Members of the Body to which they are united.[22]

The members of the body to which they are united . . . The autonomy of the parts is hard to reconcile with the neo-classical taste for symmetry and centralism; and indeed, twenty years later, the metaphor of the epic body reaches its logical conclusions:

> If these Digressions [which perhaps best deserve the Appellation of Episodes] are forc'd and unnatural, that is, if they do not evidently arise from some incident or Episode of the Action, by the Mediation of which they are connected to the Poem, they are no more a part of it, than a Worm is of an Animal, to which it adheres, or than Ivy or Woodbine are parts of the Tree, to which they cling [. . .] And if they swell to a great length, by which the main Action is forgotten and left out of Sight, they are so many Tumours and large Excrescencies, that deform the Narration, and weaken its Force.[23]

The organicist conception, as we know, has the rare virtue of being always wrong: but in this case it is even more than usually so, since an epic of the kind Blackmore wanted, completely innocent of digression, would have to exclude half of Homer and half of Virgil. So, some way must be found to save the primacy of the Action, while still recognizing the *de facto* reality of digression. And halfway through the eighteenth century the solution emerges: Henry Home subdivides the category of the subordinate episode, in such a way that he can attribute one type of event (the 'incident') to the unfolding of the action, and another (the 'episode') to its enlargement:

---

[22] The article appeared in the *Athenian Mercury* on 26 January 1695, and is included in H.T. Swedenberg Jr, ed., *The Theory of the Epic in England 1650–1800*, California University Press, Berkeley–Los Angeles 1944, p. 220.

[23] Blackmore, *Essays upon Several Subjects*, 1716, vol. 1, pp. 56–7: included in ibid., p. 224.

Every incident that promotes or retards the catastrophe . . . must be part of the principal action. This clears the nature of an episode, which may be defined: 'An incident connected with the principal action, but which contributes not either to advance or to retard it.' The descent of Aeneas into hell doth not advance or retard the catastrophe; and therefore is an episode.[24]

An episode that neither advances the action, nor retards it. And how is that possible? By leaving the stage, is the reply implicit in Home's words. By moving *into another world*: the Hades of the *Odyssey*, the *Aeneid*, or the beginning of *The Cantos*; the Witches' Sabbath of *Faust*, the Ocean of *Moby-Dick*, the Library of *Bouvard and Pécuchet*, or the Sahara of *Peer Gynt*. The interruption to the narrative is here part and parcel of a geographical extension. History becomes slower, and the world wider.[25]

So far I have spoken about the first half of the epic world: the 'independent worlds' of Eckermann, the 'autonomous parts' of Schiller and Goethe. And the second half? The incorporated, unified world of Faust and Mephistopheles? Perhaps we may turn here to a different theory of the epic form. The epic is linearity, writes David Quint:

> . . . teleology: all events are led, or dictated, by an end that is their cause. [. . .] The narrative shape of this history-as-triumph bears an affinity with the well-made literary plot – the plot that presents a whole with its linked beginning, middle and end.[26]

And here is Morton Bloomfield:

---

[24] H. Home (Lord Kames), *Elements of Criticism* (1762), Huntington and Savage, New York 1843, pp. 424–5. The quotation is taken from Chapter 23, 'Epic and Dramatic Compositions'.

[25] Not all narrative genres, incidentally, can admit this spatial and temporal expansion: the nineteenth-century novel, for example, specializing in the compact and homogeneous space of the nation-state, has very little room for digression (and contemporary narratology, constructed upon the novel, has indeed 'forgotten' the category of digression).

[26] D. Quint, *Epic and Empire*, Princeton University Press, Princeton NJ 1992, p. 33.

Behind epic is the notion of following a pattern, *serving* one's destiny [. . .] The basic notion is serving and doing one's duty, not [. . .] wondering [. . .] In short, what is lacking in the typical epic is 'adventure', the opening out to the unexpected, the encounter with the unknown [. . .] The differentiating quality of romance, however, is just the absence of rationality and its replacement by irrational or unmotivated episodes. It is these episodes which are properly adventures and which give romances their particular flavour from the point of view of narrative technique.[27]

Doing one's duty, not wondering . . . No, this is a far more closed world than that of *Faust*. And it is so, I think, because of the conception Bloomfield and Quint have of the epic ending. For them, the ending represses every alternative possibility, and thus embodies a truly 'definitive' ideology: a destiny, a duty, a linear teleology. And yet . . .

And yet you open *Faust* at the decisive line – 11581: when Faust is on the point of halting the passing moment – and discover that Goethe crosses out the original 'I shall', replacing it by an 'I might' which leaves the wager forever open, and Faust's fate wholly uncertain. *Moby-Dick* finishes in a no-man's-land, undecided between Ahab's damnation and Ishmael's progress to maturity. 'Penelope', as we shall see, reopens *Ulysses* instead of concluding it. In *The Waste Land*, the univocal character of the allegory explodes into the fragments of the final lines, then dissolves into the Sanskrit word whose meaning 'passeth understanding'. Not to speak of *Bouvard and Pécuchet*, *The Man Without Qualities*, or *The Cantos*, which never reached a conclusion at all; or *The Nibelung's Ring*, whose ending is changed four times, before settling upon the least teleological version by far . . .

All weak, indecisive endings, that neither conclude the text nor settle its meaning once and for all. Does this mean that the modern epic remains an ensemble devoid of unity, an archipelago of 'independent worlds' like that of Eckermann? No, not necessarily. It merely means that the unity of this form does not lie in a *definitive conclusion*, but in its perennial *ability to begin again*. A unified world is not necessarily a *closed* world:

---

[27] M.W. Bloomfield, 'Episodic Motivation and Marvels in Epic and Romance', in *Essays and Explorations*, Harvard University Press, Cambridge Mass. 1960, pp. 105–6.

and if *Faust* is made up almost entirely of digressions, that does not mean that it lacks any unitary Action – but that *the digressions have themselves become the main purpose of the epic Action.*

Digressions – indeed, their very proliferation – as substance and purpose of the Action. And why not? Digression, Alessandro Portelli has written, is the technique that seeks 'to fit the whole world inside a single text': just what is needed for the modern epic.[28] Faust's movement from world to world is *a sign of his power*: it indicates the freedom of movement, the spiritual mobility, the cynicism even, that are necessary in the new world-system. After all, the closed ending of Bloomfield and Quint was the appropriate conclusion for a territorial empire: for the rectilinear Action of the military campaign, which aims precisely to eradicate any alternative development. But in the case of the world-system, the teleology of this premodern plot is replaced by the perpetual digression of *exploration*: an activity that by no means excludes violence, but that operates in a system with too many variables to obtain definitive results.[29]

There remains a very solid link between epic and power, then – but it no longer takes the form of a goal to be reached, because every goal is now felt as a fetter: a *limitation* of power, rather than a confirmation of it. We can glimpse here what will be the most typical ideology of the twentieth century: ideology as an opening of possibilities, rather than their repression. We shall return to this later.

World texts. I

Back to Bloch. 'Germany in general', he observes in his 1932 essay,

> which did not accomplish a bourgeois revolution until 1918, is, unlike
> England and much less France, the classical land of nonsynchronism,

---

[28] A. Portelli, *The Text and the Voice: Writing, Speaking, and Democracy in American Literature*, Columbia University Press, New York 1994.

[29] This structure is prefigured to a great extent by the *Odyssey*, with its digressions towards an unknown that is then regularly defeated. I do not believe it is any accident that the *Odyssey*, in its turn, is the representation not of an empire, but of a world-system – the Mediterranean – where the local terror of mythical powers is 'incorporated' in the network of sea routes.

that is, of unsurmounted remnants of older economic being and con-sciousness.[30]

England and France on the one hand, Germany on the other. Non-synchronism, Bloch here suggests, is connected with a specific position within the world-system: unknown to the relatively homogeneous states of the core, it is typical of the semi-periphery where, by contrast, com-bined development prevails. And it is precisely there that we find many of the masterpieces of the modern epic form: in the still divided Germany of Goethe (and of the early Wagner); in Melville's America (the *Pequod*: bloodthirsty hunting, and industrial production); in Joyce's Ireland (a colony, which nevertheless speaks the same language as the occupier); in certain zones of Latin America.[31] All, as I was saying, sites of combined development: where historically non-homogeneous social and symbolic forms, often originating in quite disparate places, coexist in a confined space. In this sense, *Faust* is not 'German', just as *Ulysses* is not 'Irish' or *One Hundred Years of Solitude* 'Colombian': they are all *world* texts, whose geographical frame of reference is no longer the nation-state, but a broader entity – a continent, or the world-system as a whole.[32]

---

[30] Bloch, *Heritage of Our Times*, pp. 90–91.

[31] A possible geography of literary forms emerges here: while world texts are con-centrated in the semi-periphery, the novel by contrast flourishes in the highly homogeneous national cultures of France and England, at the core of the world-system. (Modern tragedy has a different geography again, about which I have written in an essay entitled 'The Moment of Truth', in *Signs Taken for Wonders*, 2nd enlarged edn, Verso, London 1987.)

[32] Russian literature presents a particular case in this respect, and one of great inter-est, in which epic and novel are intertwined with an intensity unknown to other European literatures (Pushkin, Gogol, Tolstoy, Dostoevsky, Pasternak: see F.T. Griffiths and S.J. Rabinowitz, *Novel Epics*, Northwestern University Press, Evanston 1990, pp. 1–4). There thus emerges a compromise formation between epic and novel (*Novel Epics* = 'new' epics, but also 'novelistic' epics) that is in full accord with the Russian 'nation-empire', which constitutes almost a world apart. It is interesting that the United States of America – another geopolitical reality broader than the European type of nation-state – should likewise have produced a literature rich in epic attempts. Unlike the Russian case, however, the American epic has clear cosmopolitan tendencies, and the gravitational force of the great nineteenth-century novel is almost unnoticeable in it.

The construction of national identity – henceforth required of the novel – is thus replaced, for the epic, by a far larger geographical ambition: a global ambition, of which *Faust* is the unchallenged archetype. The take-off of the world-system has occurred – and a *symbolic form* has also been found for this new reality. But what technique is to be used to represent the world?

We arrived at non-contemporaneity through a discussion of history: it was necessary to explain the smashing of linear time in *Faust* Part Two. Developing Bloch's theses, on the other hand, history has become intertwined with geography. In Reinhardt Koselleck's studies, the interdependence increases:

> [The] fundamental experience of progress, embodied in a singular concept around 1800, is rooted in the knowledge of noncontemporaneities which exist at a chronologically uniform time. From the seventeenth century on, historical experience was increasingly ordered [in accordance with these].

And again:

> The geographical opening up of the globe brought to light various but coexisting cultural levels which were, through the process of synchronous comparison, then ordered diachronically.[33]

So this is what constitutes 'the fundamental experience of progress': transforming synchrony into diachrony; taking geographical facts, neutral in themselves (social forms of a different kind), and arranging them according to an ascending teleology – which will then end by legitimizing the dominion of the 'advanced' West over the 'backward' periphery. For world texts, which likewise work upon non-contemporaneous phenomena, nothing would be more logical than to share this finalism. And some do indeed follow the model of the philosophy of history: Imre Madach's 1862 *The Tragedy of Man* (which begins with Adam and Eve, and goes on to the Pharaohs, Miltiades, patricians and Christians, Kepler,

---

[33] R. Koselleck, ' "Neuzeit": remarks on the semantics of the modern concepts of movement', in *Futures Past*, translated by Keith Tribe, MIT Press, Boston 1985, pp. 147–8.

Danton . . .); or Shaw's *Back to Methusaleh*, which is perhaps the biggest piece of trash in universal literature.[34] But *Faust* is quite another matter, and not just because it is better. The fact is that, if it is read in teleological terms, it becomes quite incomprehensible. It starts off from the Renaissance of the Imperial Court, then moves from there to the Mothers who exist before and outside time; it goes back to the Renaissance, where French Revolution *assignats* crop up; then it goes back to the Classical Walpurgis Night, on the anniversary of Pharsalus; farther back – between Homer and the tragedians – with the 'Helen' Act; forward to the Crusades; back to Arcadia; two millennia forward in the vision of Byron, then again to the Renaissance; the ghosts of mediaeval wars are evoked; it moves forward to Holland, and then to the industrial visions of the dying Faust; and ends in a Marian-Catholic atmosphere, between Middle Ages and Counter-Reformation.

This is a sequence which – as a sequence – has no meaning. Rather than a teleological development, Goethe has constructed a zigzag that leaps from one epoch to another without any consistency; and as for the destination of the whole, the 'Mountain Gorges' scene still awaits a defender adequate to the task. In Part Two, history cannot be taken literally, as history: for it to have any meaning, it must be interpreted as a great rhetorical figure. It must stand for something else. But for what?

The ideology of progress, as we have seen, privileges *non-contemporaneity* of the contemporaneous: the 'Alongside' becomes a 'Before-and-After', and geography is rewritten as history. Well, for the modern epic the opposite is true: *contemporaneity* of the non-contemporaneous moves into the foreground: the 'Before-and-After' is transformed into an 'Alongside' – and history thus becomes a gigantic *metaphor for geography*. The treasures with which Mephistopheles sets the great machine of Part Two in motion, writes Francesco Orlando, are 'a German substitute for colonial resources: derived not from the distance of adventure, but from the depths of the past'; in the early nineteenth century, adds Peter Burke,

---

[34] E.M. Butler (*The Fortunes of Faust*, Cambridge University Press, Cambridge 1952, p. 275) alludes also to a not very promising 1895 *Faust und Prometheus* by H. Hango. It remains to be explained why on earth the philosophy of history should have such a devastating effect on literature.

'the ancient, the distant and the popular were all equated'.[35] In this metaphorical field, which seems to unite more or less the whole of European culture, the shifting back and forth in time of Faust and Mephistopheles loses its senselessness: if we replace the 'ancient' by the 'distant', the zigzag then turns into a series of geographical expeditions, where arrival in far-off epochs recounts (and masks) landing on distant shores. And as for Goethe's games with the past, or those legendary personages who end up 'working' for Faust – they too are metaphors: for playing with the world, and for a concrete power over real persons in the present. And since every metaphor always involves an emotive aspect, a value judgement, let us add: once again, they are metaphors *of innocence*, which present the power of the West as something fundamentally innocuous. Doing violence to the past, when all is said and done, is of no importance. You cannot harm a phantasm.

The hypertrophy of historical culture, according to one of the most brilliant theses of the young Nietzsche, was a 'fault and defect' of the nineteenth century. It weakened and discouraged the creative instinct, so as to 'uproot the strongest instincts of youth':

> All living things need an atmosphere, a mysterious mist, around them [. . .] such a veil of illusion, such a protecting cloud. But [history, a] light too clear, too sudden and dazzling, is the infamous means used to blind [men].[36]

And if we were to reverse this hypothesis? If the history so liberally dispensed by world texts were precisely the appropriate illusion for a Europe bent on conquering the globe? The 'walking encyclopaedias' mocked by Nietzsche as grotesque outcomes of a century sick with history – here they are: *Faust, Ulysses, Cantos, Waste Land* . . . Thanks to them, the West has gained the breadth of vision consonant with its new world power –

---

[35] F. Orlando, *Gli oggetti desueti nelle immagini della letteratura*, Einaudi, Turin 1993, p. 400; P. Burke, *Popular Culture in Early Modern Europe*, Harper, New York 1978, p. 10.

[36] F. Nietzsche, 'The Use and Abuse of History', in *Thoughts out of Season*, translated by Adrian Collins, T.N. Foulis, Edinburgh and London 1909, vol. 2, pp. 4, 88 and 60–61.

while keeping itself at a safe distance from crude geographical truth. Just think (to take a little leap ahead) of one compositional detail of *The Waste Land*: the choice of epigraph. Initially, Eliot thinks of a phrase from *Heart of Darkness*. An interesting choice: it would have been the only reference to contemporary Africa in the entire poem; placing it at the beginning, moreover, would have presented non-contemporaneity (of which *The Waste Land* is a magisterial example) as a geopolitical phenomenon linked to colonial conquest. But Pound intervenes, and Conrad's phrase disappears: the definitive draft opens with a swirl of English, Latin, Greek and Italian, in which politics disappears and history replaces geography. It is the most esoteric, but perhaps also most effective, form of the rhetoric of innocence.[37]

Rhetoric of innocence: history as metaphor for geography. I have spoken of these constructions stressing their social utility: their ideological function. But what kind of ideologies are these? Who has ever heard of them? No one, I think, *and that is why they are interesting.* For, in the great concert of ideology, literature has *its own* arias: fresh, unrepeatable – not 'foreseen' by the surrounding ideologies. The epic form comes close, for example, to the ideology of progress, and even works with the same ingredients; yet it does not give us an 'epic of progress', just as – to mention an analogous case – the English and French novels of the nineteenth century never give us a 'novel of liberalism'. And in both cases the reason is the same: a society does not normally have any need for duplicates.[38] Once a thing has been said in one language, there is no

---

[37] Another example. In *The Waste Land* there are some fifty geographical references, with England (sixteen mentions, mostly to London) and the Mediterranean (seventeen mentions, mostly to its southeastern shore) predominating. The City, in other words, and the extra-European peoples caught in the Western world-system: very realistic. Apart from a couple of exceptions, however, the mentions of England all refer to the *present day*, those of the Mediterranean to *antiquity*. The encounter between the two geopolitical realities is thus transformed into an encounter between different epochs, where the historical aspect is far more visible than the geographical.

[38] About fifteen years ago, it occurred to me to study the novel of liberalism. It took me five years to understand that it did not exist, and another ten to understand why. But I succeeded.

interest in repeating it wholesale in another language (even supposing – which I do not admit, incidentally – that this would be possible).

'Unforeseen' ideologies, then. And unforeseen for a very simple reason: because they are born not as *ideologies*, but as *rhetorical experiments*. Mephistopheles permits symbolic moves of immense importance: yet, as we have seen, his own origin is accidental, and it is only by manoeuvring his figure more or less at random that the rhetoric of innocence takes shape, without any conscious project. And the same thing is repeated with non-contemporaneity. In a first moment, Goethe is merely coming to grips with the epic form: hence, as its conventions require, he makes Faust advance into the great world of the past. Here a second stage begins (likewise fundamentally rhetorical), in which Goethe starts to play with the relationship between past, present and future, thus creating those strange scenes in which different epochs meet and mingle. And finally there is a third stage, in which this work of *bricolage* shows that it can confront (and camouflage) a historical experience of immense importance: the new world dominance of the West. The form has constructed its own ideology – and a very effective one. But all this is the result of a purely formal dynamic. It was not the primary object of Goethe's work, and rhetoric met history only at the end of the process.

But does it really make much difference whether ideology precedes rhetoric or follows it? It makes an enormous difference. For, in the former case, ideology might guide form to the desired end; not so in the latter, since it comes up against the rigidity of ready-made rhetorical choices. This is why literary ideology is always somewhat askew in relation to others: because it rests upon a jumble of fortuitous experiments, rhetorical fetters and unpredictable turns. Sometimes this way of doing things actually functions better than conscious discourse: it produces Mephistopheles, and the perverse, unsurpassed intelligence of Goethean innocence. At other times, however, the chain of formal choices imposes trappings that are perhaps too cumbersome. To stay with *Faust*, this is what happens with non-contemporaneity – where classical mythology involves perhaps too many scholastic ingredients to have a really widespread effectiveness. In the next chapter, we shall see a complication of yet another kind.

CHAPTER

3

'An incredible musical pandemonium'

Let us begin with an antithesis made famous by Mikhail Bakhtin: epic monologism ('unitary language'), and novelistic polyphony ('heteroglossia'). The former, Bakhtin writes, 'accomplishes the task of cultural, national and political centralization of the verbal-ideological world'. The latter, on the other hand, which 'sounds forth [. . .] at the lower levels, on the stages of local fairs and at buffoon spectacles', belongs to the sphere of 'decentralizing, centrifugal forces'.[1] In short, centripetal epic, and centrifugal novel: up to the eighteenth century, this is a convincing counterposition. But then things change, and literary evolution seems precisely to refute it. The nineteenth-century novel, for example, with its dialectic of provinces and capital pinning the story at the centre of the nation-state, acts in the opposite way to a centrifugal force. And the same holds for novelistic conversation, or the impersonal voice of the narrator: rather than nourishing polyphony, they impose a drastic *reduction* of it, giving birth to a more compact and homogeneous 'verbal-ideological world' in each new generation.

Pace Bakhtin, in short, the polyphonic form of the modern West is not

---

[1] M. Bakhtin, 'Discourse in the Novel', in *The Dialogic Imagination*, University of Texas Press, Austin 1981, p. 273.

the novel, but if anything precisely the epic: which specializes in the heterogeneous space of the world-system, and must learn to provide a stage for its many different voices. Already in *Faust*, in fact, polyphony is the style of the 'grand' world, whose otherness it signals vis-à-vis the 'little' one (though 'narrow' would perhaps be more accurate) in which Margareta lives. Here, as the girl's first words suggest – 'I'm not a lady, and I'm not sweet' (2607) – the purest monologism holds sway: things and persons have a single, immutable name. But along comes Faust, and the semantic rigidity of the narrow world is undermined: for his seduction consists largely in persuading Margareta to listen to 'wording' with 'a difference' from that of the priest, and to accept that 'all human hearts . . . speak the same message, *each in his own speech*' ('Martha's Garden', 3461, 3464). It is a coaxing, artful polyphony, which becomes wholly sinister in the 'Cathedral' scene, where the Evil Spirit's laughter mingles with the grim Latin chorus of the *Dies Irae* and with the desperate prayer of Margareta herself. The time is past when her thoughts were all bound up in a 'little worn prayer-book' (*Büchelchen*, 3779: the diminutive of a diminutive, for a tiny, little world). Faust has taught her many other words, and many thoughts. But it is a poisoned gift:

> Oh God! Oh God!
> If I could get rid of these thoughts
> That move across me and through me,
> Against my will!
>
> 3794–7

If I could get rid of these thoughts . . . The 'Prison' scene, when madness multiplies Margareta's 'voices' and takes her to the gallows, is the fitting complement for this black-magic polyphony. And yet, Goethe suggests, that very same power that acts with devastating violence in a confined world can play quite another role in a wider space. In the crowd scenes in *Faust* Part Two, polyphony no longer has anything sinister about it: it is an index of creativity, of euphoria. Each new voice is a new presence: autonomous, self-aware, clearly delineated. Voices of today, and of antiquity; real, and imaginary; sacred, and profane; alone, in groups, in chorus. . . .

But where are all these voices to be put? And even before that, indeed, how is their sudden appearance to be explained? The poem's chronology gives the answer: by the 'Walpurgis Night'. The first polyphonic scene to

Modern Epic

be composed by Goethe – and fortuitously so, no doubt, because of its obvious links with the Faust story. A fortuitous choice. Indeed, a dubious digression ('vulgar diversions', in Faust's own words) from the tremendous crescendo of Margareta's tragedy. But the digression works, and chance is transformed into necessity. The 'Walpurgis Night' is *selected*, and becomes the model for all the polyphonic scenes in Part Two: and, thereafter, for Melville, Flaubert, Kraus, Joyce, Pound, Döblin . . . Even for a musician:

> The following Sunday, we went on the same walk with Mahler. At the fête on the Kreuzberg, an even worse witches sabbath was in progress. Not only were innumerable barrel-organs blaring out from merry-go-rounds, swings, shooting galleries and puppet shows, but a military band and a men's choral society had established themselves there as well. All these groups, in the same forest clearing, were creating an incredible musical pandemonium without paying the slightest attention to each other. Mahler exclaimed: 'You hear? That's polyphony, and that's where I get it from!'[2]

Instead of Bakhtin's dialogic polyphony, critical and intelligent, just an incredible din. Voices that talk and talk without paying any attention to one another, as almost everywhere in *Faust* Part Two, or in the chapter 'Midnight. – Forecastle' of *Moby-Dick*, or in the Basilica of Heresies in *The Temptation of Saint Anthony*. According to certain alarmed reviews, this lack of harmony is indeed already outright dissonance: *Faust*, 'a cat jumping about on the piano keyboard'; *Moby-Dick*, 'mowing, gibbering, screaming, like an incurable Bedlamite'.[3]

In short, polyphony as cacophony. A defect? No. For, as I have already

---

[2] T.W. Adorno, *Mahler*, translated by Edmund Jephcott, University of Chicago Press, Chicago 1992, p. 112. The passage is taken from N. Bauer-Lechner, *Erinnerungen an Gustav Mahler*, Leipzig–Vienna–Zurich 1923, p. 147.

[3] The judgement on *Faust*, by R. Gottschell, dates from 1855 and is quoted by H. Schwerte, *Faust und das Faustische. Ein Kapitel deutscher Ideologie*, Klett, Stuttgart 1962, p. 119; the one on *Moby-Dick* appeared in the July 1855 issue of *New Monthly Magazine*, over the signature 'Sir Nathaniel' (probably W.H. Ainsworth), and is reproduced in the appendices to the edition of *Moby-Dick* edited by H. Hayford and H. Parker, Norton, New York and London 1967.

said, the choice of the witches' sabbath *works*: it is repeated from one work to another, because it resolves – albeit in a rather odd way – a decisive problem for the modern epic form. The fact is that Goethe and the others, needing to represent the take-off of the capitalist world-system, are in search of what we might call (paraphrasing Roland Barthes) 'world effects': devices that give the reader the impression of being truly in the presence of the world; that make the *text* look like the world – open, heterogeneous, incomplete. The Babel of the witches' sabbath is not, of course, the only possible solution to the problem. In the modernist epoch, for example, many others will emerge – from collage to free verse, from the emancipation of dissonance to metonymic drift. But meanwhile the witches' sabbath was there, and it worked, because a tumult of discordant voices always suggests a large, crowded space. Never mind if the scene appears chaotic and maybe a bit incomprehensible. In the expanding universe of modernity, many things are as yet unclear; and it is necessary to learn to live with noise: to represent it – and, indeed, hear it – without too many embellishments.

So, then: thirty-odd different voices in the first 'Walpurgis Night'; another thirty in the 'Dream'; and forty in the 'Classical Night'. Polyphony, to be sure: a world effect. But *where* to put them, all these voices? On Sunday 20 December 1829, talking to Eckermann about the allegorical masquerade (forty-odd different voices here too), Goethe observes that you would need 'a theatre so large as to be almost unimaginable' ('a theatre of Mars', as Kraus will say of *The Last Days of Mankind*, with its hundreds of characters). And indeed, among all the reasons why *Faust* Part Two is 'unperformable', there is certainly also the fact that the confined space of the stage is incompatible with the expansive movement of an action seeking to give voice to an entire world. 'It is amazing', Rudolf Arnheim observes, 'how little Goethe worked for the stage, how entirely in the expressive material of verbal art.'[4]

Amazing, yes, if humankind had been created by Hegel, and accordingly set itself only such problems as it could already solve. If that is not the case, however, then there is really nothing strange. Goethe finds himself

---

4 R. Arnheim, *Radio*, translated by Margaret Ludwig and Herbert Read, Faber and Faber, London 1936, p. 182.

confronted by a completely new world order, and he tries to grapple with it by constructing a symbolic form capable of representing its essence. If the technical means at his disposal reach only so far, fine! – it will be a partial solution, imperfect as usual. And the polyphony of the witches' sabbath is precisely that. A great discovery, but a far from definitive one. So long as you read it, it works. But if you try to stage it, Arnheim goes on, then it becomes a 'museum curiosity': 'all the harder', moreover, 'if imaginary forms are to be represented which have a voice but no body [. . .] What will happen in the case of the spirits?'[5]

The answer, Arnheim concludes, arrives a century after *Faust*. It is radio: the disembodied voice that opens the gates of everyday life to polyphony.[6] Eckermann and Goethe had been on the wrong track: the masquerade did not require immense stages crammed full of yelling extras. It did not need *more* space, but a parallel space. Like that of radio, in fact – or even, as we shall see, that of the stream of consciousness. But in the meantime? Between the prophetic magic of *Faust* and twentieth-century technology, how to imagine a space for polyphony? And where to locate it?

First and foremost, far away from the nation-states situated in the core of the world-system, which are becoming ever more homogeneous, hence ever less polyphonic. To achieve their encyclopaedic dream, Flaubert's two copyists decide first and foremost – *À la campagne!* – to flee the capital that has invented the language of bureaucracy. And the author of *Bartleby*, who is likewise well acquainted with bureaucratic monologism, dispatches Ishmael to New Bedford (where 'actual cannibals stand chatting at street corners': *Moby-Dick*, 6); and then even farther away, onto the Ocean, where 'far more than in [the life of] terra firma, wild rumours abound' (*Moby-Dick*, 40).

But it is still not enough. Compared with *Faust*, the works of Melville and Flaubert do not show us what it would be reasonable to expect – in

---

[5] Ibid., pp. 181–2 (translation modified).

[6] 'I anticipated the damn thing in the first third of *Cantos*', wrote Pound to Ronald Duncan on 31 March 1940, in a letter where – what more could you ask? – radio is defined as a 'devil box' (now in D. Paige, ed., *The Letters of Ezra Pound*, Harcourt, New York 1950, pp. 342–3). 'Just as newspaper culture was endemic in *Ulysses*, the *Wake* is full of the new culture of the airwaves', adds Patrick Parrinder (*James Joyce*, Cambridge University Press, Cambridge 1984, p. 231).

other words, a development of the new polyphonic technique – but a drastic *reduction* of it. A few examples, then we shall try to understand why.

Polyphony in America. I

In Melville's novel, there is certainly no lack of polyphonic elements. There is the initial encounter between Ishmael and Queequeg, under the banner of religious tolerance and dialogue between different cultures. On a more ambitious scale, there is the ethnic heterogeneity of the crew, illustrated in the chapter 'Midnight. – Forecastle' (and saluted by Starbuck – to underline the 'Walpurgis Night' atmosphere – as 'infernal orgies' of a 'heathen crew': *Moby-Dick*, 37). On a still vaster scale, there are the 'two thirds of this terraqueous globe', the passing ships, the four continents skirted by the *Pequod*. And if we move from the story to discourse, there are the 'Extracts' that preface the novel, and the encyclopaedism permeating almost all of it. And yet . . .

And yet, the story of *Moby-Dick* is that of a lost polyphony. Ishmael and Queequeg are separated, the crew kicks up a row for one night then falls silent for ever, the wider world remains far away – as though held at a distance. Why on earth? In the first place, because of Captain Ahab's 'irresistible dictatorship' (*Moby-Dick*, 32), which imprisons the voices of the *Pequod* in a vow that brooks no objection. 'The mastering word alone can work my will', cried the aged Faust (11502, translation adapted): well, this monologic fury inhabits Ahab from the outset, and another famous line ('One mind shall move a thousand hands': 11510) sounds far truer for the *Pequod*'s crewmen than for Goethe's lemurs. This linguistic grip is complemented, moreover, by the geographical contraction of the pursuit ('and I'll chase him *round* Good Hope, and *round* the Horn, and *round* the Norway Maelstrom . . .': *Moby-Dick*, 35), which drives the *Pequod* 'round' every obstacle and onward, blind and deaf to its surroundings. No digressions on this sea journey, no curiosity or memorable encounter: Ahab is truly the opposite of Odysseus, and for him the whole universe is merely a backdrop. His world is a closed and narrow one: made up of a single creature, in whose whiteness all the colours of the universe are concentrated – and vanish.

Reduction of polyphony within the plot, therefore. And then a second reduction, at the level of discourse. Here, the monologic device is the voice of Ishmael (Ishmael as narrator): *one* voice, omnipresent and situated at a level where no other can respond to it, and thus call it into question. In the central part of the novel, roughly half the chapters are in fact concluded by the narrator's reflections – a strategic placement, investing Ishmael's words with particular authority:

> Consider all this; and then turn to this green, gentle, and most docile earth; consider them both, the sea and the land; and do you not find a strange analogy to something in yourself?
>
> *Moby-Dick*, 57

> But why say more? All men live enveloped in whale-lines. All are born with halters round their necks; but it is only when caught in the swift, sudden turn of death, that mortals realize the silent, subtle, ever-present perils of life. And if you be a philosopher, though seated in the whale-boat, you would not at heart feel one whit more of terror, than though seated before your evening fire with a poker, and not a harpoon, by your side.
>
> *Moby-Dick*, 59

> But Stubb, he eats the whale by its own light, does he? and that is adding insult to injury, is it? Look at your knife-handle, there, my civilized and enlightened gourmand dining off that roast beef, what is that handle made of? – what but the bones of the brother of the very ox you are eating? And what do you pick your teeth with, after devouring that fat goose? With a feather of the same fowl. And with what quill did the Secretary of the Society for the Suppression of Cruelty to Ganders formally indite his circulars? It is only within the last month or two that that society passed a resolution to patronize nothing but steel pens.
>
> *Moby-Dick*, 64

Melville's rhetoric, here, is always the same. To start with, he turns to the reader: questions him, teases him, forces him to reflect on the meaning of what he is reading. And then he explains it to him. To be sure, *Moby-Dick* is a sea story (especially the Cetology chapters); but the sea is like the earth, just as sailors are like townsfolk, or matter like spirit. 'Understanding' *Moby-Dick* means following its analogies: accepting the idea that the world has a meaning – because it has two. Ahab:

O Nature, and O soul of man! how far beyond all utterance are your linked analogies! Not the smallest atom stirs or lives in matter, but has its cunning duplicate in mind.

Moby-Dick, 69

Duplicate in mind: the second meaning of the analogy. But second in order of appearance, certainly not of importance. Chapter after chapter, the relationship between the two sides of the sign tilts further and further out of balance – and always in the same direction. The first term of comparison is of extremely diverse provenance: geographical, anatomical, legal, historical, commercial. The second term, however, is always the same. Whatever the point of departure, the destination remains unchanged: the moral nature of human beings. The 'duplicate' is really a centre: if we wish to be mischievous, it is a sort of black hole, capturing and swallowing up all forms of speech that pass close to it. In the last resort, the ambition of the narrator of *Moby-Dick* is precisely this: to take the multifarious codes of nature and culture, and to demonstrate that they are all to be found in the moral super-code. To take polyphony, in other words, and reduce it to a single language: ultimately, to eliminate it altogether. But without malice. In a calm, accessible, friendly way – presenting the whole process as a way of understanding one another better. Is so benevolent a monologism really possible?

Polyphony in America. II

Reduction of polyphony. Strange, if you consider the genesis of the United States. As Melville puts it in *Redburn*, 'Settled by the people of all nations, all nations may claim her for their own [. . .] We are not a nation, so much as a world.' And Whitman, in the 1855 manifesto-preface to *Leaves of Grass*: 'Here is not merely a nation but a teeming nation of nations.' The world in miniature, in short. 'Passage to India':

> Tying the Eastern to the Western sea,
> The road between Europe and Asia.

> (Ah Genoese, thy dream! thy dream!
> Centuries after thou art laid in thy grave
> The shore thou foundest verifies thy dream!)

63

In Whitman's America, non-contemporaneity has become a daily, collective reality: languages, customs and divinities from other epochs, making the New World – epically – 'the greatest poem'. An 'unrhymed' poem, the 1855 Preface goes on: as yet unsung, but also not to be 'marshalled in rhyme'. Not to be fettered, in other words, by those rigid forms that have made European poetry 'blind to the particulars and details that move in splendour among great masses': incapable, in short, of representing the variety of a polyphonic world. Allen Grossman comments:

> Whitman's policy was to establish a new principle of access that would effect multiplication, or pluralization (the getting many into one), without the loss entailed by exchange [. . .] In the chronology of Whitman's work, the 'open' line as formal principle appears simultaneously with the subject of liberation, and is the enabling condition of the appearance of that subject.[7]

A 'rhetoric of inclusivity' is thus asserted, Grossman continues, which replaces 'syntactic centralization' by the new technique of the 'sequence of equipollent lines'.[8] Sequence – or list: one of the devices most typical of the epic form. And one that allows Whitman – writes Leo Spitzer in his essay on chaotic enumeration – to construct some of the best-known effects in modern poetry: the fragment, chaotism, the magic of proper nouns, the 'democracy of things', cosmopolitanism . . .

So here they are, the space and the technique of polyphony: America, and the List. 'We must insist that it is the American continent, with its enormous size, that made the global world-view possible', Spitzer also writes. And again:

> There is no real anachronism in finding a link between Whitman's lists – *der Katalogdichter*, the bard of the catalogue, as Eulenberg called him – and the great almanacs of assorted goods. *Leaves of Grass* was

---

[7] A. Grossman, 'The Poetics of Union in Whitman and Lincoln', in W.B. Michaels and D.E. Pease, eds, *The American Renaissance Reconsidered*, Johns Hopkins University Press, Baltimore and London 1985, pp. 191–2.

[8] Ibid., pp. 193, 195.

published in 1855, and it is precisely around that date that the huge development began of the bazaars of the West – the department stores.[9]

Der Katalogdichter. And indeed, in the 1855 Preface the first description of the United States is also the work's first list, as if the latter were unimaginable without the former, and vice versa. But is it equally certain that the list is, as Grossman has it, 'the formal principle of liberation'? 'Song of Myself', Section 51:

> Do I contradict myself?
> Very well, then, I contradict myself:
> (I am large – I contain multitudes).

'I am large – I contain multitudes.' But what does this 'contain' mean? Include and shelter? Or perhaps, instead, rein in and control? And what is the list, then: a transparent medium, which leaves intact the autonomy of the things listed? – or a form in its own way dense and opaque, which imparts its colour to whatsoever falls within its orbit?

Let us start off again from Grossman (who incidentally defends the former hypothesis with intelligence). In a sequence of 'equipollent' lines, it normally happens that with each new line something changes (usually the object mentioned), and something else remains unaltered. In the simplest cases – like the Welcomes in 'Song of the Broad-Axe' – the constant element is an expression complete in itself, which accompanies the descriptive content of the list with a sort of emotive crescendo. Elsewhere a pronoun may be involved, or an adverb ('you', 'where', 'when'); and in such cases – which are also the most common – the more numerous the things listed, the more the semantic weight of the invariant element expands. In 'Song of the Open Road', for example, the many places mentioned have the 'you' apostrophizing them all gradually superimposed upon them, transforming the list from a purely descriptive sequence into an endless, tense harangue. Or again, in the thirty-third section of 'Song of Myself', the word 'where' – repeated dozens of times at the beginning of a line – eventually acquires a hypnotic force, subordinating to itself those scenes to which, at the strictly

---

9 L. Spitzer, 'La enumeración caótica en la poesia moderna', in *Linguistica y Historia Literaria*, Greidos, Madrid 1961, pp. 297 and 259 n.

grammatical level, it would itself be subordinated. You forget the bear searching for honey, and the steamship; but you certainly remember the ubiquity of that American where/everywhere, which passes from place to place without meeting any obstacles. You forget, in other words, the things listed; and you remember, instead, the *form* that holds them together and gives them meaning.

And this is the point. Whitman's list is not a neutral container, but an organizing module: a 'symbolic form', in Panofsky's sense, which subordinates the variety of America to an omnipresent and invariant poetic voice. A voice, or more precisely a grid – a *gaze*. 'I see' or 'I look' are the most common locutions used to establish the list: which, moreover, is almost always a collection of things observed. It is the 'unrhymed poetry' of the 1855 Preface: the 'democracy of things' (Spitzer), which finally makes visible the objects ignored by the old poetry. And yet, behind the egalitarian euphoria of that fine-sounding expression, something very different may be glimpsed: control, and surveillance. Bentham's Panopticon, and Polanyi's 'total inspectability'; the removal of roofs yearned for by Dickens and by Sherlock Holmes; the glass houses of Zamyatin and Orwell . . . There were some, after all, who spotted it at once:

> Above this race of men stands an immense and tutelary power, which takes upon himself alone to secure their gratifications and to watch over their fate. That power is absolute, minute, regular, provident, and mild . . .[10]

Absolute, and minute: like the list, with its abstract regularity, and its countless concrete details. And 'watching over' is truly appropriate for the Great Listmaker:

> I go from bedside to bedside – I sleep close with the other sleepers, each in turn,
> I dream in my dream all the dreams of the other dreamers,
> And I become the other dreamers.
>
> 'The Sleepers'

'I have no mockings or arguments – I witness and wait', adds the I of

---

[10] A. de Tocqueville, 'What sort of despotism democratic nations have to fear', in *Democracy in America*, vol. 2, Knopf, New York 1951, p. 318.

'Song of Myself' (section 4); 'And am around, tenacious, acquisitive, tireless, and cannot be shaken away' (section 7). Is it the voice of a poet, saying such things? Or is it not rather the Police?

> I teach straying from me – yet who can stray from me?
> I follow you, whoever you are, from the present hour.
>
> 'Song of Myself', 47

Let us conclude. Whitman's interest in oratory, pointed out in his day by Matthiessen, shows through in the extreme frequency with which he resorts to rhetorical questions: constructions, in other words, that allow a doubt – even a dialogue – to be simulated, but without their achieving actual expression. For with rhetorical questions the orator puts a second voice on the stage, rather than allowing a second orator to speak. Better: he invents a second voice *in order that* there be no second orator. This too is a rhetoric of inclusivity: of a very different sort, however, from Grossman's. The other does enter Whitman's poem, to be sure, but like a ventriloquist's doll. It is a bogus other. In short, once again, it is monologism. But a monologism that is ashamed of itself, and dresses itself up as polyphony: democratic monologism, as it were.[11] Another analytical section, and I shall return to it.

'With all the certainty of a mechanical process'

There is a short exchange near the beginning of *Faust*, whose thrust and counterthrust sum up the difficulties of the encyclopaedic ambition in the modern world. To Faust, who would like to 'embrace/The experience allotted to the whole/Race of mankind', Mephistopheles replies, with a sneer, that between the individual and the species there now exists an unbridgable gulf. Better drop it, dear 'Mr Microcosm': 'such totality/Is only for a god' (1770–72, 1802, 1780–81). A god, a superman, a being above ordinary mankind? Quite the contrary, for Flaubert:

---

[11] Similar conclusions in A. Portelli, *The Text and the Voice: Writing, Speaking, and Democracy in American Literature*, Columbia University Press, New York 1994; and D. Simpson, 'Destiny made manifest: the styles of Whitman's poetry', in H.K. Bhabha, ed., *Nation and Narration*, London and New York 1990.

to recover a relation to totality, superficiality is the answer – credulity, silliness. Encyclopaedic rhymes with idiotic.

It is the great discovery of *Bouvard and Pécuchet*: stupidity. The stupidity of the *Sottisier* ('FÉNÉLON: Water is made to support those prodigious edifices that are called vessels'): bombastic, crude, but having little to do with our theme (nor, for that matter, did it concern Flaubert himself all that much). And the stupidity of the *Dictionnaire des idées reçues*: quieter and more peaceful than the previous kind; but also more pervasive and widespread, because no longer confined to specific contents.[12] A thought, here, is never stupid *in itself*: it becomes so only after a particular treatment, which transforms it into a commonplace. And this treatment is one of the great discoveries of the mid nineteenth century: the statistical mean. Here is one of its principal theorists, Quételet, inventor of the 'average man':

> The man whom I take into consideration in this study [. . .] is the mean about which the social elements oscillate: he will thus be, if you like, an imaginary creature.[13]

Un être fictif. 'We [. . .] try to contrive to be some sort of impossible generalized man', you may read at the end of *Notes from Underground*. And in the 1880s someone even decides to photograph that average man, through an ingenious system of multiple exposures.[14] And the point is that this imaginary creature speaks only in commonplaces. René Descharmes:

> The commonplace is the synthetic resultant of an indefinite number of particular notations, isolated observations, phrases spoken by socially

---

[12] This, I think, is why *Bouvard and Pécuchet* has two characters of exactly the same importance. With a single protagonist, we might associate stupidity with a particular intellectual position; but with the two *bonshommes* championing contrary conceptions, stupidity is freed from any determinate content and located at the formal level.

[13] A. Quételet, *Physique sociale ou Essai sur le développement des facultés de l'homme* (1835), Brussels–Paris–St Petersburg 1869, vol. 1, pp. 149–50.

[14] Discussed in I. Hacking, *The Taming of Chance*, Cambridge University Press, Cambridge 1990, pp. 182 ff.

and intellectually diverse individuals, and judgements pronounced in the most varied circumstances.

Flaubert wished to preserve the *anonymous commonplace*, freed from the circumstances that produced it [. . .] In every field, it will be the measure of a certain average intellectual level, about which the individual intelligences of the bourgeois oscillate. The ensemble of commonplaces will make up the average psychology of the bourgeois type; and if Flaubert's characters give the impression of being real, it is because they approximate to this *ideal type*.[15]

An average man, about whom single individuals oscillate; an average thought, about which single ideas oscillate. But we should not be deceived by the apparent neutrality of that 'average'. We are in the presence, here, of one of the great incubi of the nineteenth century: the second principle of thermodynamics, with its thesis of an irreversible growth of entropy. In the cultural field, it means that unusual ideas and original individuals will become rarer and rarer, eventually to vanish altogether, while 'the system continues to fluctuate about the state of equilibrium'.[16] Or, to say it with the other great observer of modern stupidity:

I'll make a suggestion to you, Gerda. Let us assume that in matters of morality it is exactly the same as in the kinetic theory of gases: everything swirls about chaotically, each thing doing what it likes, but if one calculates what in a manner of speaking has no cause to arise out of it, one finds that is the very thing that does really arise! Let us therefore assume too that a certain quantity of ideas is swirling about in the present time. It produces some most probable average value. This shifts very slowly and automatically [. . .] our personal individual motion doesn't matter in the least in all this. We may think and act to the right or to the left, high or low, in a new way or an old way, wildly or with circumspection: it is of no consequence at all to the

---

[15] R. Descharmes, *Autour de 'Bouvard et Pécuchet'*, Librairie de France, Paris 1921, p. 65.

[16] René Descharmes, speaking of *Bouvard and Pécuchet*? Not quite: I. Prigogine and I. Stengers, on the second principle of thermodynamics (*Order Out of Chaos*, Heinemann, London 1984, p. 124).

average value. And to God and the universe *that's* all that matters – *we* don't count!

The Man Without Qualities, II, 103[17]

The average is thus formed outside the individual, and without bothering about him. But little by little it enwraps him, and penetrates into his very brain:

> If a young man is intellectually alive [. . .] he is continually sending out ideas in all directions. But only what produces resonance in his environment will radiate back to him and condense, whereas all the other messages are scattered in space and lost. [And thus] in the course of time one's ordinary and non-personal ideas intensify quite of their own accord and the extraordinary ones fade, so that almost every one of us steadily becomes more mediocre, with all the certainty of a mechanical process . . .

The Man Without Qualities, II, 29

Ordinary and non-personal ideas intensify quite of their own accord . . . We have entered the 'impersonal realm of the *On*'; the 'one', or the 'they'; the 'neuter'; the abstract All-Nobody that is everywhere, although it is faceless.[18] This, writes Barthes, is Racine's 'menacing pronoun': 'the grammatical

---

[17] The idea that fate has become a statistical fact seems to have been very popular in German-language literature between the two wars. The life of Franz Biberkopf (*Berlin Alexanderplatz*, 1928) is spent, for example, amid a host of little thrusts and counterthrusts entirely independent of his will: to the point where Biberkopf becomes convinced that nothing ever makes much difference in and of itself, and that you may as well float with the tide. Something similar in a novel today forgotten, *A Twentieth Century Tragedy* [*Karl und das 20 Jahrhundert*] by R. Brunngraber, which in 1933 enjoyed a resounding success.

[18] J.-P. Sartre, *The Family Idiot*, vol. 1, translated by Carol Cosman, University of Chicago Press, Chicago 1981. The 'they' descends naturally from the '*man*' of Heidegger, and is similarly (like Flaubert's commonplace and Musil's average) the result of an entropic process: 'averageness, which is an existential characteristic of the "they" [. . .] keeps watch over everything exceptional [. . .] every kind of priority gets noiselessly suppressed' (M. Heidegger, *Being and Time*, 1927, translated by John Macquarrie and Edward Robinson, Basil Blackwell, Oxford 1962, pp. 164–5).

sign for aggression'.[19] And, indeed, there have been those who have shown exhaustively how ferocious stupidity can be, without thereby ceasing to be stupid: Kraus, Döblin, Céline, Naipaul. 'I charge with murder . . .', we read in *The Last Days of Mankind*, which is the dauntless *summa* of this 'black' stupidity: 'I charge with murder all pat phrases'.[20]

Murder by pat phrases. Flaubert would probably have liked Kraus's invective; but the stupidity of *Bouvard and Pécuchet* nevertheless takes a more good-natured and consensual form, where the commonplace becomes a kind of infinite echo, in which the individual returns to society its favourite phrases, and society daily provides him with new ones. In such a blandly implacable circuit, which could go on for ever, it very soon becomes hard to grasp 'who' is speaking: everything slides towards an impersonal style, where language seems literally to speak 'of its own accord'. And this, of course, is the great Flaubertian technique: the free indirect style to which the story of *Bouvard and Pécuchet* – all résumés, simplifications, mnemonic endeavours, semi-disputes, attempts at compromise – lends itself on almost every page. Here are the two heroes grappling with philosophy:

> The facts of moral sensibility, on the other hand, owe nothing to the body: 'What is there in common between Archimedes' pleasure at discovering the laws of gravity and Apicius' filthy delight at devouring a boar's head!'
>
> This moral sensibility has four types, and the second type, 'moral desires', can be divided into five kinds, while the phenomena of the fourth type, 'affections', are subdivided into two other kinds, among which is self-love, 'a legitimate tendency, no doubt, but which, when exaggerated, is called egoism'.

---

[19] R. Barthes, *On Racine*, translated by Richard Howard, University of California Press, Berkeley and Los Angeles 1992, p. 35.

[20] K. Kraus, *The Last Days of Mankind*, II, 10. The murderous idiocy *par excellence*, in Kraus's diagnosis, is the lexicalized (hence stupid) metaphor with a violent (hence brutal) meaning: 'like a fire driven by the wind', 'to be suddenly struck dumb', 'to pour salt on the wounds', 'torn from our hands' . . . For Kraus, this mixture of banality and violence, in which the newspapers specialize, is the ideal one for making war in democratic times.

> Within the faculty of knowing comes rational perception, in which
> are found two principal movements and four degrees . . .
>
> *Bouvard and Pécuchet*, 8

Who is speaking here? Bouvard, or Pécuchet? One of them, or the philosophy manual? The manual, or the philosopher in question? The
philosopher, or the narrator? In an unstoppable crescendo, the voices of
the story all merge – indeed, the very distinction between story and
discourse is erased. A result saluted by literary historiography as a liberation from moralism, but where the decisive fact is rather Flaubert's
terrible drift towards uniformity: where it is no longer clear 'who' is
speaking, because only a single voice is left. Supreme, deadly success of
Bouvard: to have abolished the difference between a book on stupidity,
and a stupid book.

The commonplace as a result of cultural entropy. Next, the commonplace as the style of a monologic world. Finally, the commonplace – the
'maxim' [*Spruch*] as André Jolles calls it in *Einfache Formen* – as the tomb
of experience. For the maxim, Jolles writes, is a 'predicate of an affirma-
tive or apodictic type, in contradistinction to the continuous or
discursive'; one which appears in cases where 'we are clearly not making
any critical judgement whatsoever of the situation'.[21] We use it to stave
off

> all the tiresome consequences and implications to which experience
> constrains us [. . .] We feel ourselves exempted from the trouble of
> interpreting lived and perceived events: 'All's well that ends well!'[22]

On the one hand, experience: and with it arguments, consequences, interpretations, judgements – all plurals, all dynamic constructions of uncertain
outcome. On the other side, the maxim: in the singular, in the third person, so generic and abstract as to be incontrovertible. More than a line of
reasoning, Jolles goes on, this is 'a conclusion, a counter-signature': it does

---

[21] A. Jolles, *Einfache Formen*, Max Niemeyer, Tübingen 1968, pp. 163–4, 157.
[22] Ibid., pp. 167–8.

not examine what has occurred, but 'puts it on record, so to speak, without incorporating it'.[23]

In short, the maxim seems anxious to deny the very reality of experience: refuses to recognize it, pretends that nothing has ever happened. Is it a loss? No doubt. But it is a loss that *creates space*: that, in destroying, also makes possible the emergence of something new. And indeed, half a century later, in the most astonishing change of function in literary history, the commonplace will be transformed from an experience-killing mechanism into a support for the most adventurous representation of modern experience: *Ulysses*, and the stream of consciousness. For the stream of consciousness to become imaginable, I mean, a semi-catastrophe had first to happen to everyday experience: it had to go adrift, amid semi-worked impulses, confused memories, and opaque associations. Had the rich, malleable experience of, say, the Goethean *Bildungsroman* remained operative, Leopold Bloom would never have been invented (and, what is worse, there would be an extremely long novel on Stephen Dedalus's years of pilgrimage). But Flaubert killed off the novel of 'formation'; and *bêtise*, with a bit of luck, gave birth to the new man. All's well that ends well.

Literary evolution. II

Melville, Whitman, Flaubert. The techniques are different, but the tendency is always the same: from polyphony, towards monologism. Towards a monologism that, along the way, loses its personal and purely repressive features (consider the following sequence: Ahab, Ishmael/narrator, Myself, 'They'), and becomes progressively more abstract and 'democratic'. 'Messrs Bouvard and Pécuchet are the basis of democracy', wrote Pound in 1922.[24] Better, they are the living nexus between democracy and mediocrity: just as Whitman's Myself brings democracy close to

---

23 Ibid., pp. 158, 168. 'Idle talk', writes Heidegger in the same years as Jolles, 'is the possibility of understanding everything without previously making the thing one's own' (*Being and Time*, p. 213).

24 E. Pound, '*Ulysses*', in *The Dial*, June 1922; now in T.S. Eliot, ed., *The Literary Essays of Ezra Pound*, Faber and Faber, London 1954, p. 403.

social control, and Ishmael brings it close to cultural standardization. Nor ought this to surprise us, since every political form has its secret bedfellows, and Western democracy has precisely been allotted (among others) mediocrity and social control. These aspects of democratic culture were indeed *among the first* to assert themselves, because they ensure stability; and a culture at its inception, if it does not wish to disintegrate, must rest upon something solid. Against the Bakhtinian idea of a natural alliance between polyphony and democracy, in short, the advent of the latter *encouraged monologic tendencies*: a common culture, not innumerable different cultures.[25]

A trajectory which, in the course of a half century, reduces polyphony and increases monologism: a historical trajectory. But what history is this? Of *what*, exactly? And, more generally, what is 'historical', in literary history? The text? Certainly: written during specific years, reworked some time after that, published later still, every text is a veritable lump of history. And yet, even where you can really ask for no more – the sixty years put into *Faust*, say – the individual text is never enough to characterize a historical tendency: you have to move away from it, and bring other works into play. It is a bit like geometry: to draw a line, you need at least two points.

The 'line' that I have in mind, of course, is the literary genre: the true protagonist, in my opinion, of the history of literature. What is harder to understand – sticking to the geometrical metaphor – is the nature of the 'points' through which it passes. Are these points individual texts? Yes, and no. Yes, because the concept of literary genre always rests upon concrete, specific works: *Faust, Moby-Dick, Leaves of Grass, Bouvard and Pécuchet* . . . But theoretical reflection must then work on the text – and, more precisely, pull it to pieces – in order to extract from it something which, for the purposes of morphological evolution, is far more precious than the text itself: namely, the device. In these pages, polyphony, monologism, the commonplace. Later on, it will be the turn of allegory,

---

[25] And as with democracy, we may add, so too with the novel. What *Moby-Dick* and *Bouvard* have of polyphony derives from their *epic* components: it is a residue of another convention, which the voice of the novel – Melville's narrator, Flaubert's indirect style – is gradually levelling out.

or the stream of consciousness. It is the device, not the text, that is the literary genre's partner in carrying forward the history of symbolic forms. It is the device, once again, that allows us to 'see' literary change: to follow it from text to text and from year to year, measuring its transformations and analysing its complexities. And, if we are lucky, even allowing us to establish a date of birth and a date of death.

The genre, and the device. The former, much bigger than the individual text; the latter, much smaller. A literary history split in two, which has lost its measure. And that is not all. What kind of history, what kind of trajectory, is the one drawn in these pages?

Certainly not the straight line of a continuous growth. If you imagine the story of polyphony on Cartesian axes – one measuring the boldness of the device, the other indicating the passage of time – you at once obtain, with *Faust*, a rather high value; but then the curve begins to decline (*Moby-Dick*), and to decline further (*Leaves of Grass*), until it almost reaches zero (*Bouvard and Pécuchet*); it then remains steady, only to climb again suddenly around the First World War. It is an undulating curve: a discontinuous history that soars, then gets stuck. Overall, it is the conception illustrated by Gould and Eldredge with the theory of 'punctuated equilibria': evolution like the life of a soldier, made up of long periods of boredom, and brief moments of terror. Heaven knows, the history of the modern epic bears them out.[26]

A history split in two, between the very large and the very small. A history almost always still, but rocked every now and then by explosions. But is it really a *history*, then? To be sure, the curve of polyphony does take place 'in' history. But 'because of' history, as well? Scarcely at all. In the ups and downs of this device, the passage of time counts for less than

---

[26] The phrase on boredom and terror comes from the geologist Derek Ager. As for the application of punctuated equilibria to literary history, I have discussed it in 'On Literary Evolution' (see *Signs Taken for Wonders*, 2nd enlarged edn, Verso, London 1987), and sought to offer a concrete example in the essay: ' "A Useless Longing for Myself": The Crisis of the European *Bildungsroman*, 1898–1914', in Ralph Cohen, ed., *Studies in Historical Change*, University of Virginia Press, Charlottesville 1992.

movement in space. Nineteenth-century polyphony is at its peak in the German semi-periphery of Goethe, and declines progressively as it draws closer to the core of the world-system (USA, France); in England it is wholly lacking (and the new ascendant phase will, in turn, begin in the semi-periphery of *Ulysses*). The distribution of the 'very small' (the individual device) thus confirms that of the 'very large' (the different areas of development of epic and novel), and gives a glimpse of the possibility – perhaps not too distant – of a genuine literary geography.

4

Allegory and modernity. I

'Anyone who has not looked about a bit, and had a few experiences, will get nothing out of *Faust* Part Two': thus Goethe to Eckermann on 17 February 1831 – and, to judge by the misunderstandings that accompanied the poem's reception, it was a truly prophetic comment. But it was also something of a self-fulfilling prophecy, since the difficulties of *Faust* depend only to a small degree upon the reader's experiences, and to a much greater extent upon Goethe himself, who opted here for a decidedly allegorical structure.

Now, allegory is a specific rhetorical figure, which poses a problem of comprehension quite similar to that of the linguistic sign as such. For, in both cases, we have a two-sided linguistic entity (for the sign, signifier/signified; for allegory, literal meaning/allegorical meaning), and a wholly conventional relation between the two levels. From the signifier *lupa* [she-wolf], in other words, there is no way of arriving at the meaning the term possesses in the Italian language; and from this literal meaning, in turn, it is impossible to derive the allegorical meaning in Canto I of the *Divine Comedy*. It is a conventional relation, so there is just one way to move from one level of the sign to the other: namely, to know the entire code to which it belongs. 'To work at it', as Goethe would say: to study.

To study. And it is precisely this conventional nature of the allegorical sign that provides the point of departure for one of the most celebrated controversies of modern aesthetics: the clash – particularly sharp precisely in Goethe's day – between allegory and symbol. Being conventional, allegory gradually acquires a whole series of pejorative connotations. It is an artificial figure, mechanical, dead. Its instrumental use of the literal meaning (reduced to a mere signifier of the second level of meaning) is seen as a humiliation of sensuous reality – and thus of the aesthetic sphere itself – to the benefit of a somewhat pedantic abstraction. And finally (an offence that effectively says it all) allegory is a tendentially denotative, or univocal, form: reducing the semantic plurality of literature, it leaves us with the poverty of a single authorized meaning.

I could go on. But it is a fairly well known story, and I shall instead point out how the tendency has been reversed in our own century. From Benjamin's lonely attempts regarding Baudelaire and the *Trauerspiel*, to the re-readings by De Man and Culler of the symbol/allegory antithesis, and on to the recent Goethe studies of Schlaffer and Kruse, the twentieth century has decisively revoked the condemnation of allegory, and indeed seen in this figure the sign of a particular self-awareness of modern literature. Challenging a hardy critical tradition, which saw the greatness of *Faust* in its *non*-allegorical nature, Schlaffer and Kruse thus completely reformulated the terms of the problem: not only is allegory manifestly the keystone of *Faust* Part Two – it is rightly so. The fact that Goethe renounced his own theoretical convictions (favouring the symbol) is a sign of his historical intelligence: of his having understood that allegory is *the poetic figure of modernity*. And, more precisely, of *capitalist* modernity.

At the end of the first Act, Kruse writes, the paper money episode underlines the semiotic nature (conventional: allegorical) that the new form of wealth will have. And as for Schlaffer, his detailed reading of the allegorical masquerade as a great market – where everything, including people, is now offered for sale – moves in the same direction. Between the inner form of allegory and Marx's analysis of the commodity, Schlaffer continues, developing some insights of Benjamin's, there is a clear structural parallelism. Like the commodity, allegory humanizes things (making them move and speak), and it reifies human beings. In both cases, furthermore, an abstract reality (exchange value, allegorical meaning) subordinates and almost hides the concrete reality of use value and literal meaning. And then, of course, there are the 'ghosts' and 'social hieroglyphics' of the first volume of *Capital*; the 'secrets', the 'magic', the 'fetishes', the 'sensuous things transcending sensuousness' . . .

The 'critique of political economy', Schlaffer concludes, might thus properly be rechristened a 'critique of the allegorical world'. And he is right. At the level of semantic correspondences, the parallelism between allegory and commodity form really is indisputable. But when he moves from this to causal links, things change. When we read that allegory functions like the commodity, in fact, we cannot help retorting: Why not the opposite? Why start off from Marx's commodity in order to explain Goethe's allegory, rather than vice versa?

For Schlaffer, the answer lies in the primacy of social relations with respect to symbolic forms: an approach that, in general, I share. In this specific case, however, I must confess that a quite different scenario comes to my mind: the image of an economist brought up on Goethe (and on Hegel, who in the matter of allegory sees things exactly like Goethe), just getting ready to draft the preliminary exposition of his theory: a philosophical and also somewhat literary exposition, in which he wishes to highlight the enigmatic and inhuman features of the new social relations. Nothing odd, then, about his search for a guiding image to express his position effectively. Nor anything odd about his finding it in the semantic field 'overturning of the sensuous world', which – for German aesthetics – characterizes allegory: a field that is 'available' (*Capital*, in the end, is written half a century *after Faust*) and that is already oriented in a polemical direction.

Besides, when Schlaffer underlines the truly extraordinary correspondences between the descriptions of allegory and those of the commodity – well, that is an excellent argument *against* his own thesis. The construction of an aesthetic form consonant with new social relations is a long and rocky process, where cultural heritages of all kinds come into play and the most absurd attempts gain a footing. That Goethe should find – immediately – the form *perfectly* appropriate for capitalist reality is something so odd as to appear frankly unbelievable. Perfection ill becomes history – and it becomes materialism even less well. If we value both, then whenever we meet something resembling perfection, it is more reasonable to think of an *imitation* (conscious or otherwise) than of an autonomous process of duplication in different spheres.

If this is true, then the causal link established by Schlaffer is reversed, and allegory becomes the *explicans* of an *explicandum* that, of course, is not the existence of commodities, but the polemical and paradoxical formulations of the early chapters of *Capital*. Scarcely do we explore the arguments a bit more thoroughly, moreover, than the parallel constructed by Schlaffer begins to totter. For Marx, for example, commodities can be exchanged because they are qualitatively different, and quantitatively equal: in the semantic field, however, there is no way of reproducing the distinction between quantity and quality. Again, for Marx, the equivalence between commodities rests upon the equal quantities of labour embodied in them: but, once more, the idea of embodied labour has no meaning in the realm of allegory. And if this falls, the labour theory of value falls too, as does that of the fetishism of commodities. In other words, the whole of Marx's theory (whether right or wrong) collapses, and only analogies of formulation remain.

To find a link between allegory and modernity, therefore, we shall have to change course. And we may as well confront the main difficulty of the undertaking at once.

'You, I think, should know us all'

As I said at the beginning of this chapter, the same thing happens with allegory as with any linguistic sign – and, more precisely, as with the words of a foreign language. At first, they are utterly incomprehensible; then, once the code is found, they become perfectly clear. 'As is also the case with the *Magic Flute*', Goethe tells Eckermann in January 1827, 'the higher import will not escape the initiated . . .'; and the *Flute*, with its shadeless antithesis between Darkness and Light, is a really excellent example of a figure with scant sympathy for middle ways.

A clear counterposition, therefore, between ignorance and certainty. Whether this is then seen as the death of art, or as a lucid acknowledgement of its conventional nature, it is how things are for allegory. But is it how they are for *Faust*, too? Hardly. Instead of presenting us with the clear alternative of darkness or clarity, the poem is situated in a kind of no-man's-land, where figurative meanings pile up on one another with no further control. There occurs here, on a large scale, what happens in concentrated form in the allegorical masquerade of the 'Spacious Hall' scene. In principle, as the various figures successively make their entrances, a Herald explains their meaning. Indeed, he is there to re-emphasize that allegory requires an official explanation, from the person who knows the code: 'Now here come ladies you'll not know by sight . . .' (5345); 'Mysterious! But such riddles can be read . . .' (5398).

Everything seems to be proceeding as it ought. At a certain point, however, the Herald's explanatory abilities fail:

> Yet through windows, I admit,
> Airy phantoms seem to flit;
> There are ghosts and magic here
> Which I can't keep out, I fear.
> First, that spooky dwarf; and now
> A whole flood of it somehow.
> As my office bids, I should
> Give you an interpretation
> Of these shapes; I wish I could!
> They defy all explanation.
>
> 5500–5509

As my office bids, I should give you an interpretation . . . The person responsible for such perplexity, the Boy Charioteer, challenges the Herald:

> Herald, come; proclaim out loud,
> While we're with you, who we are,
> What we're like, etcetera.
> Since we're allegorical,
> You, I think, should know us all.
>
> 5528–32

Yet – nothing. The Herald tries to follow an indirect route ('To describe you I might try;/But that's not to identify': 5533–4), but it is completely useless: between literal meaning and allegorical meaning, as we know, there is a purely conventional connection, and the description of the one offers no indication as to the content of the other. In the Boy Charioteer's scornful conclusion:

> It seems your herald's role is to proclaim
> The hollow mask, but not to name
> The true reality that lies behind;
> That is beyond your shallow courtly mind.
>
> 5606–9

I shall return shortly to what trips up the Herald. But let me point out that the most programmatically allegorical scene in *Faust* opens in a climate of total faith in the univocal interpretation – and ends in the most total perplexity. And indeed, what happens when an allegory fails to be understood?

Hans Georg Gadamer, *Truth and Method*:

> [Unlike the symbol] Allegory is certainly not the product of genius alone. It rests on firm traditions and always has a fixed, statable meaning [. . .] the concept of allegory is closely bound up with dogmatics.[1]

Firm tradition, fixed meaning. Within the tradition, in short, there is certainty and univocity of the allegorical sign. But outside it? What happens (Gadamer again) 'in the nineteenth century', when 'mythical and historical tradition was no longer a self-evident heritage'?[2] How to read those signs that no longer constitute a living link with the past, but a remote, disconcerting repertoire?

For Gadamer, the answer is simple and perfectly logical. When the key to allegory is lost, the figure falls silent – to be replaced by the new signs proposed by the aesthetics of the symbol. But the exact opposite may also happen, and actually did happen:

> The many obscurities in the connection between meaning and sign [. . .] did not deter, they rather encouraged the exploitation of ever remoter characteristics of the representative object as symbols, so as to surpass even the Egyptians with new subtleties. In addition to this

---

[1] H.G. Gadamer, *Truth and Method*, translation revised by Joel Weinsheimer and Donald Marshall, Crossroad, New York 1989, p. 79.

[2] Ibid., p. 133.

there was the dogmatic power of the meanings handed down from the ancients, so that one and the same object can just as easily signify a virtue as a vice, and therefore more or less anything.[3]

Unlimited and unending subtleties. Here we encounter – Benjamin notes – the 'antinomies of the allegorical', where 'any person, any object, any relationship can mean absolutely anything else'.[4] Hardly a *silence* of allegory, then. Once Gadamer's 'firm traditions' are broken, the old signs do not fall dumb at all: if anything, they speak in even louder voices. They have been transformed into so many hieroglyphics, and seem to say to the interpreter: there is a sign, here, so there is assuredly also a meaning; but since the key is now lost, you are free to interpret it as you like. A wonderful situation: certainty of meaning – and total freedom of choice. It is a magic language, which utters only the words desired by the listener. 'When in 1822 Champollion deciphered hieroglyphics', Blumenberg writes, 'for the romantic spirit it came almost as a disappointment.'[5]

---

[3] Giehlow, *Die Hyerogliphenkunde des Humanismus in der Allegorie der Renaissance*, quoted in Walter Benjamin, *The Origins of German Baroque Drama* (1928), translated by John Osborne, Verso, London 1990, p. 174.

[4] Ibid., pp. 174–5.

[5] H. Blumenberg, *Die Lesbarkeit der Welt*, Suhrkamp, Frankfurt a/M 1981. A few decades later, Melville and Hawthorne are still insisting on the 'symbolic' interpretations of hieroglyphics that Champollion had stripped of any basis: 'For [them] the ambiguous character of the hieroglyphics was their prime significance. The hieroglyphics were the linguistic analogue of an enigmatic external world whose shape was various enough to sustain almost any interpretation [. . .] Both writers understood [. . .] that Champollion's scientific reading of the hieroglyphics had not rendered the nearly four centuries of metaphysical interpretations either worthless or meaningless' (J.T. Irwin, *American Hieroglyphics*, Johns Hopkins University Press, Baltimore 1983, p. 239). 'How may unlettered Ishmael . . .', we read in the chapter 'The Prairie', 'hope to read the awful Chaldee of the Sperm Whale's brow? I but put that brow before you. Read it if you can.' It sounds like a challenge. And it is one, if the reader wants a definite meaning. But if he is satisfied with a 'subjective' meaning, then the Chaldee of the natural world is not awful because of its impenetrability – but because of the numerous meanings that may be attributed to it. And indeed Ishmael, albeit 'unlettered', when it is a matter of reading is never one to hold back.

One and the same object that can just as easily signify a virtue as a vice, and therefore more or less anything. Modern subjectivity has taken heart, and plays fearlessly with the signs of classical antiquity. According to Blumenberg, it is an idea that must have occurred to Goethe from his earliest youth:

> While the 'Prometheus' article in Benjamin Hederich's *Gründliches mythologisches Lexicon* [Complete Mythological Lexicon], published in 1724, and accessible to Goethe [. . .] does end, like all the others, by adducing allegorical elucidations of the myth, it does not do so without the encouragement, astonishing after so much painful pedantic precision, that is given to the reader in the very last sentence: 'Everyone can produce more such interpretations for himself.' [. . .] One can imagine how Goethe, reaching this terminus, must have felt himself addressed.[6]

A chain reaction of subjective interpretations. Blumenberg's book does not develop this hypothesis in relation to *Faust*; just a few months after the poem was published, however, one of its earliest exegetes had already thought of doing so. In a truly remarkable insight, Loewe's *Commentar* decides to cut the allegory in half: it offers a punctilious mythical and historical glossary of the figures in *Faust* – but makes not the slightest attempt to define their meaning within the work. I shall confine myself to the 'literal meaning', the author at once warns: because it is inevitable, and indeed quite right, that the allegorical one should vary 'according to each reader's cultural level'.[7]

A varying allegory: not univocal at all, but *polysemous*. It is a paradoxical situation in which allegory seems, as it were, to have betrayed its own mission. And if there are some who decide to drop hermeneutics and abandon themselves contentedly 'to the pictorial moment of poetry [. . .]

---

[6] H. Blumenberg, *Work on Myth*, translated by Robert Wallace, MIT Press, Cambridge Mass. and London 1985, pp. 403–4.

[7] C. Loewe, *Commentar zum zweiten Theile des Goethe'schen Faust*, Logier, Berlin 1834, pp. 2–3.

this ineffably rich, many-coloured and sensuous ornament',[8] the most widespread reaction nevertheless is different. In a mixture of bewilderment and admiration, it is recognized that the polysemy of *Faust* will end up generating – in the prophetic image of a mid-century commentator – an ever more endless army of exegetes:

> If twenty of the most acute men were to write each his own interpretation of the second part of *Faust*, twenty more could easily be found, each of whom would bring to light something of which none of the first twenty had thought.[9]

Twenty interpretations, then twenty more, then . . . And many of these, if truth be told, really bizarre. Jens Kruse is quite right to define the reception of Goethe's poem as 'a history of misunderstandings'.[10] And yet, how shall I put it, *misunderstandings suit Faust*: instead of weakening its effectiveness, they have surrounded it with a vast semantic aura, making it into a truly unique work in Western literature. For this is precisely Goethe's great invention: to have constructed, in *Faust* Part Two, *a mechanism that allows readers to make mistakes.* A brief analytical parenthesis, and I shall return to this.

The sign run amok

In *Faust*, allegory is a message coming from antiquity; from the world of shadows. For Hawthorne and Melville, however, it is a convention still alive in the culture surrounding them, and one whose semantic vicissitudes are far from painless. In *The Scarlet Letter* and in *Moby-Dick*, the

---

8 C.H. Weisse, *Kritik und Erläuterung des Goethe'schen Faust*, Reichenbach, Leipzig 1837, p. 74. In 1844, the compiler of a commentary addressed to ladies will admit candidly to not possessing the necessary mythological knowledge to understand the 'Classical Walpurgis Night': 'So far as this part of the poem is concerned, I can thus merely counsel to enjoy that which speaks to us directly thanks to its poetic freshness . . .' (F. von Sallet, *Zur Erläuterung des zweiten Theiles vom Goethe'schen Faust. Für Frauen geschrieben*, August Schultz, Breslau 1844, p. 19).
9 A. Schnetger, *Der Zweite Theil des Goethe'schen Faust*, F. Manke, Jena 1858, p. x.
10 J. Kruse, *Die Tanz der Zeichen*, Anton Hain, Königstein/Ts 1985, pp. 1–2.

passage from the univocal to the polysemous is thus a genuine historical leap: a break with the past, whose protagonists are not so much the story's characters, as its *signs*.

This is familiar stuff. At first, Hester Prynne's 'A' is the sign of a condemnation – indeed, it is the condemnation itself turned into a sign. In the second chapter of the book, Hester can leave the prison with the heavy oak door that stands on the market square, because in reality she continues to carry it with her, pinned to her breast: it is so weighty a semiotic chain, that embroidered letter, that there is never any need (not even once, in the entire novel!) to make explicit the link between the signifier 'A' and the signified 'adulteress'. This is an allegory, one feels like saying, and then some. A univocal, inflexible sign, defining and labelling once and for all.

For a good half of the story, everything contributes to reinforcing the univocal character of the imprisoning sign: the townspeople's gossip, and little Pearl's appearance; explicit accusations, and casual glances. But then, gradually, a second semantic level emerges alongside the first. Pearl (like Queequeg after her) takes on the interrogative form of a 'living hieroglyph'. The rumours about the letter begin to become more complex, and even contradictory. The 'fantastic ingenuity' of Hester's needlework, at first confined to the level of the signifier, invades that of the signified. The scarlet letter is eventually transformed from a constitutive element of the public sphere into a private 'legend': stratified, mutable, different depending on the person and place – and, basically, no longer in anyone's interest to control. So the 'A' begins to stand for able, then admirable – and then angel.

From Adulteress to Angel. The moral antithesis here is so clear as to be unforgettable: yet it is perhaps not the most important thing. For, beyond the reversal of values, *The Scarlet Letter* points to a less spectacular, but newer and potentially far more explosive process: *a neutral semantic drift of the allegorical sign*, which passes from one univocity not merely to another with the signs reversed (as in the peripeteia of baroque tragedy), but to the polysemy of multiple paths basically equivalent to each other. This is a tendency confirmed a year later by Melville's novel, in which Moby-Dick, who is initially 'evil personified', does not subsequently become 'good' (Adulteress/Angel), but scatters his meaning between the nebula of 'The whiteness of the whale', the reflections of the chapter on 'Cetology', or the centrifugal – and equivalent – readings of 'The doubloon'.

In Hawthorne and Melville, in other words, allegory loses its univocal character. Allegory 'runs amok', in Marcello Pagnini's fine metaphor, and the clash of different meanings engenders the great and complex poetry of the American Renaissance.[11] Very true. But the victory of polysemy also goes beyond literature. When the relation between words and things opens up to so many interpretations, it means something important is escaping the control of authority. Thanks to the protean medium of oral communication, writes Alessandro Portelli, signs become emancipated from Gadamer's 'firm traditions' and allow different individuals to think in different ways.[12] When that 'A' can also mean 'Able', freedom of opinion is born.

Language is emancipated from established tradition . . . There would, of course, be a much clearer way of cutting this link:

> 'Let us not look back,' answered Hester Prynne. 'The past is gone! Wherefore should we linger upon it now? See! With this symbol, I undo it all, and make it as it had never been!' So speaking, she undid the clasp that fastened the scarlet letter, and, taking it from her bosom, threw it to a distance among the withered leaves.
>
> *The Scarlet Letter*, 18

Burying the signs of the past among the withered leaves. But at once Pearl arrives and forces her mother to take up the letter and fasten it again to her bosom. And although Hester promptly resolves to hurl it into the ocean, 'that shall swallow it up for ever!', for some reason that does not happen and the 'A' remains with her to her dying day (and beyond: it will be engraved upon her tombstone). And that is how things are in Melville too, where the ocean once again refuses to swallow up allegories, and Moby-Dick remains alive (except in abridged versions for children) to bear his enigmatic polysemy about the world.

No, old signs do not disappear. They duplicate their own meaning, betray it, distort it – but they do not go away. However free America

---

[11] M. Pagnini, 'Struttura semantica del grande simbolismo americano', in his *Critica della funzionalità*, Einaudi, Turin 1970, pp. 192 ff.

[12] A. Portelli, *The Text and the Voice: Writing, Speaking, and Democracy in American Literature*, Columbia University Press, New York 1994.

may be of the 'ruined castles' of Goethe's poem, even she does not manage to live undisturbed by the 'pointless memories and futile strife' of the past world. It is the most complex and fascinating form of non-contemporaneity: when Bloch's paradox invades the actual figurative texture of the work, and forces *meanings from different epochs* to cohabit within the same sign.

And here, once again, the difference between the two great narratives of the modern West emerges. On the one hand, the novel: which invents a new language. On the other, the epic: which produces *a new interpretation of the old language*. In the former case, we have the compactness of a world in which everybody speaks the same language, and lives in the same period. In the latter case, we have the specific *historicity* of a universe in which fossils from distant epochs coexist with creatures from worlds to come. In this huge symbolic stratification, there is no trace of that great novelistic invention which is the present: the brief span of time – a year, a youth, a generation – that contains within itself an entire destiny. The present does not exist in epics. As the last lines of *Faust* declare, 'All that must disappear/Is but a parable': a symbol, an unsteady bridge thrown between past and future – between Helen and Holland, between The Mothers and Homunculus. It is already the great modernist polarity of Archaism and Utopia – with nothing for today.

Allegory and modernity. II

Allegory run amok, I said. A defect? No, this source of perpetual misunderstandings does not indicate a weakness of *Faust* or *Moby-Dick*. If anything, it is evidence of a circumstance at first sight truly incredible: of a civilization that has recognized itself in world texts for two exactly opposite reasons. It has recognized itself in them a first time because they present themselves as great allegories, and promise the revelation typical of a sacred text: the certainty that plunges its roots into the established tradition of the most distant past. But it has then recognized itself in them a second time – with yet more durable consequences – through the limitless polysemy that opens these texts to innumerable future interpretations, making them the first open works of the modern West. In an extraordinarily effective division of labour, the sacred text dominates the reader, and reassures him; while the open work frees him and, like Melville's doubloon, 'mirrors back his own mysterious self'.

We have thus come back, by a quite different route, to the questions discussed in Chapter 3, in relation to polyphony. But there is a problem. While the history of polyphony was marked by a progressive *reduction* of the device, in the case of allegory we observe, by contrast, an *increase* of polysemy. So, world texts seem to send us two contradictory signals. Either I have made a mistake, or I must explain why.

Well then, to start with, let us say that polyphony and polysemy are not the same thing. The former constructs for itself the signs it needs; whereas the latter can emerge only from an already existing sign: Charioteer, embroidered letter, whale, or whatever. 'There's another *rendering* now', Melville tells us in 'The doubloon', 'but still *one text*'. The semantic freedom of allegory may be very extensive; but it still finds a limit in the fact (which will return to stunning effect in Franz Kafka) that its point of departure is one, and unchanging. This, I believe, is why allegory does not undergo the 'reduction' that befell polyphony: there is no need for it, because allegory bears *within itself* the mechanism that keeps it under control. It can be allowed greater freedom than polyphony – because by its very nature it is *less free*.

Is this rhetorical duality perhaps the sign of an analogous duality of social relations? Karl Mannheim:

> The modern economic system (just because economic necessities are penetrating to an increasing extent into the very fabric of our daily lives) can 'afford' to give the 'ideologists' more freedom than has hitherto been possible.[13]

Symbolic intransigence, Mannheim goes on, is typical of economically fragile societies: those that 'hold themselves together' with orthodoxy, and have to repress the autonomy of the cultural sphere. But once the silent fetter of the capitalist economy is instituted (the doubloon . . .), the ideological chains can be loosened and society can open up to

---

[13] K. Mannheim, 'On the nature of economic ambition and its significance for the social education of man', in *Essays on the Sociology of Knowledge* (1930), Routledge and Kegan Paul, London 1952, p. 246.

disparate symbolic options. It has become *stronger*: so it can also be *more free*.[14] Allegory, which contains within it this mixture of fetter and freedom, is the figure that best represents such a state of affairs, and so opens the path to every other form of polysemy. It heralds the twentieth-century art of which Edgar Wind will speak: the 'splendid superfluity' that is by now 'well received because it has lost its sting'.[15] It is the sign of a 'neutralized' cultural sphere, in which everything is possible – *poly*semy, *poly*phony – because nothing is important any longer.[16]

Obligations imposed by the economy, then; and freedom of ideologies. Well, there is one object – a very particular object – which condenses in itself Mannheim's formula, with all its paradoxes: money. On the one hand, in the bourgeois world money really is 'obligatory': it 'is the bond which ties me to *human* life and society to me, which links me to nature

---

[14] The fact that the strengthening of capitalism does not imply an 'alignment' of the cultural sphere, but exactly the opposite, is something that Hegelian Marxism – with its fondness for totality – has often persisted in denying. To cite only the best: 'At the present level of development the artist is incomparably much less free than Hegel could ever have believed at the beginning of the liberal era' (T.W. Adorno, *Philosophy of Modern Music*, Sheed and Ward, London 1973, p. 17); 'What we must now ask ourselves is whether it is not precisely this semi-autonomy of the cultural sphere which has been destroyed by the logic of late capitalism' (F. Jameson, 'Postmodernism, or the Cultural Logic of Late Capitalism', in *New Left Review* 146, 1984, p. 87); '20th-century capitalism has "re-unified" economy and culture by subsuming the cultural under the economic' (A. Huyssen, *After the Great Divide*, Indiana University Press, Bloomington 1986, p. 21).

[15] E. Wind, *Art and Anarchy*, Duckworth, London 1985, pp. 10, 8.

[16] 'The rationalism of the eighteenth century', writes Henry Kamen, 'supported toleration not because it was essential to religion but because religion itself was unessential' (H. Kamen, *The Rise of Toleration*, Weidenfeld and Nicolson, London 1967, pp. 23–4). 'So natural to mankind is intolerance', observes John Stuart Mill for his part, 'in whatever they really care about, that religious freedom has hardly anywhere been practically realized, except where religious indifference [...] has added its weight to the scale' (J.S. Mill, *On Liberty* (1859), Collins, Glasgow 1962, p. 133).

and to man', writes the young Marx.[17] But since money 'is not exchanged for a particular quality, a particular thing [. . .] but for the whole objective world of man and of nature',[18] the concrete contents it assumes remain wholly undetermined: open to the will, desire or whim of each single individual.

Obligations imposed by money, then; and freedom in its use. It is the paradox of Ernest Gellner's 'dualistic world', which we shall encounter in *Ulysses*. And it was already the strangeness of allegory run amok (obligatory nature of the inherited sign; freedom in its interpretation), and of *Faust* Part Two. In Goethe, indeed, the old allegorical decoding of the Herald breaks down precisely when it comes to Pluto, god of wealth. Spectacular wealth, at first: necklaces, jewels, precious stones. Then wealth as gold. Finally – though the transitions are all very swift – wealth as paper money. It is a whirl of signs and metamorphoses, which the Herald does not understand; and which in the late-feudal world of the Empire, as is to be expected, produces conflict and disintegration. But in the central thread of the plot, wealth waiting to be invested becomes instead a creative power: it drives 'fancy' to 'its highest flight', Faust explains to the Emperor, and places 'trust unbounded in this boundlessness' (6115, 6118). And shortly afterwards, turning to Mephistopheles:

> Let me inform you that your pranks
> Have consequences, my good friend.
> We made him rich and earned his thanks,
> And now he must be entertained.
>
> 6189–92

And now he must be entertained . . . Is it the whim of a sovereign, who has at last a bit of money to spend? Yes, but the whim is called Helen of Greece – and will take Faust to The Mothers, to the 'Classical Walpurgis Night', to Helen, to Euphorion . . . Would the boundless machinery of *Faust* Part Two ever have started, without those first banknotes?

---

[17] K. Marx, 'Money', in 'Economic and Philosophical Manuscripts', translated by Gregor Benton: see *Early Writings*, Penguin Books, London 1975, p. 377.
[18] Ibid., p. 379.

'But infinite forms do not exist . . .'

So, the more redundant literature was, for the purposes of social cohesion, the freer its form, and its interpretation, became. The sacred text declined: the book that had to keep society united, and that therefore demanded a univocal interpretation. The world text was born: which had no 'political' responsibilities, and which therefore allowed multiple readings.[19] To be sure, literature had for some time been sliding towards the periphery of the cultural system. But the *Wirkungsgeschichte* of *Faust* – in which the work's exceptional prestige has been accompanied by the most improbable elucubrations – gives the change a flavour of inevitability. In the words of Loewe's *Commentar*, everyone will find a different truth in the poem – *and they will all be valid*. And this pulverization of the world text's audience will be my point of departure for a few provisional conclusions.

The first scene of *Faust* Part One, the 'Prelude on the Stage', is almost entirely devoted to a discussion between the Poet and the Director on the nature of the modern audience. 'Do not remind me of that motley throng,' the Poet exclaims, 'Spare me the sight of them!' (59–60). The mass audience, pushing and shoving in front of the box-office in an 'unruly flood', is the exact opposite of his art: a jumble of casual impulses, whereas the latter is unity – a 'harmonious whole' that 'engulfs the world and draws it back into his soul'. The Director listens, but then tries to play it all down:

> Let many things unfold before their eyes,
> Let the crowd stare and be amazed, for then
> You'll win their hearts, and that's to win the prize;
> You'll join the ranks of famous men.

---

[19] The essential thing, of course, is not that a text should be 'sacred' in the sense of religious dogma, but that it should have a socially decisive role. Spinoza's *Tractatus Theologico–Politicus*, for example, recognizes that civil law is far more necessary than Scripture for the security of the modern state: it follows that the law requires the stable interpretation of a sacred text; while Scripture is 'neutralized', and becomes open to free individual interpretation.

Mass alone charms the masses; each man finds
Something to suit him, something to take home.
Give much, and you'll have given to many minds;
They'll all leave here contented to have come.
And let your piece be all in pieces too!
You'll not go wrong if you compose a stew;
It's quick to make and easy to present.
Why offer them a whole? They'll just fragment
It anyway, the public always do.

91–103

The Poet, of course, cannot accept such advice. And in this, as in his general attitude towards the mob, he is quite close to the voice that speaks in the 'Dedication' to *Faust*[20] – hence, people usually add, to Goethe himself. No doubt. However, the Goethe who writes *Faust* is in agreement with the Director. Read those suggestions again: many things, and amazing ones; varied registers for differing tastes; an episodic structure, where everyone will find something for themselves; a work that cannot be an organic whole, and that even the most scrupulous of directors is indeed obliged to break into pieces . . .

Was it an ironic way of preparing us for Part Two, to have it announced by a small capitalist of letters? A delightful, but implausible, hypothesis. In 1798, when he is drafting the 'Prelude on the Stage', Goethe has no inkling of what is going to happen to *Faust*. So it is far more likely that the Director is there to give expression to that tendency towards social atomization which, from the French Revolution on, has constituted one of Goethe's major preoccupations. Yet the fact remains that the author of *Faust* Part Two does follow this seemingly contemptible advice. So what has happened?

What has happened is what we have now encountered more than once in the course of our analysis: the basic components of the modern epic

---

20 'They cannot hear my present music, those/Few souls who listened to my early song;/They are far from me now who were so close,/And their first answering echo has so long/Been silent. Now my voice is heard, who knows/By whom? I shudder as the nameless throng/Applauds it. Are they living still, those friends/Whom once it moved, scattered to the world's ends?' (17–24).

93

do not emerge as *desirable innovations*, but as *problems to be solved*. The all-encompassing hero makes his appearance as an idle chatterer; polyphony as an infernal din; the episodic plot as a collapse of action; allegory as an incomprehensible legacy of the past. And now the overall structure of *Faust* is heralded in a poetics of mercantile inspiration, which emphasizes its mechanical nature. As I have said more than once, these are the visible traces of literary evolution: the signs of a constrained historical process, which must accept such materials as come to hand, and try to turn them to the best possible advantage. And there is also the evil star of an inherited form, which clings to an existence at variance with its times, and finds itself working in singularly adverse conditions. The entire structure of the world text, indeed, is an excellent example of a difficulty that two centuries of work have not yet managed wholly to overcome.

Let us return for a moment to the 'Prelude in the Theatre'. On one side, the Poet: spokesman of the work as '*ein Ganzes*', a unitary whole. On the other, the Director: advocate of the work '*in Stücken*', in pieces. Organic form against mechanical construction, as people begin to say between the eighteenth and nineteenth centuries. And *Faust* (like *Moby-Dick*, or *Bouvard and Pécuchet*), as it proceeds, tilts ever more clearly towards the mechanical. The initial impulse withers and dies; the new parts are added without being connected to one another. At the thematic level, the natural element fades away, and the stage is thronged with dead, artificial, museum forms. Figures, Spengler would say, of Civilization:

> The Civilization is the inevitable *destiny* of the Culture [. . .] Civilizations are the most external and artificial states of which a species of developed humanity is capable. They are a conclusion, the thing-become succeeding, the thing-becoming, death following life, rigidity following expansion [. . .] They are an end, irrevocable, yet by inward necessity reached again and again.[21]

The death that follows life . . . But it is an embalmed death, which ingenious antiquaries transform into a ghostly ballet:

---

[21] O. Spengler, *The Decline of the West* (1918), translated by Charles Francis Atkinson, Allen and Unwin, London 1926, p. 31.

The end is a sunset reflected in forms revived for a moment by pedant or by eclectic – semi-earnestness and doubtful genuineness dominate the world of the arts. We today are in this condition – playing a tedious game with dead forms to keep up the illusion of a living art.[22]

They are all there, the accusations levelled at *Faust*, and then at *Moby-Dick*, *Bouvard and Pécuchet*, *Ulysses*, *The Cantos*, *The Waste Land*: pedantry, eclecticism, a boring game, dead form, frivolity, artificiality, illusion . . . All true, in my opinion. Spengler makes no mistake in his analysis, or in his phenomenology of the mechanical form. On this level, a far greater mistake is made by anyone who seeks to prove at all costs that *Faust* is not allegorical, *Bouvard* is not boring, *Ulysses* is not frivolous, or *Moby-Dick* is not heterogeneous. I ask you.

'One does not detract from [Melville's] book', Richard Chase has written, 'in saying that it has a "made-up" quality, that it is a good deal "put together" . . .'[23] Quite right: instead of wasting time in denying the obvious, far better to accept the mechanical form as given, and then see what is promising about it, or even emancipatory. Edgar Morin:

> It is interesting that a system should be simultaneously something more and something less than what might be defined as the sum of its parts. In what sense is it something less? In the sense that organization imposes fetters that inhibit so many potentialities inherent in the various parts. And this occurs in all organizations, including social organizations.[24]

Organization imposes fetters; as does organic form. Mechanical form, by contrast, with its parts constructed one at a time, like the acts of *Faust*, or the chapters of *Bouvard* and of *Ulysses*, leaves more freedom – more space for experimentation. As Staiger writes:

> One cannot cut big pieces out of an organism without endangering the life of the whole. But the *Iliad* could be reduced to a half, to even

---

[22] Ibid., p. 207.

[23] R. Chase, *The American Novel and its Tradition*, Bell, London 1958, p. 100.

[24] E. Morin, 'Le vie della complessità', in G. Bocchi and M. Ceruti, eds, *La sfida della complessità*, Feltrinelli, Milan 1985, p. 51.

a third of its length, and no one who was not familiar with the remainder would miss it.[25]

A form that may be cut at will. Above all, one that may be *added to* at will. To which may be added a section experimenting with polyphony; then another about money and allegory; and yet another on the growth of the world-system . . . 'Give them more – give them excess', said the Director in the 'Prelude'. And Staiger: 'The principle of composition most truly epic in character is that of simple addition. On a small as well as on a large scale, epic brings independent elements together.'[26] And Daniel Madelénat:

> Under the banner of aggregation (of lines, episodes and themes), the monumental scale of epic space reveals its fertility: through collage, montage or juxtaposition, it opens the way to continuous growth.[27]

A form in continuous growth: one 'that wouldn't exclude something merely because it didn't fit' (Ezra Pound).[28] A form 'distending itself for centuries, like pythons swallowing sheep' (Frye), and thus becoming the 'incommensurable whole' of which Goethe speaks a year before his death. All definitions dictated by pride in a form that dares to contend in breadth with the entire world. But after the twelve thousand lines of *Faust*, Melville's cetology, and the endlessly identical adventures of *Bouvard and Pécuchet*, reservations about the technique of aggregation do begin to circulate:

> Sterne's writings [. . .] are formless because he could have carried on to infinity, and his death meant only the end of his works but not their

---

[25] E. Staiger, *Basic Concepts of Poetics*, translated by J. Hudson and L. Frank, Pennsylvania State University Press, Philadelphia 1991, p. 121.

[26] Ibid., p. 122.

[27] D. Madelénat, *L'Épopée*, PUF, Paris 1986, p. 72. On the epic as an 'encyclopaedic aggregate' (with the stress on the latter), see also the section 'Thematic Modes' in N. Frye's *Anatomy of Criticism*, Princeton University Press, Princeton NJ 1957, pp. 54–61.

[28] The phrase is recorded in H.N. Schneidau, 'Pound's Poetics of Loss', in F.A. Bell, ed., *Ezra Pound: Tactics for Reading*, Barnes and Noble, London and Totowa 1982, pp. 110–11.

completion. Sterne's works are formless because they are extensible to infinity; but infinite forms do not exist.[29]

It is the coldly brilliant indictment drawn up by the young Lukács, in which sarcasm on the formlessness of epic genres (a question that, only a few years later, will dominate *Theory of the Novel*) goes together with the suspicion of modernism, from which Lukács will never free himself. Infinite forms do not exist:

> – You forget that both books, as we have them today, are fragments. Who knows where Sterne would have taken the love story between Uncle Toby and the Widow Wadman if he had lived long enough to finish writing it?
>   – What I'm saying is that he couldn't have lived that long.[30]

That long . . . It is the sincere surprise of the aged Goethe, who apparently never expected to finish *Faust*;[31] the deaths of Flaubert and Musil, which cut short *Bouvard and Pécuchet* and *The Man Without Qualities*. Between the brief span of individual existence and the continuous growth of the social totality, the game has become unequal: the aggregation of the mechanical form seeks in some way to confront it; but vying in extent with the world, in the long run, makes no sense. It is necessary to relearn how to 'conceive a whole', writes Lukács. And here is Edgar Morin:

> Simultaneously, the organized whole is something more than the sum of its parts, because it brings out qualities that without such organization would not exist. They are emerging qualities, in the sense that they are empirically observable, but they are not logically deducible. Such emerging qualities retroact upon the parts, and may stimulate the latter to express their potentialities.[32]

---

[29] G. Lukács, 'Richness, Chaos and Form: a dialogue concerning Lawrence Sterne', in *Soul and Form*, translated by Anna Bostock, MIT Press, Cambridge Mass. 1974, p. 143.

[30] Ibid., p. 138.

[31] 'Nothing will any longer be able to distract me from *Faust*', he declares to Eckermann on 24 January 1830, 'because it would really be quite amazing if I managed to finish it! And it is possible . . .'

[32] Morin, 'Le vie della complessità', p. 51.

The organized whole: this is the task, then. But how to reverse the trend? How to transform a paratactical form into a literature of complexity? It seems an insoluble problem, and indeed it was not a writer who managed to solve it.

The
Nibelung's Ring

CHAPTER

5

'Drink first, hero, so that distant things don't escape you'

Let us begin with an oddity. George Bernard Shaw, *The Perfect Wagnerite*:

> Almost the first thing that a dramatist has to learn in constructing a
> play is that the persons must not come on the stage in the second act
> and tell one another at great length what the audience has already seen
> pass before its eyes in the first act. The extent to which Wagner has
> been seduced into violating this rule by his affection for his themes is
> startling for a practised playwright. Siegfried inherits from Wotan a
> mania for autobiography which leads him to inflict on everyone he
> meets the story of Mime and the dragon, although the audience have
> spent a whole evening witnessing the events he is narrating. Hagen
> tells the story to Gunther; and that same night Alberich's ghost tells it
> over again to Hagen, who knows it already as well as the audience.
> Siegfried tells the Rhine maidens as much of it as they will listen to,
> and then keeps telling it to his hunting companions until they kill
> him.[1]

---

[1] G.B. Shaw, *The Perfect Wagnerite* (1888), Dover Publications, New York 1967,
p. 109.

The *Ring* stories as indecorous ballast: Shaw is quite right to mock the woodenness of Wagner the dramatist. But is it equally sure that the *Ring* is above all a *drama*? Thomas Mann:

> Wagner loathed cultural pretensions. He was not a man to make such demands. Wherever he went to work the world began anew, and nobody should have need of any previous knowledge in order to understand.[2]

The world that begins from scratch every time. This, adds Mann, is Wagner's 'epic radicalism': which from the original *Siegfried's Tod* causes him to go back to the hero's youth; then still further back, to meet his parents; and finally, to the distant antecedent of *Rhinegold*. As in *Faust Part Two*, the original tragic nucleus swells into a gigantic construction; and in this new context, the autobiographical mania of the Wagnerian heroes is not in the least out of place. 'Presentation', writes Staiger, 'is the essence of epic poetry': literally, 'making present' what is past. Standing before it, filled with joy at 'being able to say: This is how it looks!':

> The greatest vitality lies in the depths of the past and no opportunity is missed to plumb these depths. When two men ready themselves for combat with each other [in Homer, but also in Wagner!] they ask for name and origin, and the man questioned relates the history of his clan back to the oldest forefathers, even to the god who founded the family [. . .] For it is precisely the merit of epic reflection that it stems the pressing flow of people and things.[3]

Stemming the flow of people and things: just think about the plot of the *Ring*, and you will understand the value of memory in Wagner's world. Everything comes to an end there: the faith of lovers, and the strength of heroes; the race of giants, that of the Nibelungs, and that of the gods. Swords are found and broken, tempered and lost; the leaves fall from the

---

[2] T. Mann, 'Richard Wagner and *The Nibelung's Ring*' (1938), in *Pro and Contra Wagner*, translated by Allan Blunden, Faber and Faber, London and Boston 1985, p. 184.

[3] E. Staiger, *Basic Concepts of Poetics*, translated by J. Hudson and L. Frank, Pennsylvania State University Press, Philadelphia 1991, pp. 104, 107, 100–101.

World Ash, the eternal youth of the gods fades . . . Well, the story-telling so derided by Shaw sustains this dying world, and is – far more than Siegfried himself – its secret protagonist. The death of the young hero, significantly intertwined with a memory potion ('Drink first, hero, from my horn:/I've seasoned a sweet-tasting drink/to stir your memory afresh,/so that distant things don't escape you!') so that Siegfried is in effect killed *by his own story*, is like a miniature of their relationship: the story takes the place of the hero. And when the dying Siegfried sees once more the smile and the eyes of Brünnhilde, *and speaks of himself in the third person*,[4] grammar itself bows down to the new lord and master: the logic of the story is so strong, it has wiped out awareness of self.

The story as a force that 'saves' the world. In what sense? In the only sense possible, given the sombre atmosphere of the *Ring*: by making it unforgettable. To keep Siegfried alive, halt the twilight, or tame the conflict between the races which destroys the Wagnerian universe – none of that is possible. But the story can ensure that its memory is not lost, and, above all, can still present the world *as a whole*. It can highlight its causal connections and secret interrelations. It can restore its unity, at least in imagination.

This is the great turn towards *concentration* impressed upon the modern epic by the *Ring*. Spatial concentration, first and foremost. In Wagner, from *Flying Dutchman* on, there is a continual allusion to boundless spaces, and to endless, aimless journeys. But the reality of things is different. '*Ein fremder Mann!*', a stranger, Sieglinde exclaims at the sight of Siegmund: but no, that man who has apparently arrived by chance at her cabin is, in fact, the brother for whom she has always been waiting. At the end of *Valkyrie* Brünnhilde, trying to save Sieglinde from Wotan's vengeance, hides her in the very wood that already harbours the Giant and the Dragon, the Ring and the Nibelung. 'My home's far away', Siegfried in turn declares at the start of the third part of the cycle: '[I'll] go forth from the forest/into the world:/I'll nevermore return' (*Siegfried*, I, 1): but then he goes off on a real pilgrimage of destiny to the sites of the preceding

---

[4] 'One came to wake you;/his kiss awakes you/and once again he breaks/the bride's bonds' (*Twilight of the Gods*, III, 2, in *Wagner's Ring of the Nibelung*, translated by Stewart Spencer, Thames and Hudson, London 1993).

operas. In *Twilight*, he will end up at the abode of the only person who is still thinking about the ring.

This is the first of the many duplicities of the Wagnerian universe: a world at once grand and narrow. Grand: five or six different races, scattered among the four elements, separated by real abysses. Narrow: because, on close inspection, the significant places in the *Ring* number about ten, and they attract the (few) important characters with calamitous force. The plot is like a maelstrom: everything in it whirls round in ever tighter, deeper and more remorseless circles, towards – a tiny circle of metal. There truly is no space here for Goethean digression, and in fact, the more remote the grasp of fate seems, the firmer it is. The story of the Volsungs, which seems a wholly autonomous episode, brings us inexorably back to the ring. The same goes for Siegfried: the 'most free' of heroes – but also the predestined one, who will weld together the links of the tetralogy once and for all.

But whatever kind of plot is this? After the first scenes of *Rhinegold*, Francesco Orlando has written:

> nothing more happens, basically, until the end of the long cycle. All we see are repercussions, or repetitions, or vain attempts at abolition, of the only thing that has really happened already.[5]

Quite true. In the overall plan of the work, the whole of *Valkyrie*, the whole of *Siegfried*, and half of *Twilight*, amount basically to just one 'move' in the plot: shifting the ring from Fafner to Siegfried.[6] And very often it even becomes doubtful whether what has happened is really an 'event' at all. Before Nothung fulfils any real function, we encounter it as a (musical) idea of Wotan's, and his pledge to Siegmund; as a wish of Siegmund's, a memory of Sieglinde's, an object illuminated by fire, a motif recalled by the orchestra . . . When Siegmund draws the sword from the Ash, therefore, it is hard to speak of an 'event' in the usual sense: more than anything else, his deed is the completion of something

---

[5] F. Orlando, 'Mito e storia ne "L'anello del Nibelungo" ', in *Intersezioni*, August 1983, pp. 351–2.

[6] On the narratological concept of the 'move', see T. Pavel, *The Poetics of Plot*, Minnesota University Press, Minneapolis 1985.

long awaited. A duplication, a closure: in a sense, already almost *an end*.[7]

A grand world, but one made up of few places; of few things and persons. A story which goes from the beginning of time to the last age, in four or five moves. And at the centre of everything, of course, a ring that contains within it power over the whole world . . . It really is impossible to imagine a structure more different from *Faust* (which Wagner greatly admired, nevertheless): more *centripetal*, in contrast to the latter's dispersion. Indeed, few things seem as essential to Wagner's poetics as the idea of concentration. As he writes in 'Opera and Drama':

> If a man's idea is bared to us convincingly only by his action, and if a man's character consists in the complete harmony between his idea and his action, then this action, and therefore also its underlying idea [. . .] gains significance [. . .] by its manifesting itself in utmost concentration.

And again:

> In the *mythos* [. . .] the vast multiplicity of surrounding phenomena, whose real association the human being cannot grasp as yet, gives him first of all an impression of unrest: in order to overcome this feeling of unrest he seeks for some connection of the phenomena among themselves, some connection which he may conceive as their First Cause. [. . .] Thus in mythos all the shaping impulse of the folk makes toward

---

[7] What is true for objects, is true also for characters: in the *Ring* (and in all of Wagner from the *Dutchman* to *Parsifal*), things abound that *one person alone* can accomplish – along with characters who exist *for that thing alone*. It is a chaining of the subject to his deed which has left an unmistakable trace in Wagnerian language, where it often happens that the character literally loses his own name, and is addressed by a verbal noun identifying him with the action he has just carried out. This goes from entirely fluent examples (*der Wanderer*, the wayfarer; *der Prahler*, the braggart) to others where language bends beneath the effort (*der Frager*, the asker; *der Verbieter*, the forbidder), and on to the unusual and somewhat excruciating *der Wecker*, with which the dying Siegfried resumes his entire life in the act of waking Brünnhilde.

realizing to its senses a broadest grouping of the most manifold phenomena, and in the most succinct of shapes.[8]

These are words drawn from a historical reflection upon Greek drama.
But when Wagner thinks about the present, things do not change:

> In the interest of intelligibility the poet has to limit the number of his
> action's moments [. . .] taking into [the chief motive] a number of
> motives which in ordinary life would only utter themselves through
> numerous moments of action. [. . .] Time and space, to let them
> appear in keeping with the movement of these figures, he will alike
> condense [. . .] The strengthening of a motive cannot therefore consist
> in a mere addition of lesser motives, but in the complete absorption of
> *many motives* into this *one*.[9]

The plot of the *Ring*, and Wagner's programmatic works, are sending us
the same message: condensation, compression, concentration. Why?

Monumental dilettantism

To answer our question, we must introduce a few new elements.
Friedrich Nietzsche:

> I have attributed the peculiar anguish that listening to Wagner's music
> provokes in me [. . .] to the fact that the eye – in order to understand –
> must forever be positioning itself differently: now as short-sighted, in
> order not to miss the sophisticated chiselwork on the mosaic; now for
> the contemplation of bold and brutal frescoes, which need to be
> looked at from a long way away.[10]

Dual optic of the Wagnerian cosmos. It is one of the themes dearest to

---

[8] Richard Wagner, 'Opera and Drama', in A. Goldman and E. Sprinchorn, eds,
Wagner on Music and Drama, Nebraska University Press, Lincoln Neb. and London
1992, pp. 88–90.

[9] Ibid., pp. 192–4. These sentences too are taken from 'Opera and Drama'.

[10] F. Nietzsche, *Werke*, ed. Giorgio Colli and Mazzino Montinari, vol. VIII.2,
Nachgelassene Fragmente. November 1887 – März 1888 (Notebook W II 3), Walter
de Gruyter and Co., Berlin 1970, pp. 376–7.

Thomas Mann, who returns time and again to the mixture of 'intellectualism and myth' in Wagner's art: 'sublime, but adapted to the world'; able to speak 'to refined needs and to simple ones', 'to the many and to the few'. 'The world success of this Bolshevik of culture', Mann concludes, 'was a tragi-comic paradox';[11] and perhaps that really was the case. Yet that success was also the fulfilment of the secret (and frustrated) desire of every world text, from *Faust* to *Ulysses* and beyond: to represent the social totality – while at the same time *addressing* it. To be innovative and popular, complex and simple, esoteric and direct: to heal the great fracture between avant-garde exploration and mass culture.

All things that Goethe does not manage, and Joyce even less, but at which Wagner succeeds. Why? Possibly, because Wagner pays heed to *Faust's* Director, and writes an opera that may easily be 'broken into pieces', with its hundred-odd *Leitmotive*: simple and highly effective unities, continually repeated so as to become deeply engraved on the listener's mind. The result is a kind of permanent publicity for the Wagnerian cosmos: a music, Pound comments, 'which is not dissimilar from that of the Foire de Neuilly'; that reminds Nietzsche of 'the art of the shop window', and Adorno of the 'phantasmagoria of the commodity'.[12] And yet, the advertiser's skill is accompanied here by something very different. Mann, in 'The Sorrows and Grandeur of Richard Wagner':

> One might say, at the risk of being misunderstood, that Wagner's art is
> a case of dilettantism that has been monumentalized by a supreme

---

[11] The quotations are taken from 'Richard Wagner and *The Nibelung's Ring*' (1938), 'The Sorrows and Grandeur of Richard Wagner' (1933), and 'Reflections of a Non-political Man' (1918). All are included in Mann, *Pro and Contra Wagner*. More cruelly, Nietzsche had spoken of the 'shrewd idiocy' with which Wagner mixes the certainties of 'the gigantic, that which moves the masses' with the fugitive seduction of 'the state of mind which precedes thought, the travail of yet unborn thoughts, the promise of future thoughts [. . .] Wagner's genius for forming clouds . . .' (F. Nietzsche, *The Case of Wagner*, T. Fisher Unwin, London 1899, pp. 20–21, 38).

[12] E. Pound, *Antheil and the Treatise on Harmony* (1924), Da Capo Press, New York 1968, p. 44; F. Nietzsche, 'Nietzsche contra Wagner', in *The Case of Wagner*, p. 78; T.W. Adorno, *In Search of Wagner*, NLB, London 1981, pp. 89–90.

effort of the will and intelligence – a dilettantism raised to the level of genius. There is something dilettante about the very idea of combining all the arts . . .[13]

Monumental dilettantism . . . This, as we know, is not just Wagner. It is the project – and the problem – of the entire modern epic, with its desire to reunite what history has divided: knowledge, ethics, religion, art; narrative, drama, lyric poetry; literature, music, painting. Wagner's own addition is the 'shamelessness' of which Nietzsche accuses him; his taking literally – with stubborn determination – the global task of his own work. Goethe plays with myth;[14] Joyce encourages foolish disciples to make extravagant claims; Eliot leaves us in doubt as to whether or not to believe in the Tarot pack. But not Wagner. Wagner is tremendously serious about everything. So serious, indeed, as to give us a glimpse, behind the semi-serious lightmindedness of the dilettante, of the more solid – and murkier – figure of the *charlatan*.

For the latter, it is not enough to reassemble what history has fragmented. He has quite other ambitions: to reduce every action, every phenomenon of reality, *to a single principle*: to the secret prime cause he has finally discovered (and perhaps even, as so often in Wagner, distilled into a magic potion). It is a contagious, ambivalent euphoria that, as the nineteenth century gives way to the twentieth, very few can resist – in reaction, I believe, to the growing intellectual division of labour. So we get the cosmologies of Spengler and Pound, Yeats and Breton: cycles, usury, the moon, dream . . . And other, less strident, traces almost everywhere: in medicine, psychology, the historical sciences. And also among the greatest: Joyce, Schönberg, Eliot . . .

And Wagner, of course. Here, his urge to concentrate takes on a new significance. It is no longer (only) a technical choice, but a magic, and even religious, principle:

---

[13] Mann, *Pro and Contra Wagner*, p. 103.

[14] 'What a contrast indeed between the Wagnerian and Goethean treatments of myth! [. . .] Each is equally great in its way, beyond a doubt [. . .] But the grandeur of Goethe's vision carries no hint of pathos or tragedy; instead of celebrating myth, he jests with it [. . .] Nothing could be less Wagnerian than Goethe's ironical manner of invoking myth . . .' (Mann, 'Richard Wagner and *The Nibelung's Ring*', ibid., p. 176).

A condensement of the shape of actual life can be comprehended by
the latter only when – as compared with itself – it appears magnified,
strengthened, unaccustomed.

And again, returning to a passage from which I have already quoted:

> To overcome this feeling of unrest [towards the vast multiplicity of sur-
> rounding phenomena] man seeks for some connection of the
> phenomena among themselves, some connection which he may con-
> ceive as their First Cause. [. . .] God and gods are the first creations of
> man's poetic force: in them man represents to himself the essence of
> natural phenomena as derived from a cause.[15]

At first sight, nothing particularly new here: all Feuerbachian ideas, widespread in mid-nineteenth-century German culture. But what is new,
and even rather incredible, is that the author of these sentences should set
about *inventing gods*. It is Wagner at his worst: a sly, false naivety. And yet,
it is exactly what is needed to breathe new life into the idea of the sacred text. It
is the Lucifer face of the modern epic: vying with, and if possible oust-
ing, the Christian faith. Challenging it with a blasphemy of colossal
dimensions: the black masses of *Faust* and the *Temptation*, of *Moby-Dick*,
Ulysses, and *Last Days of Mankind*. Or, on the contrary, inventing a new
sacredness: the redemptive virtue of *das Streben*, the Bayreuth sanctuary,
the visions of Yeats and the surrealists, Eliot's mythology. In both cases,
the world text rejects the calm agnosticism of the novel: it rebels against
the slow decline of the sacred, and seeks to restore lost transcendence.
And so, by the nature of things, it harkens to the siren songs of false
prophets.

The greatest of these was indeed Richard Wagner, who with
unscrupulous genius mingled the pagan and the Christian, bending both
to the reinvention of a simple, effective totality:

> The poet reassembles into a totality that which, to anyone who
> observes history, appears dispersed, heterogeneous and elusive. The
> artist's imagination has the task of concentrating reality, in all 'the vast
> multiplicity of its connexions' ('Opera and Drama'), so as to simplify it

---

[15] Both passages are taken from 'Opera and Drama', in Goldman and Sprinchorn,
eds, *Wagner on Music and Drama*, pp. 192 and 88.

and make it visible. For this purpose, imagination must transform known reality into images easy to comprehend. The myth of Wagnerian drama consists precisely in such images.[16]

Concentrate, and simplify. It is the decisive couplet, if you wish to understand the popularity of the *Ring,* in comparison with every other world text. For Goethe, as later for Joyce, the epic undertaking consists in *adding*: in suggesting a boundless world, populated by elusive, phantasmal forces. In Wagner, the opposite is true: cosmic war is waged between familiar figures – heroes and dwarfs, giants and gods – and in a few, continually revisited places. And at the centre of all this, the ultimate simplification: the world – in a ring.

Twofold myth

I have spoken of concentration as the basic technique of the *Ring*. Also, of concentration/simplification as the key to its mass success. Finally, concentration may well be seen as the political dominant of the Wagnerian universe. Adorno:

> In theory and in the ideology of the work [Wagner] rejected the division of labour in terms that recall National Socialist phrases about the subordination of private interests to the public good.

And again:

> He belongs to the first generation to realize that in a world that has been socialized through and through it is not possible for an individual to alter something that is determined over the heads of men. Nevertheless, it was not given to him to call the overarching totality by its real name. In consequence it is transformed for him into myth. The opacity and omnipotence of the social process is then celebrated as a metaphysical mystery . . .[17]

---

[16] A. Ingenhoff, *Drama oder Epos? Richard Wagners Gattungstheorie des musikalischen Dramas*, Max Niemeyer Verlag, Tübingen 1987, p. 113.

[17] Adorno, *In Search of Wagner*, pp. 108, 119.

Social omnipotence, and metaphysical mystery. On the one hand, the growing concentration of economic and political power, which is a constant theme of the Frankfurt School. On the other, the mythological form such a process assumes in Wagner, where it is embodied in Alberich's ring. The ring as a mask for real power, in short: as an ideological move. Which is true. But it risks distracting us from something even more interesting. Namely, that throughout the whole span of the cycle, *the ring never works*. To be sure, we are told over and over again how it confers power over the entire universe. But these words are never translated into deeds, and of all those who have the ring in their grasp (Alberich, Wotan, Fasolt, Fafner, Siegfried, Brünnhilde), not one ever obtains the promised omnipotence. Towards the end, indeed, almost no one even thinks about it any longer.

If we wish to arrive at a sociology of the *Ring*, therefore, there seem to be two basic facts to be considered: an extreme concentration of power – and its total unfeasibility. It is as if Wagner were definitively saying farewell to the idea of territorial empire: here is the world, here is the weapon that can subjugate it . . . and nothing happens. The wish for unbounded power is still very strong, and some characters sacrifice their whole beings to it. But it is useless, the world will never again belong to 'a single lord'. It is a Janus-like stance, that will recur in the world texts of the twenties and thirties: a tremendous totalitarian temptation – and the impossibility of carrying it through to the end.

The ring never works . . . In other words, if we go by the plot, the Wagnerian cycle is the story of a collapse – a cosmic failure. The myth of the *Ring*, however, is not just a story. It is also, and perhaps mainly, *an interpretive tool*. It is what (in Ingenhoff's words) makes it possible to condense human history, with 'the vast multiplicity of its connexions', into 'images easy to comprehend'. Siegfried appears – and the Volsungs and nature, the sword and destiny, are all joined together again. Wotan appears – and along with him the laws and Valhalla, twilight and the ring. The fact that Wotan then burns in Valhalla, and Siegfried is killed by treachery, is a secondary matter. Let myth as plot send the world up in flames: the other myth has still enabled us to *see it*. In the words of Eliot (who, incidentally, is attracted by myths very like the Wagnerian ones):

[The mythical method] is simply a way of controlling, of ordering, of giving a shape and a significance to the immense panorama of futility and anarchy that is contemporary history.[18]

Controlling, ordering . . . but ordering with respect to what? In *Ulysses*, in *The Cantos*, in *The Waste Land*, it is easy to answer: with respect to the chaotic fragments (let us call them that, for the moment) of modernity. But in the *Ring* saga, where there is little or no chaos? What exactly is here the grand world, to be grasped in the 'vast multiplicity of its inter-connections'?

Quite simply, it is music. Without the centripetal force of the myth, I mean, the 'infinite melody' of the *Ring* would in all probability have constituted an excessive challenge (vast multiplicity, indeed) to the perception of Wagner's contemporaries. A famous passage from *The Case of Wagner*:

> What is the characteristic of all literary decadence? It is that the life no longer resides in the whole. The word gets the upper hand and jumps out of the sentence, the sentence stretches too far and obscures the meaning of the page, the page acquires life at the expense of the whole – the whole is no longer a whole [. . .] always atomistic anarchy, disgregation of will [. . .] Everywhere paralysis, distress, and torpor, or hostility and chaos [. . .] If you want to admire [Wagner], see him at work here: how he separates, how he arrives at little unities, how he animates them, inflates them, and renders them visible. But by so doing his power exhausts itself . . .[19]

Aside from the acrimony, it is a convincing analysis, which provides an

---

[18] T.S. Eliot, '*Ulysses*, Order and Myth', in *The Dial*, November 1923. In Eliot too, the myth of the Fisher King, which lies behind *The Waste Land*, is a story of failure: it evokes a personal power that never succeeds in becoming reality. But there too, it is not the *narrative content* of the myth that is essential, but its capacity for symbolic condensation. Myth's task is not to put *an end* to the 'futility and anarchy that is contemporary history', but to give them 'a shape and a significance'. To create a *perceptual* order, not a real order.

[19] Nietzsche, *The Case of Wagner*, p. 25 (translation modified). As is well known, the image used by Nietzsche is taken from an essay by Paul Bourget on Baudelaire (*Essais de psychologie contemporaine*, Paris 1889, p. 25).

excellent basis for understanding the function of Wagnerian myth. The 'atomistic anarchy' (Eliot . . .) of the musical cells requires *a counterweight* to balance the continuous (literally, interminable) growth of the *unendliche Melodie*. The mythographer's concentrated simplicity, in other words, acts as a kind of framework and scaffolding, allowing maximum complexity and freedom for the musician. A deep, but far from obvious, relation between music and drama is thus taking shape, which we shall explore after a technical parenthesis.

Art of transition

I have spoken of the mythical plot as a counterweight to the growth of the *unendliche Melodie*. Let us have a closer look at the second side of the question. Adorno:

> [In Wagner's music] all the energy is on the side of the dissonance; in comparison the individual resolutions become increasingly threadbare [. . .] Tension is made into an absolute principle by ensuring that, as in a giant credit system, the negation of the negation, the full settlement of the debt contracted by every dissonance, is indefinitely postponed [. . .] The characteristic chord [. . .] tells both of the poignant pain of non-fulfilment and of the pleasure that lies in the tension: it is both sweet and necessary.[20]

Love for the unresolved, for the uncompleted sequence. Or, to pick up the credit-system metaphor again: Wagner's pleasure lies in a *virtually limitless* expansion, in which no development is ever excluded from the category of the possible. It is the *Kunst des Überganges*: the art of passage and transition described to Mathilde von Wesendonck in October 1858:

---

[20] Adorno, *In Search of Wagner*, pp. 66–7. This ambiguity of expression, Adorno goes on, 'did not exist before Wagner. That suffering can be sweet, and that the poles of pleasure and pain are not rigidly opposed to one another, but are mediated, is something that both composers and audience learned uniquely from him, and it is this experience alone that made it possible for dissonance to extend its range, over the whole language of music. And few aspects of Wagner's music have been as seductive as the enjoyment of pain.'

My music [. . .] prompts me to mediate and knit together all the modes of transition between extremes of mood. My subtlest and deepest art I now might call the art of transition: the whole consists of such transitions. I have taken a dislike to the abrupt and harsh. . .[21]

The whole of music consists of such transitions . . . Which means that the 'art of transition' is not just a means of moving 'between extremes of mood'. It is already *an end in itself*, whose significance (beyond its specific destination) lies in the joint presence of routes all equally possible. This is the Wagner forbidden to Schönberg by his 'old composition professor' ('a very old one, in fact he is already dead'), because he uses 'so many diminished seventh chords'. Precisely those which some beautiful pages in the *Theory of Harmony* will term 'vagrant chords':

> at home in no single key [. . . It is] entitled to reside anywhere, yet is nowhere a permanent resident – it is a cosmopolitan or a tramp! [. . . The diminished seventh chord's] decisive influence as *Modulationsmotor* comes, not so much from its own power to turn away from the key, as, far more, from its indefinite, hermaphroditic, immature character. In itself it is indecisive, it has many tendencies, and anything can overpower it. Thereupon rests its particular influence: whoever wants to be a mediator may not himself personally be all too definite.[22]

An indefinite, indecisive sound, with many tendencies, which anything can overpower . . . This is a technical passage, and yet it gives us in miniature the fundamental category of modernism: the category of the *possible*. Or rather, of the possible *as such*: where the distinction between the route actually followed, and the one merely outlined, loses all importance. This is exactly what happens with the combinations of motives in the *Ring*: not just ever richer and more complex as the opera proceeds, but, above all, ever more inclined to suggest possible connections, instead of fixing clear-cut developments. And when the paths multiply, of course, the conclusion becomes problematic: for to conclude means to *renounce* certain possibilities, and this – in a work that has increased its own

---

[21] Goldman and Sprinchorn, eds, *Wagner on Music and Drama*, p. 213 (translation modified).

[22] A. Schönberg, *Theory of Harmony* (1922), translated by Roy Carter, University of California Press, Berkeley 1978, pp. 239, 195–6.

combinatory potentialities from one scene to the next – will inevitably be felt as an undeserved *impoverishment*. It is the Wagner of Pierre Boulez: 'an "open" structure never "closed" except provisionally and unwillingly.' And again:

> This explains why Wagner's conclusions are so difficult and sometimes appear hasty, arbitrary and abrupt – almost brusque gestures of impatience [. . .] In his strongest works he boldly faces this problem and refuses artificial solutions. Doubt and suspense – the feeling that the whole drama can start all over again – are of the very essence of Wagner's endings: nothing, least of all the musical texture, is finally stopped dead and nothing can ever be absolutely completed. There is no need to go as far as [. . .] *Finnegans Wake* in order to feel that at the end of the *Ring* Wagner has set the scene for a further instalment of the drama.[23]

The epic interplay between digression and conclusion, which I discussed in Chapter 2, resurfaces here as an inverse and complementary relation between music and drama. For, if Schönberg and Boulez are right, the brutality of Wagner's plots, and especially that of the *Ring*, is the one force still capable of delimiting this expanding universe. Something is needed to impose upon the *unendliche Melodie* (from outside, and almost treacherously: like Hagen's lance-blow) that ending which, from the musical standpoint, has by now lost any justification. The conclusion of the cycle thus becomes an act at once indispensable and arbitrary. Indispensable, because the complexity cannot go on growing *ad infinitum*. But also 'abrupt and arbitrary', because it betrays the inner logic of the work.

And, indeed, the last scene of the last day is the *Ring*'s most tormented passage: rewritten four times, across the span of a quarter century. At first, it is an optimistic finale: a Feuerbachian salute to mankind bereft of its gods. Next, it is a Schopenhauerian rejection of the 'abode of greed and illusion'. Later still, it becomes an announcement of redemption, reminiscent of *Parsifal*. And finally, it acquires the form which we know today – and which is also, significantly, *the least conclusive variant of all*: an

---

[23] P. Boulez, 'Time Re-explored' (1976 Bayreuth Festival programme for *Rhinegold*), in P. Boulez, *Orientations*, translated by Martin Cooper, Faber and Faber, London and Boston 1986, p. 271.

umpteenth recapitulation, wholly incapable of fixing the work's meaning. No more philosophy here. No religion, no message of universal scope. Brünnhilde no longer even speaks to the human beings surrounding her on the stage, but to her horse. The cycle must end, of course – Wagner seems to be telling us – but do not expect its meaning to be found *in the finale*. Four banal sentences, and let the last word be left to the music.

Complexity. I

A few final reflections upon the most programmatically epic concept of the Wagnerian undertaking. *Gesamtkunstwerk*: 'total artwork'. Total, people usually add, by virtue of the parallelism between music and drama, which develop an identical message in the two different sign-systems. The result of my analysis, however – a centripetal, simplificatory plot; a polymorphous, centrifugal score – suggests a quite different hypothesis: that, in the *Ring, music and drama follow opposite logics*. From 'Music of the Future':

> The poet [. . .] will eavesdrop from the musician the secret hidden from the latter's self, the secret that Melodic Form is capable of infinitely richer evolution than the musician had as yet deemed possible within the Symphony itself [. . .] Thus where the Symphonist still timidly groped back to the original dance-form – never daring, even for his expression, to quite transgress the bounds which held him in communication with that form – the Poet now will cry to him: 'Launch without a fear into the full flood of Music's sea; hand in hand with me, you can never lose touch of the thing most seizable of all by every human being; for through me you stand on the solid ground of the Dramatic Action [. . .] Stretch boldly out your melody [. . .] since my hand it is that guides you.'[24]

---

[24] R. Wagner, 'Zukunftsmusik', in *Prose Works*, vol. 3, translated by William Ashton Ellis, Kegan Paul Trench Trübner, London 1894, p. 337. Similar ideas in 'Opera and Drama': 'the word poet has concentrated an infinitude of scattered moments of action, sensation, and expression [. . .] to a point the most accessible to the feeling; now comes the tone poet, and has to expand this concentrated, compact point to the utmost fullness of its emotional content' (Goldman and Sprinchorn, eds, *Wagner on Music and Drama*, p. 207).

Boldness, and an ocean, for music; solid, bounded terrain for drama. Wagner's metaphorics here suggests a division of labour quite similar to the one I have been outlining. Such is also the conclusion of Pierre Boulez:

> [As the *Ring* develops] there is something like a duality between the worlds of the drama and of the music. The world of the music becomes far richer than that of the drama and tends, by its sheer power of proliferation, to make an exclusive claim on our attention. The motives show a strong tendency to become autonomous, with the stage action serving perpetually as pretext and providing explanations – in fact the dramatic text becomes, literally, a musical pretext.[25]

A structure that is born as relatively unitary, but then gradually divides into a dramatic pretext, and an autonomous musical cosmos. It is a perfect example of how formal change takes place: not in a consistent and simultaneous way at all levels; but a piece at a time, at different rates, and perhaps even in different directions. In other words, evolution as *differentiation*: as the history of a work in which the dramatic plot *remains simple*, to guarantee the solidity of the ensemble; while the musical tissue *evolves towards complexity*, embarking on epoch-making experiments.

It is a Janus-like structure: semi-*archaic* and semi-*advanced*. Non-contemporaneity operates with such force here as almost to break the *Ring* in two: *mythical* content, and music of the *future*. As Boulez writes, 'Romanticism and structure – two words not usually found in alliance' (and it is hard not to be reminded of Goebbels's 'steely romanticism').[26] Or again: reaction and revolution. On the one hand, writes Francesco Orlando, 'the racist tendency, prone to permanent dissociations' of the libretto; on the other,

> the formal level of the 'continuo' which circulates tirelessly in the music, sparing no possible association [. . .] By dint of converting similarities into oppositions, and oppositions into similarities, it succeeds –

---

[25] Boulez, *Orientations*, p. 265.
[26] Ibid., p. 262.

more often than the words – in transcending and denying the mystifi-
cations of the ideology.[27]

There are structures, as I was saying at the end of Chapter 4 (quoting
Edgar Morin), which are only equal to the sum of their parts, and perhaps not even that. There are others, however, which are more than a
sum: they are a system, whose various parts interact among themselves.
Faust was an example of the former type; the *Ring*, of the latter. This is the
reason, finally, why Wagner is so fond of those wretched recapitulations
that we took as our point of departure. At a certain moment – when he
decides to compose *Rhinegold* and *Valkyrie*, i.e. the pre-history of the
Siegfried story – he really does seem determined to banish them. Here is
the manifesto-letter he sent to Liszt on 20 November 1851:

> By the distinctness of representation which is thus made possible [by
> the new compositional plan] and *which at the same time does away with
> everything of the nature of a lengthy narration, or at least condenses it in a few
> pregnant moments*, I gain sufficient space to intensify the wealth of rela-
> tions, while in the previous semi-epical mode of treatment I was
> compelled to cut down and enfeeble all this.[28]

Confine the detailed narrative to brief allusions? But if the texts are compared, as Carl Dahlhaus observes, the opposite turns out to be the case:
in *Twilight*, the Norns scene, Waltraute's prayer, Hagen's dream, are all
decidedly *longer* than the equivalent passages in the original *Siegfried's
Tod*:

> Thus the epic element plays a paradoxical role in the *Ring*: [. . .] the
> epic recapitulation of what has already been shown visually actually
> creates opportunities for passages that are particularly rich in motivic

---

[27] F. Orlando, 'Proposte per una semantica del leit-motiv nell' "Anello del
Nibelungo" ', in *Nuova Rivista Musicale Italiana*, April–June 1975, p. 245. Very
similar to the position of Boulez: 'The whole *Ring* reveals a counterpoint [...]
between ideology in the accepted sense, which does in fact become pessimistic
and even reactionary, and the musical ideology, which generates an increasingly
subversive fermentation' (Boulez, *Orientations*, p. 275).

[28] *Correspondence of Wagner and Liszt*, vol. 1, translated by Francis Hueffer, H. Grevel
and Co., London 1888, p. 173 (italics added).

development. The epic traits that Wagner the theorist wanted to banish from drama were restored out of musical necessity.[29]

They were restored; or, more accurately, they were never eliminated. Here, the mechanism of refunctionalization starts to operate once again. For the purposes of the plot, the recapitulations are laborious and unjustifiable; once the plan of the opera is fleshed out, they should simply be thrown away. But at a certain point Wagner notices that those very passages are the ideal prop for creating extraordinary *conglomerations of Leitmotive*. For the recapitulations work like so many kaleidoscopes: they shake up and reassemble the tiniest units of Wagner's music into ever richer combinations. It is the shift which concluded the first part of this work: from parataxis to interaction. From the mechanical form to *complexity*.

Drama, and music. Recapitulation, and motivic tissue. In the ensemble as in the details, the relationship is always the same: *simplicity* of the drama, and *complexity* of the music. Progress coexists with backwardness, indeed depends upon it. One level of the work can be bold, *because* the other is crude and superfluous. It is a constructional split that runs through almost the entire twentieth century. Ezra Pound:

> The correspondences [of *Ulysses*] are part of Joyce's mediaevalism and are chiefly his own affair, a scaffold, a means of construction, justified by the result, and justifiable by it only.[30]

And again:

> The parallels with the *Odyssey* are mere mechanics, any blockhead can go back and trace them. Joyce had to have a shape on which to order his chaos.[31]

---

[29] C. Dahlhaus, *Richard Wagner's Music Dramas*, Cambridge University Press, Cambridge 1979, pp. 86–7.

[30] E. Pound, '*Ulysses*', in *The Dial*, June 1922. Now in T.S. Eliot, ed., *The Literary Essays of Ezra Pound*, Faber and Faber, London 1954, p. 406.

[31] E. Pound, 'Past History', in *The English Journal*, May 1933. Now in F. Read, ed., *Pound/Joyce. The Letters of Ezra Pound to James Joyce, with Pound's Essays on Joyce*, Faber and Faber, London 1967, p. 250.

Mere mechanics, Pound is right; in *Ulysses* the scaffolding and the finished edifice are wholly heterogeneous things. The dominant tendency in criticism, of course, has devoted itself to the opposite task: to demonstrate the homogeneity of *Ulysses*, as others sought to prove the symbolic nature of *Faust*, or the harmony between music and drama in the *Ring*. All cases in which the cult of homogeneity has hidden the most interesting aspect of the question: the fact that a work of transition, technically revolutionary, *cannot avoid being internally discontinuous*. Because morphological innovation works like the *bricoleur:* one piece at a time. In some cases with good results; in others, less so. The final product may well, if fortune smiles, be a masterpiece: but under no circumstances can it be a consistent, well-amalgamated masterpiece. The world text of the twentieth century, *Ulysses*, will provide us with a matchless illustration.

PART II

Ulysses and the Twentieth Century

6

In a celebrated *film noir* from 1949, *The Third Man*, a middle-aged American writer finds himself unwillingly caught up in the mysteries of postwar Vienna. Amid vanishing witnesses, appointments on the Prater Wheel, a semi-lynching, and shoot-outs in the sewers, something else happens to the protagonist: one evening, on returning to his hotel, he is thrust into a large black limousine and borne at top speed, through streets filled with sinister shadows, to a room full of people . . . patiently waiting for his lecture on the modern novel. At the conclusion of a painful performance, a young man with an anguished expression raises his hand and asks the first question: 'Tell us, Mr Martin, do you believe in the "stream of consciousness"?' It is clearly the worst moment of the entire scene – Joseph Cotten is dumbstruck, the director of the British Cultural Centre is acutely embarrassed, a number of ladies with grotesque hats get up and walk out – and bears witness to the aura of legend surrounding the stream of consciousness, even outside avant-garde circles. This chapter seeks to understand the reason for such success.

The Ladies' Paradise

Georg Simmel, 'The Metropolis and Mental Life':

The psychological basis of the metropolitan type of individual consists in the *intensification of nervous stimulation* which results from the swift and uninterrupted change of outer and inner stimuli [. . .] the sharp discontinuity in the grasp of a single glance, and the unexpectedness of onrushing impressions.[1]

Simmel does not say so, but this is an absurd situation. On the one hand, European capitalism is at the peak of its success, which it seals by creating cities of truly epic dimensions: concentrates of the world – 'cosmopolises', as they are often called in the late nineteenth and early twentieth centuries – where the most disparate products flood in from the various parts of the globe, and become so many 'stimuli' to be enjoyed. On the other hand, however, such unprecedented abundance subjects the 'metropolitan type' to a 'nervous stimulation' that threatens his wellbeing, and even his mental health. The best that the great city has to offer is also its greatest danger: too many stimuli, too disparate and too intense, always on the point of turning into a 'shock', as Benjamin will say of the metropolitan poetry of Baudelaire.

Well, the stream of consciousness is one way – and perhaps the most successful – of confronting this situation of extreme tension. It begins as the sign of a crisis: of an Ego bombarded, divided, in difficulty. But gradually it learns to confront the countless stimuli swirling through the streets of the modern city, and to capture them. It provides the metropolis with a form, and its inhabitants with a perspective. So it is no surprise that the stream of consciousness should be the most famous technique of the twentieth century: in view of what it has done, it fully deserves to be. But it is a complicated story, and we must proceed in an orderly manner.

Nervous stimulation, we were saying. Shock. And Simmel and Benjamin are certainly not alone in recognizing the new pathology of the metropolis. There is the American doctor John Girdner, for example, who diagnoses the neurosis of the twentieth century – in its first year – as 'Newyorkitis'.[2] Or Franz Biberkopf, the hero of *Berlin Alexanderplatz*, who on his return to

---

[1] G. Simmel, 'The Metropolis and Mental Life', in *The Sociology of Georg Simmel*, translated and edited by Kurt Wolff, Collier-Macmillan, London 1950, pp. 409–10.

[2] Girdner's work is pretty flat, but a few passages – 'speed, nerviness, lack of deliberation in muscular movements' – herald, almost in so many words, certain of Simmel's descriptions two years later (J.H. Girdner, *Newyorkitis*, Grafton Press, New York 1901, pp. 119–20).

the city feels virtually paralysed: his 'head threatens to burst'.[3] But usually the atmosphere of the metropolis is rather more ambiguous, with fear and promise intermingled. If the new stimuli do cause some alarm, they are also terribly seductive: objects to be owned, products to be consumed, places to be lived in, roles to be filled . . . Or even just things to be seen. Émile Zola:

> But when she finally emerged onto the Place Gaillon, the young girl stopped short in astonishment.
>   'Oh, Jean!', she said, 'just look!'
>   [. . .]
>   'Well!', said she, after a pause, 'that's what I call a shop!'
>   Right there on the corner [. . .] stood a big drapery store, its display windows a riot of bright colours in the soft, pale, October light.
>
> *The Ladies' Paradise*, 1

It is 'The Ladies' Paradise', as Zola rechristened the more prosaic Bon Marché: a concentrate of the metropolis, just as the metropolis is a concentrate of the world. In the new space invented by it – the shop-window, where inside and outside are no longer differentiated – the commodities of the bourgeois century finally appear in their full glory. ' "Don't be afraid!" ', the proprietor Mouret – 'the best window-dresser in Paris' – says from the outset: ' "Don't be afraid; dazzle them!" ' And that is just what happens with the great white sale that marks the triumph of 'The Ladies' Paradise':

> Nothing but white, and never the same white, every shade of white, heaped up on one another, contrasting with and complementing one another, until they merged into the brilliance of light itself. It began with the dull white of the calicos and hollands, the flat white of the flannels and bedlinens; then came the velvets, the silks, the

---

[3] 'He got off the car, without being noticed, and was back among people again. What happened? Nothing. Chest out, you starved sucker, you, pull yourself together, or I'll give you a crack in the jaw! Crowds, what a swarm of people! How they hustle and bustle! [. . .] What was all this? Show stores, hat stores, incandescent lamps, saloons. People got to have shoes to run around so much [. . .] Hundreds of polished window-panes, let 'em blaze away, are they going to make you afraid or something, why, you can smash 'em, can't you . . .' (Alfred Döblin, *Berlin Alexanderplatz*, translated by Eugene Jolas, Continuum Publishing, New York 1993, pp. 4–5).

satins, in an ascending scale, the whiteness gradually catching fire to form little tongues of flame at the breaks of the folds; and with the transparency of the gauzes the white took flight, to become free radiance with the muslins, the guipures, the laces, and above all the tulles, so light that they were like the farthest, dying note, while the silver of the pieces of oriental silk sang higher than all in the recesses of the vast bay.

The Ladies' Paradise, 14

The commodity which turns into light. Here, a sheet is no longer a thing, but precisely a stimulus: a blinding, luminous ray. And Mouret is well aware of it: 'He used to say that the customers, when they left the store, should all have sore eyes.' The intensification of nervous stimulation, for him, is not a risk to be guarded against, but excellent business: if the customer loses her way, or even her mind, so much the better for 'The Ladies' Paradise':

On Saturday evening, as he was casting a final glance over the preparations for Monday's big sale [. . .] he suddenly realized that the shelf-arrangement he had adopted was clumsy. Yet it was an absolutely logical arrangement, with fabrics on one side and made-up articles on the other, an intelligent order designed to allow the customers to find their own way [. . .]

'A fine idea I had there, a land-surveyor couldn't have done better! [. . .] A woman would come in, go straight to wherever she wanted to go, move from skirts to dresses, from dresses to coats, and then leave, without losing her way even for an instant! [. . .]

[But now,] 'first of all, this continual circulation of the customers scatters them about everywhere, multiplies their number and makes them lose their heads; secondly, since they have to be guided from one end of the store to the other – if, for example, once they have bought the dress, they want the lining – these journeys in every direction make the establishment appear three times as large to them; thirdly, they are obliged to pass through departments where otherwise they would never have set foot, temptations entice them as they pass, and they succumb; fourthly . . .'

The Ladies' Paradise, 9[4]

---

[4] Here, Zola is faithfully following Boucicaut's programme for the reopening of Bon Marché: see R. Bowlby, *Just Looking. Consumer Culture in Dreiser, Gissing and Zola*, Methuen, New York and London 1985, pp. 74–5.

Three times as large . . . Perhaps 'The Ladies' Paradise' is not really a paradise – but it is certainly a *world*. It takes the most disparate branches of commerce, and unifies them into a kind of self-sufficient universe, which drives its competitors mad with anger.[5] It does with commodities what the museum has just done with art: it takes the universe, and encloses it between four walls. Moreover, as if to suggest some kinship between the totalizing ambition of the two buildings, that same Schinkel who

> had created in the 'Altes Museum' one of the principal works of the aesthetic church of the Twenties [. . .] conceived in 1827 a design for a department store, the first of its kind, which has an incredibly modern air.[6]

Incredibly modern – or postmodern? Fredric Jameson:

> I believe that, with a certain number of other characteristic postmodern buildings, such as the Beaubourg in Paris or the Eaton Centre in Toronto, the Bonaventura aspires to being a total space, a complete world, a kind of miniature city.[7]

All true: apart from the novelty of the thing. 'World buildings' have a history going back a century and a half by now, and in this – as, perhaps, in everything – the postmodern is just one more step along a route traced long ago. If 'it is quite impossible to get your bearings in this lobby [of the Bonaventura]', well, it was already like that in Zola.

---

[5] 'This number of twenty-eight departments was what particularly enraged [the old draper]. Some had doubtless been sub-divided, but others were completely new: for example, a furniture department, and one for Paris goods. Could you credit that? Goods from Paris! [. . .] they'd end up selling fish' (*The Ladies' Paradise*, 8).

[6] H. Sedlmayr, *Art in Crisis. The Lost Center*, translated by H. Regnery, Chicago 1958, p. 33. Schinkel's plan (which bears a striking resemblance to the Louvre museum – and 'Au Louvre', of course, is also the name of one of the first Paris department stores) was never put into execution; a reproduction of it can be seen in A. Grisebach, *Carl Friedrich Schinkel*, Leipzig 1924, fig. 80, p. 124.

[7] F. Jameson, 'Postmodernism, or the Cultural Logic of Late Capitalism', in *New Left Review* 146, 1984, pp. 83–5.

Let us go back, then, to *The Ladies' Paradise*. We were just examining Mouret's new sales strategy, 'organized disorder':

> Mme Marty, with dilated pupils and intoxicated by this parade of rich objects dancing before her gaze, was repeating under her breath:
> 'Heavens! Whatever will my husband say? You're quite right, there's no order in this shop. One gets lost and behaves like a fool.'
>
> *The Ladies' Paradise*, 9

This is what happens when the grand world of modern capitalism is concentrated within a confined space. At first, a blaze of stimuli. But then, dilated pupils, loss of control, intoxication . . . Madame Bovary comes to mind, who with feverish anxiety surrounds herself with exotic goods, then kills herself because she cannot pay for them. And if tragedy is avoided here, there is still enough to warrant a proper medical diagnosis:

> It is impossible to spend even just a few hours in these monstrous places [. . .] without feeling a quite particular sensation of debilitation, fatigue, and bewilderment [. . .] It is necessary to bear in mind the host of solicitations and stimuli that assail women, and that by virtue of their number, variety and intensity are not slow to produce [. . .] an effect quite similar to that produced by liquor upon brains whose resistance is low. This 'store-itis' [. . .] until it passes a certain threshold, is for many women nothing more than a pleasant sensation, like that which a glass of champagne might procure. [. . .] But this poison behaves no differently from others: just as it produces slow, gradual intoxications, so does it cause others which are sudden and devastating.[8]

'Store-itis': there speaks the man of science. But then Dubuisson calls the strategy of Bon Marché by its true name: seduction. 'Paris belongs to women', Mouret exults at a certain point; 'and women belong to us!'[9]

---

[8] P. Dubuisson, *Les Voleuses des Grands Magasins*, Stock, Paris 1902, pp. 181, 187–8.
[9] This is what Michael B. Miller has to say about the seduction exerted by the department store: 'Mass marketing demanded a wizardry that could stir unrealized appetites, provoke overpowering urges, create new states of mind. Selling consumption was a matter of seduction and showmanship [. . .] Dazzling and sensuous, the Bon Marché became a permanent fair' (*The Bon Marché. Bourgeois Culture and the Department Store, 1869–1920*, Allen and Unwin, London 1981,

'Take care,' his cautious assistant Bourdoncle warns him; 'Take care! [. . .] the women will have their revenge.' And even if that does not happen, the ladies seduced by Mouret do eventually do something strange. They steal. They steal everything, continually. This is why I quoted Paul Dubuisson, who is not just any old doctor, but medical consultant to the Tribunal de la Seine, and whose book tries precisely to explain the unprecedented epidemic raging in the respectable society of Paris: ' "kleptomania" ' – a new word, then – 'or monomania for theft'.[10]

Dubuisson's title – 'Women who Steal from Department Stores' – already contains the essence of his diagnosis: the new pathology is the product of *a new space*. Everywhere else 'kleptomaniacs lead an absolutely irreproachable existence'; but inside the department store everything is so seductive that conscience is put in abeyance, and even the most honest woman finds herself literally *compelled* to steal. But if that is how things are, then theft from department stores should not be seen as a crime, but as the triumphal coronation of a truly brilliant commercial strategy. Mouret was right to blind the customers: and kleptomania is the shining confirmation of his bold insights.

A shining confirmation . . . *Too* shining, in fact. And not for economic reasons (the thought of all those thieves strolling through his store does not worry Mouret in the least), but because of the symbolic reaction it can provoke. If a few earrings, and tons of handkerchiefs, disappear – no problem. But if the idea catches on that department stores encourage immorality . . .

What a delightful paradox: a bourgeois institution, which perverts bourgeois morality, impelling a Professor from the University of Lyons to demand 'police measures, to prevent minors under eighteen, of either sex, from entering' – and even 'a gendarme close to every sales

---

p. 167). The eroticism of the department store was something of which Zola was well aware (*The Ladies' Paradise* [*Au Bonheur des Dames*] . . .). For him, the typical customer of this new space (Mme Marty, with her dilated pupils) is precisely the one who has switched her erotic investment from people to things: 'she was virtuous, utterly virtuous, incapable of yielding to a lover; but she would yield at once, without any resistance, when confronted by the least trifle'.

[10] Dubuisson, *Les Voleuses*, p. 3.

counter'.[11] The inventors of consumer society were too clever, and ended up going too far. This overkill of consumers must be remedied, by situating them – like Faust in the witch's kitchen – at the right distance from the magic mirror of the commodity. Not too far, so that distance cools their minds and may induce them to pass on without buying; but not too close either, so as to avoid scandals. Rosalind Williams:

> The merchandise itself is by no means available to all, but the *vision* of a seemingly unlimited profusion of commodities is available, is, indeed, nearly unavoidable.[12]

A vision that multiplies commodities: what we are talking about, clearly, is advertising. An 'inevitable' vision, Williams calls it. An insidious one, Vance Packard adds with great forcefulness:

> The most serious offence many of the depth manipulators commit, it seems to me, is that they try to invade the privacy of our minds. It is this right to privacy in our minds – privacy to be either rational or irrational – that I believe we must strive to protect.[13]

Protect the privacy of the human mind. 'The business man's hunt for sales boosters is leading him into a strange wilderness: the subconscious mind' – reads an article from the *Wall Street Journal*, quoted in *The Hidden Persuaders*. And it is all true – except for the historical perspective. For what we know about Bon Marché and kleptomania suggests that advertising, rather than committing new 'offences', if anything succeeds in *limiting* the violations feared by Packard. It is like moving from the world of adultery – 'The Ladies' Paradise': gendarmes, swoonings, angry husbands, courts, suicide attempts – to that of flirtation. Because advertising does, to be sure, conquer the customer, but it does not dishonour her. It weakens the resistance of the Super-ego, and the reality principle;

[11] A. Lacassagne, 'Les Vols à l'Étalage et dans les Grands Magasins', lecture delivered to the Geneva Congress of Criminal Anthropology and later published in the *Revue de l'Hypnotisme et de la Psychologie Physiologique*, July 1896, p. 82.
[12] R.H. Williams, *Dream Worlds. Mass Consumption in Late-Nineteenth-Century France*, California University Press, Berkeley 1982, p. 3.
[13] V. Packard, *The Hidden Persuaders*, Penguin Books, Harmondsworth 1960, p. 216.

but it does not produce that army of 'real mental cases' described by Dubuisson.

'I used to see everything as if through a mist', one kleptomaniac confesses; 'every object used to excite my desire, every one would cast an extraordinary spell.'[14] Well, advertising is precisely this enchanted mist: but composed solely of *images*, with no more things left. It is a magic mirror, where desire merges with the object, as in the shop-windows photographed by Atget, with their fantastic superimpositions between the objects on display and the passer-by gazing at them. And like the shop-window (to whose development it is significantly linked), advertising protects the merchandise from the consumer, and vice versa: it allows looking, but prevents theft, thereby allowing desire to expand freely, without offence to morality or penal consequences.

Advertising as a force which 'saves' the individual from the excessive power of commodities, in other words. Absurd? Not at all. This is in fact why advertising works, and has survived for so much longer than the jungle magic of the first department stores. Simmel again:

> The development of modern culture is characterized by the preponderance of what one may call the 'objective spirit' over the 'subjective spirit' [. . .] The individual in his intellectual development follows the growth of this ['objective'] spirit very imperfectly and at an ever increasing distance. If, for instance, we view the immense culture which for the last hundred years has been embodied in things and in knowledge, in institutions and in comforts, and if we compare all this with the cultural progress of the individual during the same period [. . .] a frightful disproportion in growth between the two becomes evident.[15]

---

[14] Dubuisson, *Les Voleuses*, p. 53.
[15] Simmel, 'The Metropolis and Mental Life', p. 421. There is an interesting parallel with Jameson's essay: 'We ourselves, the human subjects who happen into this new space, have not kept pace with the evolution [of built space itself]: there has been a mutation in the object unaccompanied as yet by any equivalent mutation in the subject [. . .] this latest mutation in space – postmodern hyperspace – has finally succeeded in transcending the capacities of the human body to locate itself' ('Postmodernism, or The Cultural Logic of Late Capitalism', pp. 82, 85). Here again, does the mismatch between subject and object really begin with postmodern hyperspace? Or with Simmel's metropolis? Or with Zola's department store?

The individual follows at an ever increasing distance . . . It is the message of *The Ladies' Paradise*, where the individual plods along behind the 'objective spirit', haphazardly grasping and pocketing a bit of everything. Well, advertising is the mechanism that remedies such a 'frightful dispro-portion', and makes the grand world of bourgeois commodities accessible to all. Or rather, advertising – and the stream of consciousness.

Stream of consciousness

The metropolitan type of man [. . .] develops an organ protecting him against the threatening currents and discrepancies of his external environment [. . .] He reacts with his head instead of his heart. In this an increased awareness assumes the psychic prerogative [. . .] Intellec-tuality is thus seen to preserve subjective life against the overwhelming power of metropolitan life.[16]

This is Simmel in 1903. Twenty years go by, and Joyce offers a diagnosis that is exactly the opposite. The person who 'developed the organ of the brain', Stephen Dedalus, is not really in tune with the big city: he prefers peripheral or enclosed places. And as for Bloom, who is the true metro-politan hero of *Ulysses*, here is how 'Ithaca' summarizes his day:

What were habitually his final meditations?

Of some one sole unique advertisement to cause passers to stop in wonder, a poster novelty, with all extraneous accretions excluded, reduced to its simplest and most efficient terms not exceeding the span of casual vision and congruous with the velocity of modern life.

Ulysses, XVII, 1769–73

Here, Simmel's 'increased awareness' really counts for little or nothing. It is all an interplay of irrational elements: hyperboles, fleeting encounters, fantasies, casual associations. 'There is nothing so "romantic" as Advertisement', writes Wyndham Lewis a few years after *Ulysses*, '[. . .]

---

[16] Simmel, 'The Metropolis and Mental Life', pp. 410–11. Spengler too goes in the same direction: 'These final cities are *wholly* intellect [...] replacement of uncon-scious living by exercise in thought' (*Decline of the West* (1918), vol. 2, translated by Charles Francis Atkinson, Allen and Unwin, London 1926, pp. 99 and 103).

the apotheosis of the marvellous and the unusual [. . .] a world of hyperbolic suggestion [. . .] the trance or dream-world of the hypnotist.'[17]
And Spitzer, in what is still the finest essay on the subject:

> It may be noted that the first advertisements to appear regularly in
> American newspapers (in the middle of the 19th century) were those
> of patent medicines, with their claims of miraculous efficacy. It is
> highly significant that the industry of advertising had its inception in an
> appeal to the age-old craving to be saved by magic from the ills and
> shortcomings of the flesh.[18]

Well then. Georg Simmel's rationalized metropolis: a city of the brain, of the
intellect. And Leopold Bloom's enchanted metropolis: a city of dream and
magic. But they are both right, because they are talking about different
things. Simmel is thinking about the city of production; Joyce, about that of
consumption. In the former, Max Weber's harsh 'disenchantment' holds
sway; in the latter, by contrast, Ernest Gellner's 'need for re-enchantment':

> A really advanced industrial society does not any longer require cold
> rationality from its consumers; at most, it may demand it of its produc-
> ers. But as it gets more advanced [. . .] more consumers, fewer producers;
> less time at work, more at leisure. And in consumption, all tends towards
> ease and facility of manipulation rather than rigour and coldness.[19]

---

[17] W. Lewis, *Time and Western Man*, Chatto and Windus, London 1927, p. 27.
[18] L. Spitzer, 'American Advertising Explained as Popular Art' (1949), in his *Essays on English and American Literature*, Princeton University Press, Princeton NJ 1968, p. 275, n. 35. In France too, advertising was long dominated by miracle cures (see K. Varnedoe and A. Gopnik, *High and Low. Modern Art/Popular Culture*, Museum of Modern Art, New York 1991, p. 243). As for England, the mingling of adver-tising, medicine and magic was already present in a (mediocre) 1909 novel by H.G. Wells, *Tono-Bungay*: 'What I like about it is its poetry [. . .] And it's not your poetry only. It's the poetry of the customer too. [. . .] the magic philtre! Like a fairy-tale [. . .] None of us want to be what we are, or to do what we do [. . .] What we all want to be is something perpetually young and beautiful.' Impossible not to think of Faust's philtre of youth, and Wagner's love philtres. Indeed, the special predilection that advertising has always shown for drinks of every kind may well derive originally from the idea of the magic potion.
[19] E. Gellner, *Spectacles and Predicaments*, Cambridge University Press, Cambridge 1979, pp. 61–3.

Ours, Gellner concludes, is a dualistic world, split between 'standardiza-tion' and 'anomie'. A splendid image, already hovering in Spitzer's essay,[20] and that perfectly expresses the paradox of advertising: taking standardized products, and making them seem unique. Let us see.

Among the inventions of Bon Marché there was one – the price ticket – which would have delighted Karl Marx. It seems quite trivial – four figures on a piece of cardboard – yet, from that moment on, commodities really do become fetishes, because they have actually learnt to speak. They begin with numbers; then they learn their own names – and finally all the rest of the alphabet. And every spot is good for this new language: walls, buses, newsstands, lavatories, fences, apartment buildings, boats, stations . . . In many paintings from the early years of the century, and especially in cubism (the best example: *City*, by Otto Möller, from 1921), the omnipresence of the word indeed stands out as the dominant feature of the urban landscape: as if Paris, or Berlin, were by now genuine *cities of words*.[21] And, basically, the stimuli/shocks about which we have said so much are just that: words. Coloured words, literally, which is how it should be if they are to touch the emotions, and 'cause passers to stop in wonder'. Words made of light, like the electric signs that so frighten Franz Biberkopf. Exaggerated, enormous words, to stand up to 'the velocity of modern life'. Words of smoke, like those traced by an aeroplane in the sky in *Mrs Dalloway*. Living words, which walk along the street chewing chunks of bread, like the letter Y from Hely's stationery shop (*Ulysses*, VIII, 126–8).

Words words words words. It is a bombardment that no one expects, and that nineteenth-century grammar is incapable of withstanding. Attention, clarity, concentration: the old virtues are worse than useless. Instead of harmonizing with advertising, they perceive it as an irritating noise. A different style is required, in order to find one's way in the city

[20] 'It is an interesting paradox that the same [American] civilization that has per-fected standardization to such a degree is also characterized by this intense need for the recognition of one's personal existence' (Spitzer, *Essays on English and American Literature*, p. 272).

[21] For two recent collections of visual materials, see Varnedoe and Gopnik, *High and Low*, and J. Clair, ed., *The 1920s. Age of the Metropolis*, Montreal Museum of Fine Arts, Montreal 1991.

of words; a weaker grammar than that of consciousness; an edgy, discontinuous syntax: a cubism of language, as it were. And the stream of consciousness offers precisely that: simple, fragmented sentences, where the subject withdraws to make room for the invasion of things;[22] paratactical paragraphs, with the doors flung wide, and always enough room for one more sentence, and one more stimulus.

In an extraordinary complicity between social phenomenon and literary form, therefore, advertising and the stream of consciousness pursue and implicate one another throughout *Ulysses*. The former is the inexhaustible transmitter of the capitalist metropolis; the latter, the receiver that captures and organizes fluctuating stimuli. But organizes them how? Really, into a 'flow', into a *stream* of consciousness? Let us try and go back to the source of the metaphor. William James:

> It is the fact that in each of us, when awake (and often when asleep), some kind of consciousness is always going on. There is a stream, a succession of states, or waves, or fields (or of whatever you please to call them), of knowledge, of feeling, of desire, of deliberation, etc., that constantly pass and repass, and that constitute our inner life.[23]

Stream – fields. Waves – states. It really seems as though James were undecided, here, between opposite cognitive metaphors. And although the lecture is indeed entitled 'Stream of consciousness', if you read it carefully the opposite metaphor – of the 'field of consciousness' – turns out to predominate by far. Indeed, 'successive *fields* of consciousness', in the plural:[24]

---

[22] The clearest example of this way of proceeding consists in placing the predicate before the other parts of the sentence: 'Devil of a job it was collecting accounts of those convents'; 'Strong as a brood mare some of those horsey women'. See the article by E. Steinberg, 'Characteristic Sentence Patterns in Proteus and Lestrygonians', in F. Senn, ed., *New Light on Joyce from the Dublin Symposium*, Indiana University Press, Bloomington 1976.

[23] W. James, *Talks to Teachers* (1899), Henry Holt, New York 1921, p. 15.

[24] The expression recurs twice in the course of the lecture, on pp. 16 and 17. Immediately afterwards, the only 'technical terms' that James entreats his listeners to bear in mind – 'focal object', and 'marginal object' (pp. 18–19) – likewise refer to the image of the field, far more than that of the stream. (As for the term 'consciousness', in James it obviously has a far broader meaning than the one current today, and includes elements that we define for various reasons as unconscious.)

just as in Bloom's experience – discontinuous, segmented. Made up of discrete, and almost absolute, moments.

Made up, more precisely, of discrete and almost absolute *paragraphs*. For, in *Ulysses*, the paragraph loses the fortuitousness that normally characterizes it, and becomes a genuine formal element: a stylistic 'quantum', whose regular pulse sustains and organizes the whole first part of the novel. In it, a great insight of late nineteenth-century experimental psychology takes on a verbal form: *the present*. James's present, which is 'no knife-edge, but a saddle-back [. . .] from which we look in two directions into time'.[25] The present, others say, which crosses our perceptive field like a kind of comet, with a vivid basic nucleus and a gradually fraying tail behind. The present as an empirical, measurable, reality – timed, indeed, more than once at the turn of the century, at around twelve seconds. Read silently, the paragraphs of *Ulysses* require perhaps a few seconds more.

The stream of consciousness as the form of the present: the present as the duration of advertising. A few seconds and no more, since the light of the advertisement is really like that of the comet: all in its velocity. If it were to last, it would lose its magic. And as in time, so too in space: the words of advertising are everywhere, to be sure, but everywhere *at the margins* of the perceptual field. Fragmented, as in cubism, or in collage. Elusive, to be glimpsed out of the corner of your eye. 'A sidelong glance with the head half-turned [that] cannot last longer than a few seconds', as Simmel writes of flirtation, '[. . .] consent and refusal are inseparably combined in it.'[26]

Advertising is flirtation with commodities, I said earlier. And now we see why: both advertising and flirtation seek to remedy a paradox of the modern world. On the one hand, Simmel writes, we find ourselves confronted by 'a large increase in the number of provocative phenomena'; on

---

[25] W. James, *Principles of Psychology* (1890), vol. 2, pp. 608–9; quoted by S. Kern, *The Culture of Time and Space. 1880–1918*, Harvard University Press, Cambridge Mass. 1983, pp. 82–3. The following references too are taken from the third chapter ('The Present') of Kern's book.

[26] G. Simmel, 'Flirtation' (1923), in his *On Women, Sexuality and Love*, Yale University Press, New Haven and London 1984, p. 134.

the other, however, we find that: 'It is simply not possible to possess all the attractive women.' Well:

> Flirtation is a remedy for this condition. By this means, the woman could give herself – potentially, symbolically, or by approximation – to a large number of men, and in this same sense the individual man could possess a large number of women.[27]

A woman could give herself, a man could possess . . . We no longer divide the world in this way. But the abstract framework of the argument remains valid. And if you replace 'men' or 'women' by the word 'stimuli', the idea put forward twenty years earlier in Simmel's essay on the metropolis reappears. On the one hand, there is a wish to enjoy the countless 'provocative phenomena' of the big city; on the other, 'it is not possible to possess all the attractive [things]' around us. And so, while flirtation takes care of the human beings, advertising takes care of the things. It keeps them ever present, it makes them even more exciting, perhaps – but it does not force us into anything. It multiplies every kind of bewitching prospect, but allows us not to take them literally. Its promises are neither true nor false: they are located beyond the true and the false. It is the world, Simmel says, of the 'great Perhaps'.

Sociology of absentmindedness

Up and down the Dublin streets, between advertising and stream of consciousness, the hero of *Ulysses* is learning a new art: to see, and not to see. Bloom notices everything, but focuses on nothing; a glance, then on again. It is the metropolitan way: the way to avoid being overwhelmed by the big world that is concentrated in the big city. But what has made it possible?

The brain, Simmel answers: the life of the intellect. Joyce, however, suggests the opposite: not an 'increased awareness', but instead an increased absentmindedness. Or rather, an absentmindedness that is not just increased (Bloom is perhaps the most absentminded character in world literature), but has also changed its function. Instead of being a *lack*, an absence, it has become an active tool: a kind of switchboard,

---

[27] Ibid., p. 150.

simultaneously activating a plurality of mental circuits, and allowing Bloom to pick up as many stimuli as possible. To take just one example, consider the beginning of Chapter V: Bloom, who has just left the post office, runs into M'Coy (stimulus 1: unpleasant), who forces him into a very boring conversation. But Bloom can put up with it, because his mind is only half with M'Coy: the other half wanders, goes to his jacket pocket and tries to work out (stimulus 2: uncertain) what Martha Clifford's letter may contain. A few more lines, and a third Leopold Bloom looks abstractedly across the street, where a pretty guest from the Grosvenor Hotel is about to climb aboard an open carriage (stimulus 3: pleasurable); and Bloom, who wants to see her legs, manages to be sufficiently 'absent' during his conversation to pursue this other possibility. Once the woman has vanished, his absentmindedness switches target, and while M'Coy goes on talking Bloom 'unrolled the newspaper baton idly and read idly' an advertisement (stimulus 4: neutral) that will then come up again several times in the course of the day (*Ulysses*, V, 82–147).

The absentminded individual, and the metropolis. It brings to mind a little classic of cognitive psychology, formulated in the fifties: the so-called 'cocktail-party problem'. For anyone entering a place where a party with lots of guests is taking place . . .

> the first sensation [. . .] is simply one of confusion, undifferentiated noise. But very quickly, and without any great difficulty, you succeed in following just one of the various conversations taking place simultaneously, in spite of the noise and confusion. You manage to understand what your interlocutor is saying, even if someone else, standing between you, goes on talking about something else, perhaps very loudly. But if you try to follow both your interlocutor and the stranger simultaneously, you find that it is very difficult. You lose too much in the former case, and do not manage to grasp the meaning in the latter.[28]

All true. But is it equally certain that, at a cocktail party, attention plays such an important role? Do you go there to 'concentrate' on a single interlocutor, or rather – like Bloom with M'Coy – to 'follow simultaneously' more than one, even at the cost of superficiality and confusion? And the

[28] S. Bagnara, *L'attenzione*, il Mulino, Bologna 1984, p. 23.

same wish, on a vastly larger scale, holds also for the metropolis – whose fascination does not lie in any specific promise, however seductive, but in the *many* choices that appear equally possible there. For Julien Sorel, for example, in thrall to a single dream, there is no great difference between the provinces and the capital; for Lucien de Rubempré, however, undecided between a career as journalist, poet, or even nobleman, Paris is already very important; and by the time we reach Frédéric Moreau, flirting with every woman and every idea, it is indispensable. With Bloom, another step is taken in this direction. Here is a paragraph initiated by the usual casual glance at an advertisement:

> He looked at the cattle, blurred in silver heat. Silverpowdered olive-trees. Quiet long days: pruning, ripening. Olives are packed in jars, eh? I have a few left from Andrews. Molly spitting them out. Knows the taste of them now. Oranges in tissue paper packed in crates. Citrons too. Wonder is poor Citron still in Saint Kevin's parade. And Mastiansky with the old cither. Pleasant evenings we had then. Molly in Citron's basketchair. Nice to hold, cool waxen fruit, hold in the hand, lift it to the nostrils and smell the perfume. Like that, heavy, sweet, wild perfume. Always the same, year after year. They fetched high prices too, Moisel told me. Arbutus place: Pleasants street: pleasant old times. Must be without a flaw, he said. Coming all that way: Spain, Gibraltar, Mediterranean, the Levant. Crates lined up on the quayside at Jaffa, chap ticking them off in a book, navvies handling them barefoot in soiled dungarees. There's whatdoyoucallhim out of. How do you? Doesn't see. Chap you know just to salute bit of a bore. His back is like that Norwegian captain's. Wonder if I'll meet him today. Watering cart. To provoke the rain. On earth as it is in heaven.
>
> *Ulysses*, IV, 201–17

As *Ulysses* proceeds, certain themes from this passage (the Levant, the olives, Gibraltar, the price of goods) will be significantly developed; while others (the citrons, Succoth, whatdoyoucallhim) will remain relatively inactive. This page, however, in no sense seeks to prefigure the hierarchy that will be established in the course of the novel. Its paratactical structure, multiplying developmental directions and making them independent of one another, conveys the opposite sensation: an open present, where *the various developments are still all equally possible.* The possible, here, has become interesting as such: in and of itself, irrespective of

*Det mulige
er interessant
i mit felt.*

any future realization. And in doing so, a recent German scholar argues, *Ulysses* rebels against the reality principle of the modern world:

> Art is, in principle, a phenomenon belonging to the realm of imagination and fantasy; the art of the stream of consciousness – and especially that of *Ulysses* – takes this state of affairs as its own content, and with artistic means represents a resistance to the reality principle.[29]

On the one hand, Schönheich goes on – following Ernst Bloch's *The Principle of Hope* – we have precisely the reality principle. On the other, the *Tagtraum*: fantasy, expressed in the stream of consciousness, and which embodies 'a desire for change, for improvement of the world'. And he concludes, returning to *Ulysses*:

> Advertisements are a fairly banal form of fantasy, which aims to seduce the viewer with banal expectations. The illusion intentionally fostered by advertising, however, comes into conflict with the reality of daily existence [. . .] Advertising makes it possible to extract an economic profit from the discrepancy between real and imaginary life, and contains – along with all its banality – also a hint of aspiration towards a better world.[30]

Verbesserung der Welt: is this what advertising seeks, with all its attendant fantasies? A transformed and improved world, in contrast to the prosaic reality of capitalism? Not at all, the world is still the same – it has only become accessible to our gaze. In fact, the light-hearted nature of the stream of consciousness, its fantasizing possibilism, is precisely what puts Bloom at ease in the world of commodities, because it allows him to pick up hundreds and hundreds of stimuli, and play freely with them. Far from being a resistance to the reality principle, advertising, the stream of consciousness, absent-mindedness, fantasizing – are all *so many versions of that principle*.[31] And highly

---

[29] C. Schönheich, *Epos und Roman: James Joyces 'Ulysses'*, Carl Winter, Heidelberg 1981, p. 137.

[30] Ibid., pp. 140, 147.

[31] The expression 'reality principle' has numerous meanings in Freud, not always very close to one another. It may allude to a precise knowledge of external reality, for example; or again (which is quite different), to the ability to adapt yourself successfully to the latter. Here, 'reality principle' will always have a pragmatic meaning: the ability to be at ease in the world, whether its laws of operation are known or not.

effective versions. Where the severe, serious bourgeois of the nineteenth century would have been shipwrecked, the fantasizer moves safely among shop-windows and advertisements. Absentminded – and socialized.

Joyce the cynic. Bloom's prosaic wanderings dissolve one of the great literary myths of the twenties: the Surrealist Promenade, with its aimless roaming, which looks to absentmindedness – the 'passive and receptive' state celebrated by the 1924 and 1930 Manifestos – for an unprecedented freedom:

> a miraculous hunt stretched in front of us, a landscape of experiences which could not but hold in store a multitude of surprises and – who knows? – some great revelation which would alter life and destiny.[32]

Revelations which change our destiny? No, that is not *Ulysses* (but then, if the truth be told, it is not *Le Paysan de Paris* either). During Bloom's walks, chance brings to light an endless quantity of things and ideas: but there is no journey to unknown lands – everything is familiar, earthly, bathed in a noonday light. In Bloom's mind, even when it is distracted – indeed, *precisely* because it is distracted, hence particularly receptive – we find only *what already exists in the world*: a whole host of things, but no miracles. In this, the effects of advertising chime with those of the radio. Rudolf Arnheim:

> [That] the listener can only listen, but not answer [. . .] is due to the technical character of wireless [. . .] It has carried to an extreme the passivity which, with the principle of specialization and division of labour, has divided the productive community more and more definitely into an active and a passive part [. . .] The wireless apparatus has only been able to obtain such immense importance because with all its advantages and disadvantages it is so admirably suited to present-day social forms. Wireless is one person speaking without hearing and all the rest listening without being able to speak.[33]

---

[32] Louis Aragon, 'The feeling of nature in Buttes-Chaumont', in *Nightwalker* [*Le Paysan de Paris*], translated by Frederick Brown, Prentice-Hall, Englewood Cliffs NJ 1970, p. 110.

[33] R. Arnheim, *Radio*, translated by Margaret Ludwig and Herbert Read, Faber and Faber, London 1936, pp. 271–2.

An active part, and a passive part . . . Bloom certainly belongs to the latter. And the stream of consciousness – which receives but does not transmit – is a portable radio *ante litteram*, with its stations, its programmes, and even its discharges of static energy. And how many things it receives, in just one day! Here, passivity is not simply a void, but rather – as Boulez says of Gustav Mahler, a composer more akin than any other to Joyce, who used to speak of his symphonies as long walks – 'a passivity that enriches'.[34] A strange formula, and not one to be taken quite literally, but which does finally suggest – after a century of attempts – the solution to a problem that has accompanied us since the start of this work.

In a world – we read in Hegel's *Aesthetics* – where there exist the state, law, division of labour, and the separation of powers, the social totality can no longer be embodied in the action of a hero. It is necessary to change tack: to rely on the 'passive hero', as I was saying of Faust. This is a figure possessing certain advantages – its 'innocence', above all – but that nevertheless never manages to be wholly convincing. Goethe, indeed, although he is the first to embark on this route, is already thinking about bringing his hero back 'to the enjoyment of deeds' of the 1800 outline (and, in any case, flanks him with the hyperactive Mephistopheles). As for Melville and Wagner, they remain undecided: between the reflective Ishmael and the ferocious Ahab; between Wotan, 'fettered by contracts', and Siegfried, with his invincible sword. In Flaubert, encyclopaedic indolence rebounds upon itself; in *Peer Gynt*, Ibsen suddenly takes his distance from his hero's superficiality.

It really does seem a blind alley: as if too many shadows were closing in about the passive hero to find in him the principle of a new totality. And at first, not even Joyce sees in him a point of departure. In his original intentions, Bloom is a conclusion: the last story of *Dubliners* –

---

[34] 'How then are we to listen, to "perceive" these works? Are we simply to allow ourselves to be carried on the flood of the narrative, to float with the different psychological currents? [. . .] Yes, that is possible! The music is forceful enough to permit such a purely passive attitude, but is such an attitude really a source of enrichment? Ideally we should be able to trace precisely every strand in the dense musical complex' (P. Boulez, 'Mahler our Contemporary', in *Orientations*, translated by Martin Cooper, Faber and Faber, London and Boston 1986, p. 299).

the culmination, possibly, of that collection's 'paralysis'. But in a dramatic change of function, Joyce places Bloom under the microscope, and discovers that in his passivity there is not just *in*-activity and *lack* of action. There are also positive quantities: receptivity, variety, openness to the world. In Bloom, as we have seen, absentmindedness itself is a mobile, active force: even if it does not 'produce' anything in the strict sense, it nevertheless enables him to find his bearings in a very complex situation, and to organize it.

A passivity that enriches, Boulez was saying: a world of things, as in every instant of Bloom's day. A selective, intelligent passivity: one that no longer has anything weak or lazy about it. And finally, here too, an innocent passivity: one that sees the wealth of the Western metropolis as a *given*, for which it bears no responsibility. The modern epic has finally found its hero: and found with him that immediately visible totality, for which it has been searching since Goethe's day: the world – the truly *grand* world – of *consumption*. After the century of *Faust*, that of *Ulysses* begins.

The great Perhaps

Up to this point I have, as it were, been working with a series of Chinese boxes. First, the metropolis as a concentrate of the world. Next, the department store as a concentrate of the metropolis. Next, advertising as a concentrate of the department store. Finally, the stream of consciousness as a concentrate of advertising. In these successive shifts, the stimuli that opened this chapter have gradually changed their nature, becoming more and more abstract. Things; then commodities; then images; then words; and finally *possibilities*. The stream of consciousness, as I was saying earlier, is the technique of possibility as such, irrespective of its realization. And, indeed, it is the technique that turns possibility into what is possibly the most typical ideology of the twentieth century.

An ideology – of possibility. But can this be possible? Is not ideology a discourse made up of laws and sanctions: a mechanism *that limits* the field of the possible? It is certainly that, if you argue as the Hegelian left did in its day, and conceive of ideology as the bourgeois form of monotheism. But that state of affairs was changed by the very development of capitalism; by its inventive technology; by a production that wants more and more consumers; by a middle class that wants more and more things. And the possible was thus transformed from an enemy of the bourgeois order into its legitimate horizon. As the *Revue des Deux Mondes* writes in 1896, 'l'âge de l'affiche' has begun:

> The monuments of other times used to exhort the people to prayer, to obedience [. . .] By contrast, the advertising poster speaks to us only of ourselves, our pleasures, our tastes, our interests, our food, our health, our life. It does not say: 'Pray, obey, sacrifice yourself . . .' No, the poster whispers into our ear: 'Enjoy things, think of yourself, eat, go to the theatre, go dancing, or to a concert, read a novel, have a good beer, a tasty soup, a proper cigar, eat all the chocolate you want . . .'
> Let the architects go on building their churches [. . .] the true architecture of our time is the ephemeral facade of the advertising poster, demolished every evening and reconstructed every morning, with its innumerable colours beneath which the old monument of stone vanishes . . .[35]

The monument of stone, and the facade of paper: two styles, two phases of European culture that intertwine and clash throughout *Ulysses*. On the one hand, Judaeo-Christian duty; on the other, the possible of advertising. The former, an explicit, intolerant, educated, strong ideology; the latter, an allusive, indulgent, superficial, *weak* ideology. And yet, one more suited to the times. More appropriate, because of its light-heartedness, for a metropolis that in peacetime has no real need of strong values, and prefers the siren whisper of the advertising poster to the seriousness of prayer. Indeed, it ends up imposing advertising upon religion itself: upon 'Dr John Alexander Dowie restorer of the church in Zion', who relies on throwaways (*Ulysses*, VIII, 5 ff.); or upon the Birmingham firm manufacturing luminous crucifixes for bedrooms (VIII, 17–20). When Bloom rewrites the Mass in his heart as though it were an advertising campaign – 'Good idea, the Latin. Stupefies them first.'[36] – the embrace of the

---

[35] M. Talmeyr, 'L'âge de l'affiche', in *Revue des Deux Mondes*, September 1896, pp. 208–9.

[36] 'The priest bent down to put it into her mouth, murmuring all the time. Latin. The next one. Shut your eyes and open your mouth. What? *Corpus*: body. Corpse. Good idea the Latin. Stupefies them first' (*Ulysses*, V, 348–51). And further on: 'Mass seems to be over. Could hear them all at it. Pray for us. And pray for us. And pray for us. Good idea the repetition. Same thing with ads. Buy from us. And buy from us' (*Ulysses*, XIII, 1122–24).

advertising poster really does seem to have smothered the old monument of stone.

Possibility, then. In the universe of consumption, this term means something very simple: it is a desire, a wish for new things. In the literature of the twentieth century, a very strong sense of *multiplicity* is added to this first meaning. Freedom no longer to do *something*, but rather *anything*: the idea that human beings are plural, indeterminate, realities: an intersection of existences, all equally possible. It is the thought entertained by D'Annunzio's Stelio Effrena, contemplating 'his infinite powers to feel and to dream'; by Tonio Kröger, who 'bears within himself the possibility of countless forms of existence'; by Lafcade, in *The Vatican Cellars*, who 'feels within himself the most extraordinary possibilities'. There are the characters from *Tarr*, who put themselves to the test with absurd experiments; those from *Törless* and *The Counterfeiters*, who impose them on others; the fortuitous case of Pirandello, who practises on anyone he can get his hands on. In Paris there is Monsieur Teste, 'the demon of possibility'; in Christiania, the hero of Hamsun's *Hunger*, driven by some unknown force to invent the most absurd stories; in Petersburg, Bely's characters, who cannot carry out two coherent actions in succession; in Moscow, the world of Mephistopheles/Woland, where everything really is possible; in Prague, in Meyrink's *Walpurgisnacht*, 'men possessed at every moment by a different demon'; in Vienna, Ulrich Anders (*anders* = otherwise), the 'man of possibility', with his refusal to 'give greater importance to what is than to what is not'; and in Dublin, of course, Stephen Dedalus, who reflects privately on the 'actuality of the possible as possible'.

Enough examples, though. Let us try, instead, to give some thought to a difference. In almost all the novels cited, the sphere of the possible basically functions as a preamble to action. The 'infinite powers to dream' do certainly move away from reality: but only as though they were taking a run-up, so as to collide with it all the more forcibly. And we get Gide's gratuitous murders, the sudden rage of Hamsun and Lewis, Broch's 'sleepwalking', the ruthless cruelty of *Törless*, Bely's terrorism, Meyrink's slaughter, Pirandello's madness . . .

In Joyce, by contrast, nothing of all this. With the appearance of the stream of consciousness, contact between the two worlds begins to fail; and the possible leads an independent life, alien and indeed hostile to any form of realization. Because realization is always also renunciation: by confirming one possibility, it excludes all others. And so, instead of turning into action, the stream of consciousness finds itself *competing* with it and growing at its expense: from that first strange word ('Chrystostomos'), almost lost in the opening page of the novel, up to the great blocs of 'Proteus', Bloom, and 'Penelope'. A page from the 'Lotus Eaters':

> Brings out the darkness of her eyes. Looking at me, the sheet up to her eyes, Spanish, smelling herself, when I was fixing the links in my cuffs. Those homely recipes are often the best: strawberries for the teeth: nettles and rainwater: oatmeal they say steeped in buttermilk. Skinfood. One of the old queen's sons, duke of Albany was it? had only one skin. Leopold, yes. Three we have. Warts, bunions and pimples to make it worse. But you want a perfume too. What perfume does your? *Peau d'Espagne*. That orangeflower water is so fresh. Nice smell these soaps have. Pure curd soap. Time to get a bath round the corner. Hammam. Turkish. Massage. Dirt gets rolled up in your navel. Nicer if a nice girl did it. Also I think I. Yes I. Do it in the bath. Curious longing I. Water to water. Combine business with pleasure. Pity no time for massage. Feel fresh then all the day. Funeral be rather glum.
>
> *Ulysses*, V, 494–506

Molly naked in bed, the relationship with Martha, the girl from the Turkish bath, the idea of masturbating. It seems like a page from a textbook: erotic desires, and daydreams. But it is all very different from the stories of emotional compensation that we associate with this combination, and which Freud himself was thinking about when translating the German *Tagtraum* by terms (*petit roman*, story) with a clear narrative dominant.[37] In *Ulysses* (with the exception of Gerty in 'Nausicaa'), there is nothing of the kind: for every narrative imposes choices, or exclusions – while the stream of consciousness seeks to keep the field of the possible wide open. And so, instead of a well developed fantasy, it

---

[37] S. Freud, *The Interpretation of Dreams* (1899), Penguin Books, Harmondsworth 1976, pp. 631–2. Freud's other two suggestions (*rêve*, daydream) are mere linguistic calques.

gives us four drafts of ten words: one in the past, one in the present, one in the future, and one purely hypothetical. None of them is placed in the foreground; and none is excluded from the foreground. They are, precisely, possibilities in the pure state: to be enjoyed as such, without any further consequence. As chance will have it, in the Turkish bath Bloom does not even masturbate.

Before concluding, let us take a quick step back: to the distant origins of the literature of the possible. The *Bildungsroman*: story of a young man, a bundle of potentialities, and an exploration of many different futures. A wide-ranging, and often fascinating, exploration – but never limitless. Youth is exempt, for a certain while, from the restraining grip of social relations: but it must still always return to contend with them – and usually it loses. Wilhelm Meister will not found the German national theatre; Julien Sorel will not follow in Napoleon's footsteps; Lucien de Rubempré will not be a poet; Tertius Lydgate will not be a great scientist . . . The high hopes have faded: *illusions perdues*. Possibility has not become reality. And in this hard, 'realistic', world an unrealized possibility is, very simply, a failure: an end – nothing. It is not, as Musil will say with an air of defiance, 'a possibility, minus its realization'. It really is nothing any more: no longer even felt to be a possibility. Stephen's phrase – 'actuality of the possible as possible' – would have seemed meaningless to Balzac.

In a novel of the last century, I mean, Bloom would be the archetypal failure: a trivial job, semi-educated, commonplace aspirations, an inner life made up of silences and humiliations. He would be a sort of Oblomov. But how does Joyce present him to us?

> I looked back over Bouvard and Pecuchet last week – Pound writes to him in November 1918 – Bloom certainly does all Flaubert set out to do and does it in one tenth the space, and moreover there is the sense all the time that something might happen, in fact that anything might happen at any moment, while in *Bouvard* they are anchored in the mud and even when some thing does happen you keep on feeling that nothing can.[38]

---

[38] The letter is included in F. Read, ed., *Pound/Joyce. The Letters of Ezra Pound to James Joyce, with Pound's Essays on Joyce*, Faber and Faber, London 1967, p. 145.

Anything may happen at any moment. In reality? Certainly not, nothing at all happens there: it is blocked, it is the paralysis of *Dubliners*. But in *Ulysses*, this is the point, *reality recedes into the background*. As Iser writes:

> The everyday Bloom is merely a collection of individual moments in the course of his life – a collection which is infinitely smaller than that of the unlimited possibilities of the Bloom that might be.[39]

Unlimited possibilities. Yes, it is the experience of every paragraph in the novel: a horizon always open, which gives sense and colour to Bloom's day, *and which therefore binds him to the world despite everything*. The existence of the 'potential' Bloom, I mean, contributes to the re-enchantment of social relations: to adopt the definition of ideology given by Lévi-Strauss and Althusser, it acts as an imaginary solution to the poverty of the real Bloom. This is what I meant earlier, when I spoke of an ideology of the possible. And, let us be clear, what is involved here is a *good* ideology: happy, flexible, curious. But it is certainly not the emancipatory challenge dreamed up by a type of criticism perpetually searching for myths.[40] Indeed, if you take a closer look . . .

Think about this: the genius of possibility, Ulrich Anders, lives in a country where nothing is possible any more; and he is bewitched by

---

[39] W. Iser, *The Implied Reader*, Johns Hopkins University Press, Baltimore and London 1974, p. 217. 'The real is nothing but a chance track left by the possible', Iser also says, echoing Musil. 'And if reality is nothing but one chance track, then it pales to insignificance beside the vast number of unseen and unfulfilled possibilities' (ibid., p. 206). ' "And what then would you do, [. . .] if you were the ruler of the world for one day?" – "I suppose [Ulrich replies] I would have no choice but to abolish reality!" ' (*The Man Without Qualities*, I, 69). And again: ' "I told him [Arnheim] that realisation always attracts me less than non-realisation [. . .] every time we fulfil just a little of an idea, in our delight we leave the greater part of it undone" ' (ibid., I, 66).

[40] 'Here begins a reading of Joyce which will point out [. . .] how Joyce's work has contributed to the discrediting of the subject; how today one can talk about Joyce's modernity by situating him "on that breach of the self" (Kristeva) opened up by other writings whose subversive force is now undermining the world of western discourse' (H. Cixous, 'Joyce: the (r)use of writing' (1970), in D. Attridge and D. Ferrer, eds, *Post-Structuralist Joyce*, Cambridge University Press, Cambridge 1984, p. 15). The least that can be said is: wrong guess.

Moosbrugger, the murderer who feels 'unable to act differently'. Leopold Bloom, the most open character in twentieth-century Europe, leads a suffocating life in a country with little freedom and no independence. It is a reality that Musil and Joyce have sought to place in parenthesis, devoting all their energies to the sense of possibility. And yet, beneath the great vaults of the Collateral Campaign and the stream of consciousness, that hard initial core can still be glimpsed. 'In spite of its ironies and para-doxes', one is tempted to repeat with Carl Schmitt, 'a consistent dependence is manifest [that] unconsciously submits [the ideology of the possible] to the strongest and most proximate power.'[41]

A freedom based upon *un*freedom. We shall return to this.

Epiphany, madeleine, Leitmotiv

Joyce and Zola, Joyce and the advertising poster, Joyce and Musil . . . And Joyce and Proust, of course: from Edmund Wilson to Joseph Frank and Giacomo Debenedetti, a parallel that by now is a little classic of contem-porary criticism. But is it really so certain that what is of most interest is the *similarity* between *Ulysses* and *À la recherche*? Think of Molly's mono-logue, and of the Guermantes reception: two episodes, at first sight, quite similar – two finales, swollen and arched back to recover time past. But if the starting point is the same, the episodes develop quite differently. In Molly's vigil, Iser writes, the past recovers that openness that it had long ago lost: time is regained because it is *reopened*: freed from all fixity, all certainty.[42] By contrast, the happiness pervading Marcel has quite another origin. It consists in recognizing with certainty: discovering 'the permanent essence of things'. Time regained is time *fixed*: carved once and for all – immobile.

Instead of Joyce 'and' Proust, in the following pages I shall therefore

---

[41] C. Schmitt, *Political Romanticism*, MIT Press, Cambridge Mass. 1986, p. 162.

[42] 'The past now is liberated from all restrictions of time and space, and so situations flow into one another elliptically, regaining the openness of outcome which they had been deprived of long ago in the past [. . .] Thus the past remembered sug-gests completely new combinations, and Molly's own life comes back to her with a surplus of possibilities . . .' (Iser, *The Implied Reader*, p. 224).

speak of Joyce 'against' Proust. It is not a matter of hierarchies (even if I have my own preferences, of course). It is that I want to highlight a feature of literary evolution: the fact that creative moments (such as the time of Proust and Joyce) are characterized by radical splits – and *for that very reason* are creative moments. What I have in mind is a bush-like history, with unequal, asymmetrical branches growing as best they can – and even, perhaps, trying to get the better of one another. A long way from Hegel's spirit of the times, in the singular, recurring in every picture, every novel, and every symphony! Literary history is a battlefield – and especially, as we shall see, in the years of modernism. For now, however, a bit of stylistics:

> Proust takes particular delight – writes Spitzer – in dependent clauses, because they illustrate the dependence (and this is not just a play on words) of man upon chance, of the individual upon the whole and so on, in a kind of acoustic and architectonic imitation.[43]

Chance – but translated into an architectonic form. 'This tightening and condensation', we read at another point in the essay,

> and this ability to accumulate the sentence, seem to me to spring above all from Proust's ability to see connections between the most disparate things. In these complex representations there is an enormous mastery and dominion over things, which knows all about precedence and subordination, and can put important and trivial things in their appropriate places . . .[44]

Total dominion over the most disparate things: a splendid metaphor. Could we possibly apply it to *Ulysses*?

> *One of those chaps would make short work of a fellow. Pick the bones clean no matter who it was. Ordinary meat for them. A corpse is meat gone bad.* Well and what's cheese? Corpse of milk. *I read in this* Voyages in China *that the Chinese say a white man smells like a corpse.* Cremation better. Priests dead against it. Devilling for the other firm. Wholesale burners and Dutch oven dealers. Time of the plague. Quicklime feverpits to eat

---

[43] L. Spitzer, 'Zum Stil Marcel Proust's' (1944), in *Stilstudien* 2, Max Hueber Verlag, Munich 1928, p. 420.

[44] Ibid., p. 368.

them. Lethal chamber. Ashes to ashes. Or bury at sea. Where is that Parsee tower of silence? Eaten by birds. Earth, fire, water. Drowning they say is the pleasantest. See your whole life in a flash. But being brought back to life no. Can't bury in the air however. Out of a flying machine. *Wonder does the news go about whenever a fresh one is let down.* Underground communication. We learned that from them. *Wouldn't be surprised. Regular square feed for them.* Flies come before he's well dead. *Got wind of Dignam. They wouldn't care about the smell of it. Saltwhite crumbling mush of corpse: smell, taste like raw white turnips.*

Ulysses, VI, 980–94

The sentences in italics constitute the first draft of the paragraph, published in *Little Review*, in September 1918; all the rest is added later, between '18 and '21, actually doubling the original length. Great is Joyce's delight, we might repeat with Spitzer, in multiplying dependent clauses – except that those clauses are clearly *not* dependent. Even where a degree of subordination can be glimpsed ('*If* a corpse is meat gone bad, *then* cheese is corpse of milk'), Joyce's parataxis functions to the opposite effect: it constructs separate, independent sentences. Nothing is 'in its appropriate place', here: or rather, the appropriate place for things and thoughts is no longer, as in Proust, a matter of 'precedence or subordination', but always equal and independent.[45]

No dominion over things, here. Every sentence, and almost every word, of the stream of consciousness is a world in itself: complete, independent.

---

[45] The two different syntactical choices produce also two opposite representations of possibility. In Proust, possibility is expressed in the weakening of the main sentence by the subordinate clauses: it is an attenuation of certainty, a specification that branches out and relativizes. It is a possibility that speaks in the subjunctive: the verbal form that 'limits the validity of assertions' (Weinrich), and evokes 'insecurity and negation' (Vossler); that tends to 'interiorize and sentimentalize sentences, burdening them with nostalgia, fear, doubt, and desire' (Spitzer). In Joyce, by contrast, the world of the possible is wholly in the indicative. Each clause is a direct assertion: perhaps mistaken, because Bloom makes every kind of blunder, but never weakened by doubt. The sense of the possible here relies upon a quantitative, even crude, fact: that the things mentioned are constantly increasing, in a never-ending addition in which everything is equivalent, clearly visible, in the foreground . . .

Every paragraph, a digression in miniature – which continues to expand, like the one we have just read, because there exists no 'organic' fetter to hold it in check. It is the logic of mechanical form: the potentially infinite addition of Goethe, Flaubert, Kraus, Pound, Dos Passos, Musil . . . And indeed, for Joyce, 'to work' at *Ulysses* basically means *to extend Ulysses*, until the day when the printer loses patience, and sends the proofs – scribbled over for the nth time – back to him: '*trop tard*'. Too late, time has run out, an astrological idiocy wants the Book to be born on the same day as the Author, and an extrinsic fact (like death, more seriously, for others) thus assumes responsibility for putting an end to the infinite form.

But if even *Ulysses* comes to a halt, one question still remains. In this universe entirely made up of independent sentences, where everything is in the foreground and every working day adds new details, what meaning can the individual page, or the individual sentence, have? Indeed – does it still have one?

In realist texts, Roland Barthes has written, 'residues of functional analysis' are often encountered:

> The irreducible residues of functional analysis have this in common: they denote what is ordinarily called 'concrete reality' (insignificant gestures, transitory attitudes, insignificant objects, redundant words). The pure and simple 'representation' of the 'real', the naked relation of 'what is' (or has been), thus appears as a resistance to meaning.[46]

Insignificant gestures, transitory attitudes, redundant words . . . No doubt about it, it is the world of Leopold Bloom. And if Barthes is right, it is a world extraordinarily *poor in meaning*. Quite the opposite, in fact, from the one foreseen by the poetics of 'epiphany'. Here is Joyce, twenty years before *Ulysses*:

> [The object's] soul, its whatness, leaps to us from the vestment of its appearance. The soul of the commonest object, the structure of which is so adjusted, seems to us radiant. The object achieves its epiphany.
>
> *Stephen Hero*, 25

---

[46] R. Barthes, 'The Reality Effect', in *The Rustle of Language*, University of California Press, Berkeley and Los Angeles 1989, p. 146.

The soul of objects – 'their essential secret, their meaning [. . .] the second reality that is the only quality which makes things worth
representing'[47] – is this what we find in *Ulysses*? The *claritas*, the 'radiance'
of the young Joyce? On the contrary, the great novelty of the stream of
consciousness consists in its proceeding for pages and pages *without the
slightest revelation*. It is the true world of prose: detailed, regular, rather
banal. The view is determinedly earthbound, with nothing taking flight –
as in the grand vision of the *Portrait* – towards a higher reality. And as in
space, so too in time. Parataxis offers a reliable, mechanical grid, where
each present is at once followed by another – different, but no more
important. No instant ever stands out from the others, unrepeatable
(Proust: 'and suddenly the memory revealed itself'), to fix the meaning of
the story once and for all.

In short, a *Ulysses* without epiphanies. It is a point over which the
mature Joyce parts company with his own early work, and with most of
his contemporaries. It is not Dublin, the city of revelations: it is Paris.
The Paris of *Nadja*, all 'sudden parallels, petrifying coincidences, [. . .]
flashes of light that would make you see, really *see* . . .'; where people go
for a walk always hoping to come across the 'event from which each of
us is entitled to expect the revelation of his own life's meaning'. Or the
Paris of Aragon, who senses 'the wonder inherent in commonplace
things', and in his *Paysan de Paris* aims precisely to show 'the places
where the divine manifests itself'.[48] And even before the surrealists, of
course, Proust's Paris: where, one unforgettable day, 'the souls held cap-

---

[47] G. Debenedetti, *Il romanzo del Novecento*, Garzanti, Milan 1981, pp. 427, 295, 303
(notebooks dating from 1962–3 and 1963–4).

[48] This idea of the ordinary/marvellous is very widespread at the beginning of the
twentieth century, from Rilke ('[Mother and I] had a different conception of the
wonderful. To us, things that happened naturally would always be the most wonderful.' *Notebooks of Malte Laurids Brigge*, Part One) to Woolf ('To be on a level
with ordinary experience, to feel simply that's a chair, that's a table, and yet at the
same time, It's a miracle, it's an ecstasy': *To the Lighthouse*, III, 11). In the terms of
Erich Heller's great hypothesis on modern poetry, it is as though all these authors
harboured a very intense nostalgia for the miracle of the Eucharist – daily bread,
divine presence – which is, moreover, the fairly obvious model for Proust's
madeleine.

tive in some inferior being [. . .] start and tremble, they call us by our name, and as soon as we have recognized their voice the spell is broken'.

The *madeleine*: that is a true epiphany – soul, death, summons, resurrection, miracle . . . But it is precisely the sacred connotations of the episode, so akin to the language of the *Portrait*, that underline the distance of *Ulysses* from every form of revelation. For memory to re-emerge, Proust writes, 'I shut out every obstacle, every extraneous idea, I stop my ears and inhibit all attention against the sounds from the next room [. . .] I clear an empty space in front of it.' An empty space: quite right, the formula of the sacred, precisely what epiphany needs. But empty space is also completely impossible in the crowded world of *Ulysses*, all noise and interference. It is as if the stream of consciousness never managed to extricate itself from the close-knit fabric of metonymy, whereas the *madeleine*, and the epiphany of *Portrait*, can always leap from the latter into metaphor. From prose, to poetry:

> And soon, mechanically, dispirited after a dreary day with the prospect of a depressing morrow, I raised to my lips a spoonful of the tea in which I had soaked a morsel of the cake. No sooner had the warm liquid mixed with the crumbs touched my palate . . .

So far, we are in the world of prose, of metonymic details – lips, spoonful, cake, crumbs, palate . . . All things that are also in Joyce. But then, the symbolic continuity is broken:

> than a shudder ran through me and I stopped, intent upon the extraordinary thing that was happening to me. *An exquisite pleasure* had invaded my senses [. . .] having had on me *the effect which love has* of filling me with *a precious essence*; or rather this essence was not in me, it was me. [. . .] What did it mean?[49]

Que signifiait-elle? 'What did it mean?' (*Portrait of the Artist as a Young Man*, 4). 'What does it mean then, what can it all mean?' (*To the Lighthouse*, III,

---

[49] The first draft of this episode (the planned preface to *Contre Sainte-Beuve*) presents a far more homogeneous symbolic fabric – and perhaps this is just why Proust modified it. For the divergence between metonymy and metaphor is not just a sign of epiphany, it actually *is* epiphany: it accomplishes the vertical emergence of meaning from the horizontal world of prose.

1). A question that is like an alarm-bell: we are leaving the world of mimesis, to enter that of meaning. But it is also the question that Bloom, for all his curiosity, never asks himself. Because Bloom really speaks a one-dimensional language: made up of simple additions, where things coexist without strain and without secrets. Around him, only the 'insignificant gestures' of Roland Barthes: the 'insignificant objects' and 'redundant words' of his essay on 'The Reality Effect'. Superficial, resistant to meaning. Very well – but why? What can be the meaning of this absence of meaning?

A bit of vulgar materialism. In the Gabler edition, the fourth chapter of *Ulysses* (Bloom's first) numbers about 550 lines. The fifth, 570. The sixth, 1030. In all, some fifty pages, and two thousand odd lines. Well, in this space, Bloom receives more than *three thousand* assorted stimuli, of which around two thirds are internal (memories, reflections, emotions), and one third external (visual, verbal, olfactory and tactile stimuli). To pile vulgarity upon vulgarity: more than sixty heterogeneous elements per page, or one and a half per line. In short: one stimulus every ten words.[50]

There it is, Simmel's metropolis. At last, it has taken linguistic form. But it has also created a far from simple problem: is it really possible to

---

[50] I extrapolate these results from nine samplings which seem to me representative of the chapters as a whole (IV – lines 1–30, 111–39, 369–96; V – lines 27–59, 279–310, 510–41; VI – lines 1–28, 229–59; 995–1026). It should be added that while the internal stimuli remain fairly constant from one chapter to the next, the external ones change considerably in both quantity and quality (as is only logical, given their dependence upon the context). One of the most surprising facts about the survey is the minimal quantity (about one per cent) of stimuli connected with strong emotions: sign of an emotional neutrality that distinguishes the Joycean stream of consciousness from that of his contemporaries, and to which I shall return in the Excursus appended to this chapter. At the other extreme, the commonest datum (around thirty per cent of the total) is represented by miniature encyclopaedic 'entries' crossing Bloom's mind, which indicate the close kinship between *Ulysses* and *Bouvard and Pécuchet*.

In general, quantitative analysis might be an appropriate interpretive key for the 'mechanical form' of the stream of consciousness. Where the whole is (almost only) the sum of the individual parts, doing the sum is always a good start.

make those three thousand stimuli *meaningful?* Yes, of course – if you are willing to *reduce them.* If you make an 'empty space' in front of them, as in front of Proust's crumbs, and restrict the field of observation:

> When suddenly, in she came, stood for a moment silent (as if she had been pretending up there, and for a moment let herself be now), stood quite motionless for a moment against a picture of Queen Victoria wearing the blue ribbon of the Garter; and all at once he realized that it was this: it was this: – she was the most beautiful person he had ever seen.
>
> *To the Lighthouse*, 1, 1

. . . it was this: it was this. A revealing stylistic feature, this syncopated and almost feverish use of the deictic. One colon, then another, then a dash: a triple focusing, which brings things closer, and squeezes out their meaning. But the meaning is precisely the result of exclusion: of a field that contracts and again contracts – this: this – and relegates everything else to the background. But in the stream of consciousness there is really no background: all sentences are main, all is foreground. And where all is in the foreground, nothing is ever really close – never a 'this'. It is a broad perception, but unfocused: able only to slide over things.

Well then, what is the meaning of this absence of meaning? Simple – it helps Bloom to live. It helps him to live *in the metropolis:* a place that requires more intelligence, to be sure – but also more stupidity. Where he must learn to see and not see, to understand and not understand. 'Unfocused interaction', as Erving Goffman has called it: 'civil inattention'.[51] A neutrality, opacity, and emotional mediocrity, that enable millions of human beings to live side by side without exterminating each other. If on that June day everything were meaningful, Bloom's head would burst – and so would the reader's. Consequently, when we read *Ulysses* we learn to accept the fact that thousands of things gradually become familiar to us, but never more than familiar. We see them again, and know they are there; but are never sure of their meaning, or why they are there.

Such are the 'themes' of the stream of consciousness, which recur

---

[51] E. Goffman, *Behaviour in Public Places*, Free Press of Glencoe, New York and London 1963, passim.

innumerable times without ever being fixed in a sure form. Here, too, we are at the antipodes to Proust: 'This time he [Swann] had distinguished quite clearly a phrase which emerged for a few moments above the waves of sound . . .' He had distinguished quite clearly – well, in *Ulysses* there is never such sureness of identity: 'I saw that picture somewhere I forget now old master or faked for money. He is sitting in their house, talking. Mysterious' (*Ulysses*, V, 289–91). Or again:

> Yet they say, who was it told me, there is no carnal. You would imagine that would get played out pretty quick. Yes, it was Crofton met him one evening bringing her a pound of rumpsteak. What is this she was? Barmaid in Jury's. Or the Moira, was it?
>
> *Ulysses*, VI, 245–8

Yet they say, who was it told me . . . Adorno's Mahler comes to mind:

> The concept of the theme as a given, then to be modified, is inadequate to Mahler. Rather, the nucleus undergoes a treatment similar to that of a narrative element in oral tradition; at each telling it becomes slightly different. [. . .] To this extent the variants are the countervailing force to fulfilment. They divest the theme of its identity [whereas] the fulfilment is the positive manifestation of what the theme has not yet become.[52]

The last sentence more or less sums up what I have been trying to say. On the one hand, 'fulfilment' of the theme, the 'positive manifestation' of the *madeleine*, the epiphany of meaning. On the other, the 'variants' in Mahler and Joyce, the 'oral tradition' of the stream of consciousness: themes that 'become slightly different at each telling'. But that in the meantime, as I was saying, become familiar. And here a second musical analogy is called for:

> Wagner's work [is endowed] with an enigmatic quality and even today, in contrast with almost all other music, the listener is left with the sense of a blind spot, of something unresolved – notwithstanding his familiarity with the music. Wagner denies the listener who accompanies

---

[52] T.W. Adorno, *Mahler*, translated by Edmund Jephcott, University of Chicago Press, Chicago 1992, p. 88.

him the satisfaction of a thing clearly defined and it is left in doubt whether the formal meaning of a given moment has been rightly apprehended. Sachs's words – 'I can't hold on to it – but nor can I forget it' – are an allusion to this.[53]

It is the paradox of the *Leitmotiv*: you recognize it without ever perhaps having known it. Armed with Max Chop's booklets, Wagnerian audiences are bewitched from the outset by the urge to identify it, and thrilled by its reappearance. But this pleasure relegates musical understanding to the background. Adorno again:

> Among the functions of the *Leitmotiv* can be found, alongside the aesthetic one, a commodity-function, rather like that of an advertisement: anticipating the universal practice of mass culture later on, the music is designed to be remembered, it is intended for the forgetful.[54]

Learning by heart replacing comprehension: for Adorno, it is an unforgivable regression. But in the context of our discourse, something else comes into play as well. Staiger:

> [In Homer] the happiness that the return of the familiar brings, the triumph of knowing that now life no longer flows on without stopping but is something lasting, and that objects have a firm, stable existence and can be identified – all this is so powerful that even today every unspoiled reader experiences in it an inspired feeling for the early days of mankind.[55]

Perhaps it is not just a feeling for the earliest days. In so far as the metropolis is itself a world – vast, complicated, dangerous – then the happiness conveyed by the return of the familiar is by no means inappropriate to the twentieth century. In the unending melody of *Ulysses*, for example (which surpasses even the *Ring* in the number and variety of its themes),

---

[53] T.W. Adorno, *In Search of Wagner*, NLB, London 1981, p. 43.

[54] Ibid., p. 31. The fact that the advertising slogan remains engraved 'like a Wagnerian *Leitmotiv*' had already been observed in 1911 by P. Raveau, 'La Guerre à l'affiche', in *La Publicité*, May 1911 (quoted in Varnedoe and Gopnik, *High and Low*, p. 249).

[55] E. Staiger, *Basic Concepts of Poetics*, translated by J. Hudson and L. Frank, Pennsylvania State University Press, Philadelphia 1991, pp. 102–3.

the return of the *Leitmotiv* is the only thing that helps us, if not actually to understand – what is there to *understand*, in a stream of consciousness paragraph? – at least to get our bearings. When things and individuals from the city of Dublin, places and gestures and words, begin to reappear – always overdetermined by their new contexts, but also, just like the Wagnerian *Leitmotiv*, always clearly recognizable – well, their return makes *Ulysses* feel like a world you can live in. Its extent remains vast, and its laws almost incomprehensible. At the same time, however – just as in a big foreign city – here and there the first fixed points are established: a bee sting, a cake of soap, a phrase from Mozart . . .

Not much? True enough, not much – from the point of view of *meaning*. But in a different perspective, it is truly *a world of things*. It is the language of the big city.

World texts. II

So warm. His right hand once more slowly went over his brow and hair. Then he put on his hat again, relieved: and read again: choice blend, made of the finest Ceylon brands. The far east. *Lovely spot it must be: the garden of the world, big lazy leaves* to float about on, cactuses, flowery meads, *snaky lianas they call them. Wonder is it like that. Those Cinghalese lobbing about in the sun* in dolce far niente, not doing a hand's turn all day. Sleep six months out of the twelve. Too hot to quarrel. *Influence of the climate.* Lethargy. Flowers of idleness. The air feeds most. Azotes. Hothouse in Botanic gardens. Sensitive plants. Waterlilies. Petals too tired to. Sleeping sickness in the air. Walk on roseleaves. Imagine trying to eat tripe and cowheel. *Where was the chap I saw in that picture somewhere? Ah yes, in the dead sea floating on his back, reading a book with a parasol open. Couldn't sink if you tried, so thick with salt. Because the weight of the water, no, the weight of the body in the water is equal to the weight of the what? Or is it the volume is equal to the weight? It's a law something like that.* Vance in High school cracking his fingerjoints, teaching. The college curriculum. Cracking curriculum. *What is weight really when you say the weight? Thirty two feet per second per second. Law of falling bodies: per second per second. They all fall to the ground. The earth. It's the force of gravity of the earth is the weight.*

Ulysses, V, 27–46: the phrases in italics are those
originally published in *Little Review*, July 1918

Leopold Bloom, and a shop-window: an ideal situation for the stream of consciousness. In this case, moreover, in front of the Belfast Oriental Tea Company, the device really does function as Mephistopheles' cloak: it makes it possible to fly through space, into those 'other worlds' – here, the Orient – of which epic digressions are made. It is a situation recalling Faust's reverie on the seashore – but with one important difference. At the time of *Ulysses*, the conquest of extra-European space is a *fait accompli*, and Bloom's geographical stereotypes – 'secondhand abstractions', as Edward Said has called them[56] – are the proof of it: testimony to a dominion so self-confident that it parades its very ignorance as indisputable knowledge. It is as if, in *Ulysses*, the grand world were suddenly shrunk. Let us take a closer look.

London, late nineteenth century. The reading room of the Reform Club, seen by a French novelist:

> 'Well, but where can he [the thief] fly to? [. . .] No country
> is safe for him.'
> 'Pshaw!'
> 'Where could he go, then?'
> 'Oh, I don't know that. The world is big enough.'
> 'It was once . . .' [. . .]
> 'What do you mean by "once"? Has the world grown smaller?'
> 'Certainly . . .'

Smaller, because you can travel round it more quickly, of course ('That is true, gentlemen, only eighty days, now that the section between Rothal and Allahabad, on the Great Indian Peninsular Railway, has been opened'). But there is something that shrinks the world even more than speed, and that is *predictability*:

> 'Yes, in eighty days! But that doesn't take into account bad weather,
> contrary winds, shipwrecks, railway accidents, and so on.'
> 'All included', returned Phileas Fogg, continuing to play . . .

---

[56] E. Said, *Orientalism*, Penguin Books, Harmondsworth 1985, p. 252.

'But suppose the Hindus or Indians pull up the rails? Suppose they stop the trains, pillage the luggage vans, and scalp the passengers!'
'All included . . .'

Jules Verne, *Around the World in Eighty Days*, 3

Tout compris: Phileas Fogg does not know it, but he has just christened modern tourism. For that clause with its glorious future promises a journey that can be calculated in advance, like every other economic investment: twenty thousand pounds, exactly; eighty days, and not a second more.[57] And that is not all. For material security is very soon supplemented by a semiotic protection that enables the tourist to encounter signs, and nothing but signs, everywhere – and signs that he already knows. Thus Mark Twain, in a book entitled – how perfect – *Innocents Abroad*:

> In a little while we were speeding through the streets of Paris and delightfully recognizing certain names and places with which books had long ago made us familiar. It was like meeting an old friend when we read 'Rue de Rivoli' on the street corner; we knew the genuine vast palace of the Louvre as well as we knew its picture . . .
>
> *Innocents Abroad*, 12

Re-cognition. It is the tourist's supreme wish. A desire so strong that the journey becomes truly complete only when, with photography, it is in turn fixed in a sign: into a good – and if possible perfect – likeness of the original signs. A person travels, here, not in order to see the world, but in order to see once more – *through* the world – his own encyclopaedia. On the semiotic level, Jonathan Culler has written: 'Tourism reveals the difficulties of appreciating otherness except through signifying structures that mark and reduce it.'[58]

---

[57] In general, *Around the World in Eighty Days* is a wonderful allegory of the nineteenth century: on the one hand, the economy and technology (or, more accurately, the pound sterling and the railway train), which help Fogg to complete his journey; on the other hand, politics and religion, which create every kind of obstacle for him. (The most perilous adventures, incidentally, take place on the site of the 1857 Indian Mutiny, and in the central United States: in both cases, Englishmen against Indians, in the vicinity of a railway line.)

[58] J. Culler, 'The Semiotics of Tourism', in *Framing the Sign*, Basil Blackwell, Oxford 1988, p. 167.

Reducing otherness . . . These are the right words with which to return to Leopold Bloom, and his thoughts on the Orient: garden of the world . . . sleep six months out of twelve . . . influence of the climate . . . walk on roseleaves . . . Sound familiar, these phrases? Of course, they are old acquaintances: they are the *idées reçues* of Bouvard and Pécuchet – who had themselves travelled around culture in (just over) eighty days. And, in one way, Joyce's commonplaces still function like Flaubert's: they reduce the unknown to the known; they know everything, they *close* everything. They shrink the world, as I was saying earlier: they bring the distant closer, and make it familiar.[59] But to this old function the commonplaces of *Ulysses* have added a new one. They have become the scaffolding for Bloom's random associations: the support for the new metropolitan perception. In more radical terms, they are the *extremely banal* basis, without which the *extremely audacious* technique of the stream of consciousness could not exist.

It is the same interweaving of regression and development (simplified plot, complex score) already encountered in the *Ring*, where it was facilitated by the presence of two different languages. In Joyce, of course, there is only one language, but the twofold level survives, to be exploited with equal intelligence. What, after all, is the stream of consciousness for? As I have said (only too often): for opening up to the stimuli of modernity; and for keeping them all present, in the foreground, without losing a single one of them. But such an endeavour has its cost. Arnold Gehlen:

> Man's world-openness might appear to be a great burden. He is flooded with stimulation, with an abundance of impressions, which he must somehow learn to cope with [. . .] Man must find *relief* from the burden of overwhelming stimulation.[60]

---

[59] While checking the geographical references in the fifth and eighth chapters of *Ulysses*, I realized that commonplaces are more frequent in so far as the place mentioned is *more distant* – and, indeed, in so far as it is *more unknown*. The maximum scores are registered by Asia, of which we saw an example in the passage on the Belfast Tea Company, and Africa, which almost automatically evokes the thought of cannibals. The minimum scores are registered by Dublin and Ireland, to which Bloom usually reacts in a rather personalized way.

[60] A. Gehlen, *Man. His Nature and Place in the World* (1950), Columbia University Press, New York 1988, p. 28.

Relief and coping: this is what Bloom's commonplaces are for. A technical detail reveals it to us: their position in the Joycean paragraph. Almost never at the beginning – which is the moment of world-openness, when it would be absurd to have a closed mind. Often at the end, in order to file away what has happened with a formula, as in *Bouvard and Pécuchet*. And almost always around the middle of the paragraph: in order to hold together the associative galaxy of the stream of consciousness. A 'banality rate' is thus established in Bloom's mind: a regular, constant rhythm – two or three stimuli, one commonplace, two or three stimuli, one commonplace – that accompanies him throughout the day, offering firm support amid the throng of external and internal impulses. These are Bloom's certitudes. The moments in which the meaning of things is revealed to him: clear, indisputable.

The moments in which the meaning of things . . . Yes, indeed, commonplaces are *Bloom's epiphanies.* The only ones appropriate for *Ulysses*: metaphors, yes – but dead metaphors, covering the metonymic fabric with a blanket of obviousness that makes it still more opaque.[61] But this is quite all right, as we have seen: the world-city requires more lucidity *and more stupidity*. Or rather, a new kind of stupidity: curiosity, plus the impersonal; the anomie of *disparate* stimuli, and the standardization of *common*places. The expanse of epic space is here welded to the novelistic theme of malleability, and the project initiated with *Faust* is finally accomplished: an epic of socialization. For this is the meaning of that day in 1904. What does Bloom do – from when he gets up to when he finally goes to sleep? Nothing. He walks, he looks round, he remembers, he dreams, he thinks. But in this *dolce far niente*, Bloom reviews his own receptive apparatus, and refurbishes his own imaginary. He harmonizes with the social that is outside him, and with the social that is inside him.

But where, inside?

---

[61] That epiphany should be revealed by the *in*-significant had been Joyce's original insight, at the end of *Stephen Hero*; but it was probably too paradoxical an idea, and Joyce beat a rapid retreat, to devote himself (like Proust, or the surrealists) to the 'deeply deep' epiphanies of *Portrait*. It is only with *Ulysses* that the meaningless returns to the centre of his work, to be represented *as meaningless*. An idea that critics have never much appreciated, nor perhaps understood: whence their vain attempts to save Joyce from himself, by attributing to *Ulysses* all manner of deep messages. But there are so many deep novels already, and the beauty of *Ulysses* is just the opposite . . .

Free association

Where, inside? As usual, that famous label – stream of consciousness – offers no help: it is not a stream, and it is not consciousness. What, then? 'The Depth Approach' is the title of Chapter 1 of *The Hidden Persuaders*; and one of Wenders's characters, at the end of *Kings of The Road*, says: 'The Americans have colonized our subconscious.' The link with the world of *Ulysses* seems self-evident. But is it really the *subconscious* speaking, in Bloom's 'stream of consciousness'?

Let us begin with a technical detail. The similarity has often been noted between the stream of consciousness and the psychoanalytic technique of 'free association'. Well, Freud writes, the 'higher degree of freedom of association' is achieved when:

> I may, for instance, require the experimenter to allow a proper name or a number to occur to him freely. What then occurs to him would pre-sumably be even more arbitrary and more indeterminable than with our own technique. It can be shown, however, that it is *always strictly determined* by important internal attitudes of mind [. . .] The associa-tions to numbers chosen at random are perhaps the most convincing; they run off so quickly and *proceed with such incredible certainty to a hidden goal* that the effect is really staggering.[62]

'Free' associations? Certainly, free from any conscious selection. But the italics (added by me) make it clear that for Freud the really staggering thing is the *lack of freedom* of the associative process. The true protagonist, here, is not freedom, but psychological determinism: the 'important internal' – or subconscious – 'attitudes of mind' that steer the associations to their necessary conclusion. 'Psychical events are determined. There is nothing arbitrary about them . . .' writes Freud in *The Interpretation of Dreams*; and a few years later, *The Psychopathology of Everyday Life* (which examines phenomena that are indeed very Joycean) aims precisely to

---

[62] S. Freud, *Introductory Lectures on Psychoanalysis*, translated by James Strachey, Penguin Books, Harmondsworth 1974, pp. 136–7 (my italics).

eliminate chance from even the tiniest behavioural and linguistic mishaps.[63]

Very well. And here is Joyce:

> Makes them feel more important to be prayed over in Latin. Requiem mass. Crape weepers. Blackedged notepaper. Your name on the altarlist. Chilly place this. Want to feed well, sitting in there all the morning in the gloom kicking his heels waiting for the next please. Eyes of a toad too. What swells him up that way? Molly gets swelled after cabbage. Air of the place maybe. Looks full up of bad gas. Must be an infernal lot of bad gas round the place. Butchers, for instance: they get like raw beefsteaks. Who was telling me? Mervyn Browne. Down in the vaults of saint Werburgh's lovely old organ hundred and fifty they have to bore a hole in the coffins sometimes to let out the bad gas and burn it. Out it rushes blue. One whiff of that and you're a doner.

Ulysses, VI, 602–12

Latin, mourning, food, the priest's face, Molly, gas, butchers, the organ in the crypt . . . These really are free associations: they move in ten different directions, without any objective or logic. And why are they so free? Because there is no 'hidden goal': no force that intervenes to deflect their course; no 'important internal attitude of mind' that 'strictly determines' their direction. Because, in other words, in the course of the associative process *the subconscious never comes into play*.

But if the stream of consciousness has nothing to do with consciousness, then, nor yet with the subconscious, who the devil *is* speaking in Bloom's stream of consciousness?

It is the 'preconscious': a 'system' to which Freud, after some initial interest, attributes rather little importance. Within it, we find quite different wishes from those that belong 'to the suppressed part of the mind and become active in us at night'.[64] No, the wishes of the preconscious

[63] S. Freud, *The Interpretation of Dreams*, translated by James Strachey, Penguin Books, Harmondsworth 1976, p. 659; *The Psychopathology of Everyday Life*, translated by Alan Tyson, Penguin Books, Harmondsworth 1975, pp. 300–344.
[64] Freud, *Interpretation of Dreams*, p. 702.

are always daytime, waking, acknowledged ones: if they remain 'not dealt with', Freud adds with uncharacteristic vagueness, it is always because of 'external reasons'. *External*: implying that conflict with other psychological forces is not involved here. And twenty years later, in *The Ego and the Id*: 'The latent, which is unconscious only descriptively, not in the dynamic sense, we call *preconscious*.'[65]

Descriptive, not dynamic. It was undoubtedly this symbolic neutrality of the preconscious that very quickly made it boring to Freud (but not to us, who have had plenty of practice with boring things). I am thinking of one word in particular, the abracadabra of the stream of consciousness and of *Ulysses*: 'Yes'. The first and last word of Molly's monologue: the last in the book, then, but also the one that reopens it, carrying us back to the beginning of the chapter – or even to the beginning of the beginning, seeing that the last letter of 'Yes' is likewise the first letter of 'Stately', which is the first word of the first chapter . . . And since we are on the subject, let me add that 'Yes' is the opposite of 'No', and it places the Joycean stream of consciousness at the opposite pole from Freud's 'negation'. As Francesco Orlando would say, it makes it into a world with a 'low figurality rate':[66] one in which nothing is forbidden, and there is therefore no need to mask anything. The prevalence of metonymy over metaphor is the rhetorical consequence of this state of affairs, supplemented – to complete the picture – by the role of the 'insignificant' within the stream of consciousness.[67]

Lack of dynamism. Neutrality. Meaninglessness. Low figurality rate. Defects? I do not know. Perhaps so, for a symbolist aesthetics. But to a

[65] S. Freud, 'The Ego and the Id', in *On Metapsychology: the Theory of Psychoanalysis*, translated under the editorship of James Strachey, Penguin Books, Harmondsworth 1984, p. 353.

[66] F. Orlando, *Towards a Freudian Theory of Literature*, translated by Charmaine Lee, Johns Hopkins University Press, Baltimore and London 1978, pp. 164 ff.

[67] When salvation appears on the horizon, I find myself confronted by a metaphor, and *I must* interpret it in a figurative sense, otherwise I shall fail to comprehend the phrase. But when a sail appears on the horizon, *I can* interpret the expression in a figurative sense (synechdoche for a ship), but I can also content myself with the literal sense of 'sail'. Texts dominated by metonymy thus usually possess a lower figurality rate than those dominated by metaphor.

sociology of literary forms, this opaque limbo appears to be the ideal instrument for surviving in the big city. Therein, finally, lies the whole difference between Bloom and Biberkopf. Biberkopf is the man of the Id and the Super-ego: he takes everything dreadfully seriously, and so eventually snaps amid all the complications of Berlin. Bloom is the man of the preconscious, and he survives: receptive, tolerant, always able to recover. His rather banal wishes, with nothing illicit about them, will be boring for psychoanalysis, but not for advertising: which thrives precisely upon such lawful desires, which have nevertheless – due to 'external reasons': lack of money, or time, or whatever – remained as yet 'not dealt with'. And finally the preconscious – ever open, and extendable at will – is the ideal space for the category that has underpinned this whole chapter: the space of the possible – *as possible.*

Stadtluft macht frei, runs an old German proverb: city air makes you free. Free from your own lord, it used to mean in its day. But today it seems instead to suggest: free as a breath of air, or a fantasy, can be. The billions of human beings who have ended up in big cities – have they really lived better? Hard to say. But they have *dreamed* better, of that I am sure. And the credit, if credit it is, goes to these: advertising, the stream of consciousness, the preconscious.

EXCURSUS

STREAM OF CONSCIOUSNESS – EVOLUTION OF A TECHNIQUE

In the previous chapter, I proposed two intertwined hypotheses. The first, derived from Simmel, is of a sociological and historical kind: with the advent of the metropolis, the modern individual is subjected to an extremely intense, and perhaps excessive, stimulation. The second, of a rhetorical kind, maintains that the stream of consciousness is able to pick up those stimuli, and organize them in a singularly effective way. What a fortunate technique, one is tempted to say, what a providential technique. On closer inspection, however, the evolution of the stream of consciousness is a bit too bizarre to have been guided by Providence. Let us follow its oddities, then, in pursuit of a genealogy that excludes all teleological assumptions.

'Why, it's I!'

Anna Karenin's last day begins:

> 'Who's that?' she thought, gazing in the mirror at the feverish, scared face with the strangely glittering eyes looking out at her. 'Why, it's I!' she realized all at once, and looking at herself full length she suddenly seemed to feel his kisses on her, gave a shiver and moved her shoulders. Then she lifted her hand to her lips and kissed it.
> 'I must be going out of my mind!' she said to herself, and went to her bedroom, where Annushka was tidying up.

168

'Annushka!' she said, stopping before the maid and staring at her, not knowing what to say. [. . .]

'Annushka, dear, what am I to do?'

Anna Karenin, VII, 27

Take your mind off things, Annushka replies. And, in the pages that follow, Anna's carriage trip gives, in effect, a foretaste of Leopold Bloom's absentmindedness:

> '**Office and Warehouse** . . . **Dental Surgeon** . . . Yes, I will tell Dolly everything. She doesn't like Vronski. It will be painful and humiliating, but I'll tell her all about everything. She is fond of me and I will follow her advice. I won't give in to him. I won't allow him to teach me . . . **Filipov, Pastry Cook** . . . I've heard he sends his pastry to Petersburg. The Moscow water is so good. Ah, the springs at Mytishchi, and the pancakes!' [. . .] 'How proud and self-satisfied he will feel when he gets my note! But I will show him . . . How nasty that paint smells! Why is it they're always painting and building? **Dressmaking and Millinery** . . .' [. . .] 'And we all hate each other – I Kitty, and she me. Yes, that is the truth. **Tyutkin, Coiffeur**. *Je me fais coiffer par Tyutkin* . . . I'll tell him that when he comes home.'
>
> *Anna Karenin*, VII, 28 and 29

Signs, wandering memories, smells, foreign words . . . It really could be Dublin. Yet, Tolstoy and Joyce are aiming at very different things. In the first chapters of *Ulysses*, the stream of consciousness occupies the centre of the picture: it is the voice of Stephen and Bloom, the style of the metropolis. In *Anna Karenin*, however, it is made up only of fleeting, peripheral moments: involuntary symptoms of that terrible question – 'Surely I can live without him?' – which overwhelms Anna to the point of making her lose her self-control.[1] Her fragmentary sentences make us think, not so much of Bloom's easy 'world-openness', as of a convulsive – and vain – flight:

> At that same instant she became horror-struck at what she was doing. 'Where am I? What am I doing? Why?' She tried to get up, to throw

---

[1] ' "Surely, I can live without him?" And leaving the question unanswered she fell to reading the signboards. "**Office and Warehouse** . . ." ' (*Anna Karenin*, VII, 28).

herself back; but something huge and relentless struck her on the head and dragged her down on her back. 'God forgive me everything!' she murmured, feeling the impossibility of struggling.

Anna Karenin, VII, 31

A fierce, unequal, struggle to keep control of herself: from the initial question ('Who's that? Why, it's I!'), to the final one ('What am I doing? Why?'), this is the meaning of Tolstoy's passage. We are approaching a 'kernel', a narrative bifurcation: will Anna Karenin live without Vronski – or will she end up killing herself? It is the decisive bifurcation in the novel: so extreme as to unhinge Anna's mind, and cause the stream of consciousness to burst violently forth from it. But this very narrative constellation confines the new technique to the interstices of the story: makes it into a *symptom*, a signal, but little more. Before Leopold Bloom is reached, there is still a long way to go.

From Tolstoy's novel, to a novella written in 1900 by Arthur Schnitzler: *Leutnant Gustl*. On the way out of a concert, a young officer behaves arrogantly to his baker, is publicly humiliated by him, and decides to kill himself before dawn. The novella tells the story of Gustl's last night, in a stream of consciousness rendered more and more disjointed – 'I am already quite mad' – by the fear of imminent death. It fills several dozen pages: compared with those few sentences in *Anna Karenin*, a notable change. On closer inspection, however, a change more quantitative than anything else. For, structurally, Gustl's stream of consciousness too is only a parenthesis – however swollen – between two narrative bifurcations: the scene that has just occurred ('What a happy man I was, an hour ago . . .'), and the irreversible event ('Who knows if they will bury me in Graz?') that will take place at the first light of dawn.

At the last moment, an apoplectic fit carries off the baker, and everything returns to normal. But only just. Twenty-five years later, with *Fräulein Else*, Schnitzler returns to the stream of consciousness, and makes a clean sweep of everything: respectability, affections, modesty, reason, life. If Anna Karenin and Gustl are afraid of going mad, Else really does go mad: compelled to lose her own honour in order to save her father's, she is overwhelmed by this double bind and eventually dies of it. The association glimpsed in *Anna Karenin* and in *Gustl* is thus fixed: the stream of consciousness, as the style of madness. Joseph Warren Beach:

The stream-of-consciousness technique is almost invariably applied to persons of an extremely 'introverted' type, to neurotics and those of unbalanced mind, or to occasional states of mind of normal individuals bordering on obsession or delirium.[2]

True. True also for such long-forgotten works as *Blue Voyage* (with the tormented insomnia of its protagonist Demarest); or *5,000* (story of a long-distance race, at the end of which the runner Monnerot falls to the ground in a faint); or *Quinze rounds*, where the boxer Battling ends up in an asylum, after being knocked out.[3] In these cases, the intensity of the stream of consciousness can actually be 'measured', since its formal characteristics – parataxis, random associations, incorrect grammar, extension of the present moment – far from remaining constant throughout the story, fluctuate continually. And they grow as *the suffering grows*: the more blows Battling takes, the more interesting his style becomes: the greater the danger, the more vivid the stream of consciousness. A brief list will suffice: Anna, Else, Septimus in *Mrs Dalloway*, Quentin in *The Sound and the Fury*, Broch's Virgil, Jean Schlumberger's man buried alive (*L'enseveli*, 1928): all die, often by their own hand. And then again: Gustl, Monnerot, Benjy, Franz Biberkopf, Battling, all of whom come very close to death. As if the stream of consciousness were the victim of its own radicalism: a poisoned style, that can lead only to extreme conclusions.

The Sound and the Fury, part one: Benjy's stream of consciousness. Uncertain identities, jumps in time, high figurality rate. And a brutal story: Benjy is an 'idiot', hated by his own family, mocked, scorned, castrated. It makes exhausting reading, of a doubly radical nature: terrible events, and an impenetrable style. But then . . .

Then Faulkner, as he put it a few years later, wrote the Quentin and Jason parts to explain the Benjy part. And he is quite right: from Benjy

---

[2] J.W. Beach, *The Twentieth Century Novel: Studies in Technique*, Apple–Century–Crofts, New York 1932, p. 529.

[3] C. Aiken, *Blue Voyage*, Scribner's, New York 1927; D. Brage, *5,000. Récit sportif*, NRF, Paris 1924; H. Decoin, *Quinze rounds. Histoire d'un combat*, Flammarion, Paris 1930.

to Quentin, from Quentin to Jason, from Jason to the narrator of the finale, *The Sound and the Fury* moves away from its initial extremism, and returns to more traditional techniques. It does so with intelligence, of course: Jason, who helps us to understand what is going on, is also a rabid racist; the clarity so long desired thus reveals itself as the enemy of justice. Be that as it may, though, the novel begins with the stream of consciousness – and it ends with a third-person narrative. Albeit with a few complications, it has changed track.[4]

With Virginia Woolf and Thomas Mann, the counter-trend to the stream of consciousness goes even further: the new technique is not merely explained, but completely rewritten. If, at certain moments, Lily Briscoe is seized by panic and on the point of losing control, Woolf's syntax is able to check any such drift, and give form to chaos:

> It was in that moment's flight between the picture and her canvas that the demons set on her who often brought her to the verge of tears and made this passage from conception to work as dreadful as any down a dark passage for a child.
>
> *To the Lighthouse*, I, 4

Nothing ungrammatical, here; no levelling parataxis, or random associations. In sentences woven into a lucid sequence leading towards their goal – Proust after the stream of consciousness, as it were – narrative consciousness has regained the upper hand. There is still suffering, but no bewilderment. And here is Thomas Mann:

> Alas, that it should vanish! That my bright vision of the depths must so soon be gone away – as though the whim of a genie gave it and as suddenly snatched it away – it fades into nothing, I emerge. So lovely it was! And now what? Where are we? Jena? Berka? Tennstadt? No, this is the Weimar coverlet, the silken one, here the familiar hangings, the

---

[4] *U.S.A.*, the epic trilogy by Dos Passos, operates in a similar way: the stream of consciousness sections ('Camera Eye'), quite hard to understand, are usually put in perspective by news items, biographies of historical characters, and long naturalistic narrative passages. Likewise in *The Death of Artemio Cruz*, by Carlos Fuentes, where the stream of consciousness parts are always followed by narrative passages providing us with a retrospective key.

bell-pull . . . What, what? Here's a brave showing, forsooth! Good for you, old man! Be not dismayed, blithe oldster that thou art!

Lotte in Weimar, 7

This is the only instance of the stream of consciousness that György Lukács liked. Which makes sense, since it sounds like a textbook: the Reconstruction of Reason. It opens with a 'vision of the depths', an erotic one: the it/Id of the first sentence. But it is an Id destined to disappear, as in the famous Freudian maxim, so that the conscious Ego of the aged Goethe may emerge strengthened from it. There is nostalgia for the lost vision ('Alas, that it should vanish!'), but no turning back. Sentence after sentence, the Ego literally returns to itself (*Wo kommst du zu dir?*), rediscovers its own spatial coordinates ('Jena? Berka? Tennstadt? No . . .), and positions itself determinedly at their centre. When the Id makes itself felt anew, in the erection discovered soon after this ('What? What?'), the conscious Goethe is by now so sure of himself that he can turn to the erotic dreamer as to another self, to be treated with indulgence (*Brav, Alter!*), but not taken too seriously. The divided Ego has been reunited.

Lost opportunities

From *Anna Karenin* to *Gustl,* to *Else,* to the beginning of *The Sound and the Fury;* from Benjy's monologue to Lily's, and then to Goethe's. We have followed the stream of consciousness from an episodic, uncertain beginning to a maximum of complexity; and then back again, from Faulkner's harshness to the nineteenth-century revenge of *Lotte in Weimar.* A whole trend, a whole counter-trend – and *Ulysses* not even touched upon! And the same goes for the metropolis: a hint in Tolstoy, then nothing more. So, what has become of the stream of consciousness discussed in the last chapter?

Nothing has become of it. It is still where we left it, in *Ulysses.* The problem lies elsewhere: not in the texts, but in the (implicit) assumptions of this Excursus. For the argument so far developed presupposes that there exists *only one form of stream of consciousness*: so that *Ulysses* is a stage, perhaps the culminating one, in its evolution. Starting off from *Anna Karenin,* in other words, sooner or later we were bound to reach Joyce.

And instead, nothing of the kind. We have found one form of stream of consciousness, with its own quite interesting and diversified history – but of the stream of consciousness of *Ulysses,* not a trace. From Tolstoy to Mann, the new technique takes shape, develops, and practically disappears, without ever turning into the Joycean stream of consciousness.

What is to be done, then? Simple: it is necessary to change our starting point. To hypothesize that there exist not one, but *two distinct 'strains' of the stream of consciousness* – and that *Ulysses* belongs to the one we have not yet spoken about. A hypothesis which is not as obvious as it may seem – and which has some notable consequences for our image of literary history. First, however, a closer look at the differences between the two types of stream of consciousness.

However disparate they may be, the versions of the stream of consciousness discussed so far all have something in common. They are a style *for exceptional circumstances*: fainting, delirium, suicide, death-agony (or, more innocuously: waking, drunkenness, sleeplessness, panic). In Joyce, by contrast, the stream of consciousness is the style *of absolute normality*: of an ordinary individual on an ordinary day. An everyday, calm stream of consciousness: free to look around, and to play with the stimuli that arrive from all sides. It is the metropolitan stream of consciousness, as I have said more than once, and a metropolis indeed is its birthplace: not Dublin, however, but Paris – in 1887, in a novella by Édouard Dujardin, *Les Lauriers sont coupés.* Daniel Prince, the protagonist, has to spend several hours waiting for his lover: empty time, in which he has nothing to do, and so allows his thoughts to wander about in countless different directions (with a predilection for food and pretty passers-by that clearly heralds Leopold Bloom).[5]

---

[5] Resemblance becomes identity in the translation by the Joycean Stuart Gilbert, who abolishes almost all relative clauses, and suppresses numerous verbal forms, thus making Dujardin's prose far more paratactical and ungrammatical than it really is. The odd line left here and there in French (whereas, obviously, Dujardin's text is *entirely* in French) completes the picture, giving the impression of a mind that does not entirely control its own verbal materials (E. Dujardin, *We'll to the woods no more*, New Directions, Norfolk Conn. 1938: see, for example, the scene in the restaurant, in Chapter 2).

Here, everything is ready for the take-off of the 'everyday' stream of consciousness: everything is ready for *Ulysses*. And yet, nothing happens. For Prince, so to speak, feels *forced into* the stream of consciousness by his lover's lateness, and he does not like it one bit: 'What a lot of foolish thoughts!' Indeed, the more the novella goes on, the more weary Prince grows of his 'inconclusive' thoughts. He would like *to be rid* of the stream of consciousness, and Dujardin gratifies his wish: he puts an end to his waiting, has the girl arrive, and so brings the novella back on to more familiar tracks. Then he starts writing for the theatre, and forgets all about the stream of consciousness.

In short, Dujardin discovers the technique of the century . . . and does not know what to do with it. It is true that more or less the whole of French culture is ill at ease with the stream of consciousness, yet the thing remains odd.[6] Still more odd, of course, is the fact that a few years later the event is exactly repeated on Austrian soil. Schnitzler reads Dujardin, likewise chooses an ordinary hero, and opens *Gustl* with a situation of waiting ('Oh, really, how much longer will it last? [. . .] Now, now, have a little patience! Even oratorios come to an end!'): once again, all ready for the everyday stream of consciousness. And yet, once again, nothing. As with Dujardin before him, an 'inconclusive' stream of consciousness does not convince Schnitzler, who moves swiftly on to the highly coloured plot we saw earlier. A second opportunity lost. And this is not yet the end. A couple of years after Schnitzler, Joyce too reads Dujardin. He is struck by it (or so he says) – but then he too does nothing with it. He writes *Stephen Hero*, and does not use the stream of consciousness. He

---

[6] Larbaud, although he adored Joyce, constructs his 1923 novella *Amants, heureux amants* upon the revenge of consciousness after a night of revelry ('Wonderful, to come back to your senses, your spirit cleansed and tranquil, lucid, after the confusion and the delirium . . .': Gallimard, Paris 1952, p. 129). Even the sporting heroes of Brage and Decoin are conscious strategists ('You see a few things, I can tell you, during that minute of interval; and you have a few thoughts!': *Quinze rounds*, p. 70). As for the other texts mentioned by Dujardin in his *Monologue intérieur* (Mossein, Paris 1931), such as Max Jacob's *Le Cabinet noir*, or Jean-Richard Bloch's *La Nuit kurde*, they present none of the syntactical or grammatical features typical of the stream of consciousness.

writes *Dubliners*, and does not use the stream of consciousness. He writes *Portrait*, and again . . .[7]

Dujardin, Schnitzler, Joyce. And then again: *Stephen Hero, Dubliners, Portrait of the Artist as a Young Man*. What a lot of labour, before the stream of consciousness of *Ulysses* finally manages to take root! It is a very different scenario from that heroic search for the new which critics like to see as the essence of literature. Here, *inertia* prevails: not the desire to change. We see novelists stumbling over the new, and then resisting it with all their might: distorting it, watering it down, forgetting it . . . Far from being the key to literary history, in short, morphological change seems to be an *extremely unlikely* development, which is in great need of being explained in its turn. If we found ourselves in 1914, and had followed the vicissitudes of the stream of consciousness from *Les Lauriers* to *Portrait*, which of us would expect *Ulysses*? And yet, *Ulysses* is coming. But why? Why does Joyce not miss the opportunity too – like Dujardin and Schnitzler before him?

Why Joyce

Let me try to proceed in an orderly fashion. The first striking thing is the variety of forms in which the stream of consciousness presents itself. There is the highly 'narrative' stream of consciousness of *Anna Karenin* and *L'enseveli*. Then, Schnitzler's psychosis, Faulkner's idiot, Biberkopf's befuddlement. The reunification of the subject, in Woolf and Mann. The moderate digression of Dujardin and of *Gustl*. The philosophical intoxi-

---

[7] Or, actually, he does use the stream of consciousness in the very first pages of *Portrait* – those closest to the language of childhood – and then abandons it, as though the new technique were a kind of growing ailment. The thesis is upheld by Melvin Friedman, among others, in one of the first studies on the stream of consciousness (*Stream of Consciousness: a Study in Literary Method*, Yale University Press, New Haven 1955, pp. 215–17). I confine it to a footnote because, although I should really like to believe that Friedman is right, I am not convinced that it is correct to speak of a stream of consciousness for the beginning of *Portrait*.

cation of Broch.[8] The 'lyrical' tendency, to which I shall allude in a moment. And then, of course, *Ulysses*, which itself offers us at least three distinct versions of it – with Stephen's logic, Bloom's fantasizing, and Molly's monologue. To sum up: two basic 'strains', and within them a dozen variants (and I have kept, with a couple of exceptions, to absolutely canonical examples). In other words, an *embarras de richesses*. Why so many attempts?

Because, at the turn of the century, Western individuals have lost their unity, and it is necessary to find a language for the divided Self. But what language? No one knows. And so, all sorts of attempts are made.[9] Blindly. Throwing in a few fragments, like Tolstoy, and then dropping it. Or beginning in one way, like Schnitzler and Faulkner, and then ending in the opposite way. Or again, like Joyce, making a simultaneous attempt in three different keys. An almighty confusion, in short, but with its own quite simple logic: that of *random innovation*. 'Random', however, does not mean 'causeless': there is always a reason for technical choices, and I have tried to describe it. 'Random' should be understood here in the sense of Darwinian theory: as a way of proceeding that cannot foresee what would be advantageous for the stream of consciousness, and that may therefore either succeed – or fail. Hence, die out.

Yes, die out. Many titles mentioned in Dujardin's little treatise, or in Beach's study – published, respectively, in 1931 and 1932 – are now totally unknown. In current studies, still fewer examples are usually found. And as for general culture, the stream of consciousness is associated with

---

[8] *The Death of Virgil* is literally dominated by the combined forces of Metaphysics and Subjectivity. Here are the subjects of the main sentences of a passage that continues uninterrupted for some two pages: 'Life [. . .] the immutable [. . .] he [. . .] the enigma [. . .] he [. . .] the past [. . .] the wide-planed wind of the sea [...] the sea-surfed lands [. . .] he [. . .] everything [. . .] he . . .' (H. Broch, *The Death of Virgil*, translated by Jean Starr Untermeyer, Vintage International, New York 1995, pp. 30-31).

[9] And very hastily: five, ten, almost simultaneous variations. It is the brief moment of morphological experimentation predicted by the theory of punctuated equilibria: the creative explosion of the twenties, included between a century and a half of tiny preparatory drafts (on which see D. Cohn, *Transparent Minds*, Princeton University Press, Princeton NJ 1978) and the substantial stability of the rest of the twentieth century.

Ulysses and maybe – maybe – with a couple of other names. The morphological explosion of the twenties was thus followed by a very rigorous selection, which erased from the picture Brage and Decoin, Nathan Asch (*Pay Day*) and Schlumberger, Waldo Frank (*Rahab, Holiday*) and Aiken – and who knows how many others. It is a minor bloodbath, and perhaps not even such a minor one. It is the ruthless, Malthusian aspect of canon formation: many called, and few chosen. But chosen by whom? And chosen why?

By whom, in this case, is fairly clear. The protagonist of the selection process is no longer the middle class that decreed the success of nineteenth-century realism, but a narrow group of super-readers: avant-garde authors, the odd Maecenas, a few publishers; later on, critics; still later, academics. It is Pierre Bourdieu's 'intellectual camp':[10] a special audience, which rewards what the wider market rejects, and vice versa. A well-defined audience, easily identifiable.

But it is not so easy to answer the second question: why Joyce, and not Schnitzler? or Broch? or even Schlumberger? Is it because the stream of consciousness is more daring in *Ulysses*, and breaks more decisively with the 'horizon of expectations' of the period?[11] That is a lovely notion, made to please everybody, halfway between old-fashioned edification (*fortuna audaces iuvat*) and planned obsolescence (*new is beautiful*). It has only one defect: it is wrong. The stream of consciousness of Faulkner and Dos Passos is further away than Joyce's from the conventions of the period (however you like to define these); *The Death of Virgil* goes further still. And yet, it is the stream of consciousness of *Ulysses* that survives. And it survives because the selection process does not reward novelty as such (Jauss's violation, or the 'estrangement' of the formalists), but *novelty that is able to solve problems*. Moving beyond the horizon of expectations of the period, in itself, is of little interest. Constructing *a new perceptual and symbolic horizon*: this is indeed a comprehensible undertaking, and one with a clear social value.

---

[10] P. Bourdieu, *Les Règles de l'art*, Seuil, Paris 1992.

[11] See H.R. Jauss, 'Literary History as a Challenge to Literary Theory', in *Toward an Aesthetic of Reception*, University of Minnesota Press, Minneapolis 1983: especially sections 6, 7 and 8.

That the stream of consciousness of *Ulysses* is precisely such a new horizon, able to cope with some major problems of modernity, I hope I have shown in the previous chapter; and if I have not succeeded, it would anyway be pointless to repeat myself. So I shall merely add a few words, here, about one final question. Just why was Joyce the one to give the stream of consciousness its canonical form? Why not somebody else?

Because, I believe, all the others yielded to the temptation to give the stream of consciousness an ancillary function. The new technique was ideal – *for making a crux in the story more dramatic*. Or else, it was perfect – *for making everyday reality poetic again*. As Mallarmé writes to Dujardin in 1888, 'You have succeeded in finding a sinuous mode of representation, full of twists and turns . . .'[12] *Virevoltant et cursif:* splendid. But then Mallarmé goes on, and we realize that – for him – the *monologue intérieur* has 'as its sole *raison d'être*, to express everyday reality, so precious and so hard to grasp'.[13] *Précieux*. Something of great value, but hidden, hard to get at, eventually brought to light. There we are again, back to epiphany: to the lyrical temptation that the Joyce of *Ulysses* – against his old self – decides to reject. But that does, by contrast, inspire a whole current of the stream of consciousness: from the visions of Woolf, to the truths of Broch; from the emotions of Dos Passos, to certain images in Faulkner or Larbaud.

One stream of consciousness disguised as lyric; another subordinated to the plot. In both cases the new device gains something very important: a function – a *meaning*. In exchange, however, it renounces its freedom. Mallarmé's 'immense possibilities', poured into pre-existing forms, remain also imprisoned within them: new means to old ends. We saw it in *Anna Karenin* and in *Les Lauriers*, where narrative motivation subordinates and eventually suffocates the stream of consciousness. It is inertia: a major force in literary life, as in life *tout court*. It is the weight of a tradi-

---

[12] The letter, dated 8 April 1888, is quoted by Dujardin in *Le Monologue intérieur*, p. 15.

[13] Ibid. Referring to Mallarmé's ideas, Dujardin then claims quite candidly to be 'saluting in the interior monologue one of the manifestations of that dazzling entry of poetry into the novel, which is one of the signs of the time' (ibid., p. 51).

tion that promptly swallows up what is new, so does not even notice *how new* it is. In the last resort, it is for this very reason that *Ulysses* achieves its canonical status. Its stream of consciousness is the only one that is not ashamed of itself. It does not try to be poetry. It accepts banality, and insignificance too. It does not seek ennoblement, so avoids adulteration.

Very well. Let us even admit this is how things are. But what kind of prodigy is this *Ulysses*, to succeed where they all fail? A generation of great writers is led astray by the wish to give an immediate meaning to the stream of consciousness, but Joyce takes the right path, calmly accepting its scant narrative functionality, and its immense banality. Why?

Perhaps because Joyce is the only one to have a partial structural failure behind him – *Portrait of the Artist as a Young Man* – in the process of whose composition he has come to realize the limits, and perhaps indeed the uselessness, of the 'lyrical' poetics of epiphany.[14] Everyday existence resists the young artist who would like to transfigure it: it remains inert, opaque – *meaningless*. Joyce combats this inertia throughout the entire novel, and at a certain point, in the vision at the end of Chapter 4, he seems even to have succeeded. But the prosaic reality of the world regains the upper hand, and, in the last chapter of the novel, Joyce's Flaubertian half carries the day once and for all. No more attempts to transfigure meaninglessness: if anything – as in Flaubert, precisely – it must be made to speak *as such*. And since there is a new technique around, in which meaningless details proliferate, he tries with that.

Yes, perhaps this is how Joyce arrives at the stream of consciousness. At the stream of consciousness, I repeat, as a technique of the *meaningless*: of banal everydayness, not of precious everydayness. And then, Joyce has decided to write an epic work, so he is in no hurry to balance his accounts: he can accept page after page of superficial impressions, with little or no constructional value. And the hero of *Ulysses* is an ordinary man, to whom nothing extraordinary happens: his style can remain at a low level of intensity, a bit boring, always the same. Always the same.

---

[14] On the failed *bricolage* of *Portrait*, and its consequences for Joyce's work, see the last part of my essay ' "A useless longing for myself": the Crisis of the European Bildungsroman', in R. Cohen, ed., *Studies in Historical Change*, University of Virginia Press, Charlottesville 1992.

Basically, Joyce's whole success lies in this. *Giving the new technique time.* Not binding it immediately to a meaning, or a precise function, thereby leaving it free to develop and change. Not exerting an immediate pressure that would risk atrophying it. Giving it time to release its immense possibilities – if it has them.

And the stream of consciousness did indeed have them. However, if the truth be told, they really emerged by chance.

CHAPTER

7

The other Ulysses

September 1922. A few months have passed since the publication of *Ulysses*, and Thomas Stearns Eliot is paying Virginia Woolf a visit:

> [Tom said] the book would be a landmark – Woolf notes in her diary – because it destroyed the whole of the nineteenth century. It left Joyce himself with nothing to write another book about. It showed up the futility of all the English styles.[1]

All the English styles. So, in conversation with a friend, this is what Eliot highlights: the stylistic pluralism, the polyphony of *Ulysses*. But then, in his famous review in *The Dial*, not a word: as if he could not define what he saw, or had nothing to say. And, like him, more or less all Joyce's great contemporaries: Schnitzler and Woolf, Lukács and Faulkner, Mann and Musil and Curtius . . . All bewitched by the stream of consciousness, and silent about polyphony.

For us, today, the opposite seems to be true: stylistic pluralism has moved to the centre of work on *Ulysses*, and will probably stay there for a long while yet. A sign of Mikhail Bakhtin's importance for contemporary

---

[1] V. Woolf, *A Writer's Diary*, Harcourt Brace, New York 1954, p. 49.

criticism; but also, I think, a shift of interest that basically follows the development of the novel itself. Exaggerating a bit, we might indeed say that the protagonists of *Ulysses* are not Stephen Dedalus and the Bloom couple, but two techniques – the stream of consciousness, and polyphony – that intertwine and clash throughout the novel, in a kind of technical drama in which the novel's initial style (the stream of consciousness) is gradually flanked, challenged and eventually defeated by the newcomer, which ends up imposing itself as master of the Joycean universe.

A quick summary. That the beginning of *Ulysses* gravitates round the stream of consciousness is fairly obvious. First with Stephen, then with Bloom, the device grows in extent and depth, retaining a clear supremacy up to the sixth chapter, and perhaps up to the eleventh. From the seventh chapter on, however, the stream of consciousness is no longer alone: with increasing emphasis, it is flanked by polyphonic devices of various kinds. First, the title/story counterpoint of 'Aeolus'; further on, chapters devoted to a plurality of ideological ('Cyclops'), sentimental ('Nausicaa') and literary ('Oxen of the Sun') positions. And when polyphony *within* individual chapters diminishes, heterogeneity *between* one chapter and another, by contrast, is intensified. So, after the expressionism of 'Circe', the naturalism of 'Eumaeus', and the catechism of 'Ithaca', even Molly's great monologue, rather than reinstating the initial technique, seems to perhaps indicate its definitive relativization – one voice, and one language, among many – within the new stylistic framework.

The first six chapters dominated by the stream of consciousness; the last seven dominated by polyphony. There is a first *Ulysses*, easily recognizable, which I discussed in the previous chapter; and a second *Ulysses*, with equally distinctive features, about which I shall speak here. And then, in the zone of transition from one to the other – when Joyce is abandoning his first great technique (but does not yet know it), and is seeking his second (but has not yet found it) – there is even a third *Ulysses*, albeit far more indistinct than the other two. An inevitable indistinctness, because – between 'Aeolus' and 'Sirens' – Joyce is undecided as to the path to follow, and so he tries more or less all of them: the (semi) polyphony of 'Aeolus', the hoaxing 'essay-style' of 'Scylla and Charybdis', the urban collage of 'Wandering Rocks', the musical composition of 'Sirens'. It is the most experimental moment in *Ulysses* – and the least successful. Because it involves *true* experiments, as in so many of Klee's paintings – and true experiments sometimes succeed, but sometimes not.

In the case of 'Aeolus', for example, everything works very well – and, indeed, we find similar solutions in the remainder of the novel. In 'Wandering Rocks' too, the experiment succeeds, and is indeed repeated on several occasions: though by Döblin, or Dos Passos, and not by Joyce – as if the latter had stumbled over it by chance (like Dujardin with the stream of consciousness), without grasping its potential. Finally, in other cases – 'Scylla and Charybdis', and above all 'Sirens' – the attempt may simply be regarded as a failure: it is repeated neither by Joyce nor by others.

Successful experiments, misinterpreted experiments, failed experiments . . . If Joyce were the Great Planner of critical legend, this is not how things would go. From the first *Ulysses* he would move straight to the second, without fumblings or mistakes. But technical change cannot be planned, and this middle section – this third *Ulysses*, which turned out so much worse than the other two – is one further confirmation of the Darwinian model: morphological innovations are the fruit of a random experimentation, which proceeds gropingly for a long while before finding the right road.[2] Not really the right one, either, just better than the

---

[2] 'The decision to move beyond the monologue technique', writes Michael Groden, 'seems not a preconceived plan but a result of his episode-by-episode progress on his work, progress that never extended very far beyond the immediate episode at hand' (*Ulysses in Progress*, Princeton University Press, Princeton NJ 1976, p. 33). Quite right, there is no prearranged plan in *Ulysses*, and this is shown precisely by those 'schemata' so often taken as proof that one does exist. 'The finished "Ithaca" barely resembles the [Linati] schema entries', Groden later observes (p. 176); and as for the schema sent by Joyce to Larbaud in November 1921, it is full of facile metaphors – 'narcissism' (for Chapter 5), 'incubism' (6), 'labyrinth' (10), 'hallucination' (15) – but as for any explanatory value, little or nothing. The love for symmetry (symmetry is order, and therefore suggests the existence of a conscious plan) induces Joyce, among other things, to establish parallelisms – like the one between the (personal) 'catechism' of 'Nestor', and the (impersonal) 'catechism' of 'Ithaca' – whose only effect is to conceal the originality of 'Ithaca'. And symmetry also decrees that the term 'monologue' should be used only for 'Proteus' and 'Penelope': as though Joyce's plan did not provide for Bloom's stream of consciousness . . . All this, I repeat, in a schema drawn up in November 1921 – when *Ulysses* was already finished! It remains a mystery why on earth these insignificant sheets, which demonstrate only Joyce's high-school fixations ('Menton = Ajax'; 'Incest = journalism'), should ever have been taken so seriously.

others – which still all remain there, in full view, at the centre of the novel, like a kind of stylistic crossroads where *Ulysses* might have gone off in quite another direction. 'Art is [. . .] something that has become,' writes Arnold Schönberg in his *Theory of Harmony*. 'It could then also have become other than it is.'

A transition from the stream of consciousness to polyphony, therefore. And then a second transition, no less important, *within* the new device. For, in certain cases, stylistic pluralism has its *raison d'être* in the narrative material itself: in 'Nausicaa', the romance style is motivated by Gerty's reading; in 'Cyclops', epic hyperbole is the rhetorical weapon appropriate to Irish nationalism. Developing an idea of Walton Litz's, Umberto Eco has spoken in this connection of a 'poetics of expressive form':

> The 'dramatic' technique eliminates the continuous presence of the author and substitutes for his point of view that of the characters and the events themselves. Modern journalism is told from the point of view of modern journalism; the noises around Bloom are perceived as Bloom would perceive them; Molly's passions are defined as Molly, in suffering them, would define them.[3]

It is an intelligent thesis, and in some cases works well. But already in 'Cyclops' there are problems, because it cannot explain the presence of passages in medical jargon (XII, 468–78), or in baby talk (XII, 846–9). Further on, with 'Eumaeus' and 'Ithaca', things become still more complicated: quite similar situations, which should therefore be 'expressed' in the same form, are instead presented in the two chapters in very different ways. Finally, in 'Aeolus' and 'Oxen of the Sun', a wholly homogeneous narrative material can in no way motivate the dozens upon dozens of different styles that appear in the two chapters. Rather than expressing the material, the form has made itself independent of it: the many styles of polyphony seem to descend from the clouds, without rhyme or reason. What is going on?

---

[3] U. Eco, *The Middle Ages of James Joyce: The Aesthetics of Chaosmos*, translated by Ellen Esrock, Hutchinson Radius, London 1989, pp. 37–8. Litz had spoken of 'expressive form' ('The form "expresses" or imitates qualities of its subject') in *The Art of James Joyce*, Oxford University Press, Oxford 1961, p. 44.

Literary evolution. III

The Waste Land, lines 60–62:

> Unreal City,
> Under the brown fog of a winter dawn,
> A crowd flowed over London Bridge, so many. . .

In the original draft of the poem, these same lines (I, 114–16) ran as follows:

> Unreal City, *I have sometimes seen and see,*
> Under the brown fog of *your* winter dawn,
> A crowd flow over London Bridge, so many. . .

As in other similar passages in the manuscript (II, 22; III, 145–9), Pound intervenes here with great energy. Rings of disapproval, crossings out: 'your' disappears, as does the narrating I of the previous line. *The Waste Land* has to be depersonalized: it must become an utterance that tells its own story – voices without a body. In the last resort, fragments.

Fragments. It is Eliot's version of polyphony – and, to be fair, it is also an idea that Eliot came to without Pound's help (and long before *The Waste Land*): as early as *Gerontion*, and above all in *Prufrock*. In these two poems, indeed, thinking in fragments is placed by Eliot at the centre of the picture, as if to make it the characteristic feature of the modern individual. Gerontion and Prufrock are two 'walking encyclopaedias', as Nietzsche would say, who have read too much, and lived too little. Too many stimuli, as always, and too little integration:

> The ordinary man's experience is chaotic, irregular, fragmentary. The latter falls in love, or reads Spinoza, and these two experiences have nothing to do with each other, or with the noise of the typewriter or the smell of cooking . . .[4]

Fragments as symptoms of the contemporary disorder, in short. But if fragments are symptoms, then they are still fully motivated: they are indeed the 'expressive form' of modern indecision. The polyphony

---

[4] T.S. Eliot, 'The Metaphysical Poets' (1921), in *Selected Prose*, Penguin, Harmondsworth 1951, p. 110.

created by them may present local difficulties, just like the stream of consciousness: but the form *as such* would have a clear *raison d'être*. It would be *motivated*: this is how human beings feel and speak in the modern world. And in Eliot's original intentions, the polyphony of *The Waste Land* was still going to operate in a similar way. There was *Gerontion*, which was to serve as an 'overture'; then, in the first section ('He do the police in different voices'), a ventriloquist narrator, presenting polyphony as a piece of individual bravura; and finally, the new walking encyclopaedia, Tiresias, right at the centre of the work (and with a more extensive role than he now has). The polyphony of the manuscript, in other words, was still largely motivated: the fragments almost always had 'bearers', in that they could be traced back to this or that character – even to the dying Kurtz of the original epigraph. But Pound eliminates Kurtz, eliminates Gerontion, eliminates the initial voice, and cuts down Tiresias: motivation is weakened, and the new technique radicalized. The fragments become more and more visible – and the reason for their presence less and less so.

I have talked about *The Waste Land* because it is a short text, where the relations between device and motivation can be grasped more easily. But in *Ulysses*, exactly the same thing occurs. Here too, the point of departure is a walking encyclopaedia (walking, and encyclopaedic: what better definition, for Leopold Bloom?), who shows himself incapable of integrating the data of experience. Umberto Eco:

> In the flow of perceptions during Bloom's walk along the streets of Dublin, the boundaries between 'inside' and 'outside' become extremely vague. Since individual consciousness is reduced to an anonymous screen that registers the stimuli that bombard it from all directions [. . .] in the open sea of the stream of consciousness one finds no individual minds that think the events, but only events flowing in uniform distribution which are gradually thought by someone.[5]

Events – usually *linguistic* events – that settle on an anonymous screen: in Bloom's stream of consciousness pieces of undigested language are

---

[5] Eco, *The Middle Ages of James Joyce*, pp. 42–3.

constantly surfacing: fragments of other people's speech.[6] They are mixed up with innumerable other things – noises, commonplaces, memories, onomatopoeias – and at first sight are barely even distinguishable. In the long run, however, they will have a quite different significance, because *it is precisely from this undigested language that the polyphony of* Ulysses *develops.*[7] Bloom reactivates discourses formed outside him, writes Topia. True: and then Joyce reactivates those reactivated discourses, without any longer passing through Bloom's mind. He reactivates them, in other words, *without motivating them any longer.* Like Pound with *The Waste Land,* Joyce eliminates the bodies and keeps the voices: he erases the original motivation, and allows the new technique to take off freely.

Freely, but not abruptly. Like nature, literature does not make jumps, and new techniques are never born already perfectly formed. They begin in a minor key, somewhat at random, and usually in marginal places. Like the polyphony of *Faust,* initiated during a digression ('A Walpurgis Night') from the tragedy of Margareta. Or like the allegory of Goethe's poem, suggested by court entertainments that Goethe cannot have taken too seriously. And history repeats itself a century later. At first, the stream of consciousness is just the emotional accompaniment to a narrative situation: a consequence, and nothing more. But the consequence solidifies, and becomes the most celebrated technique of the twentieth century. And, after a bit, the undigested language existing within it solidifies in turn – consequence of a consequence – and engenders modernist polyphony.

There is enough here to risk a hypothesis. Viktor Shklovsky: 'The artistic device, artistic invention, are the final crystallization of a slippage, of a chance mutation.' And again:

---

[6] 'The disappearance of quotation marks [from the stream of consciousness] is crucial [. . .] Nothing permits to know *a priori* if the sentence "belongs" to Bloom or not [. . .] Bloom reactivates discourses formed outside him' (A. Topia, 'The Matrix and the Echo', in D. Attridge and D. Ferrer, eds, *Post-Structuralist Joyce,* Cambridge University Press, Cambridge 1984, p. 108).

[7] In the fourth chapter, other people's speech (not counting commonplaces, which are, so to speak, shared speech) makes up between five and ten per cent of Bloom's stream of consciousness. In Chapters 5, 6 and 8, this percentage is roughly doubled: a very notable increase, not repeated for any other aspect of the stream of consciousness. But they are data to be taken with caution, because, as Topia rightly points out, it is not easy to know if a sentence 'belongs to Bloom or not'.

Literary forms possess a specific toughness that ensures their passage through a whole series of epochs; at the same time, literary form finds itself under the influence of definite tasks, and the new accumulates quantitatively upon the old [. . .] The quantitative changes become qualitative, and that moment is the birth of a new genre. The new genre is born from the entrails of the old, initially as an unplanned accumulation of details.[8]

An accidental slippage, the new accumulated upon the old, an unplanned accumulation of details, a final crystallization . . . It is just like *Ulysses*. And it is also, once again, the logic of *bricolage* and refunctionalization. To which we may add a final detail: if Shklovsky is right, and formal innovation proceeds 'in a quantitative way' – then it will happen more easily in those texts that have *a larger quantity of space at their disposal*. I do not believe it accidental that Shklovsky should formulate his hypothesis while discussing *War and Peace* (or that it should find full confirmation in *Ulysses*). Large dimensions are probably favourable to formal innovation. They allow more time, more chances, greater freedom.

And the epic form allows greater freedom for another reason, too – a structural one, this time. The epic, as we saw with *Faust*, is a form prone to digressions: full of episodes flanking the basic Action. Marginal episodes – and, for that very reason, favourable to experimentation. Because a truly innovative attempt usually begins in an uncertain, and perhaps even quite unpromising, fashion: if located in the foreground, it would be frozen by the immediate requirements of the plot. But if the experiment is at the margins of the text, the author is freer to play with the form. Even if things go as badly as can be (as in 'Scylla and Charybdis', or 'Sirens'), the catastrophe will have a limited effect, leaving the overall structure of the work intact. The textual periphery functions as a kind of protected space, where an innovation has time to develop, and consolidate its own peculiarities. Then, once it is ready, the new technique crystallizes: it rids itself of the old motivation, and it moves to the foreground.

---

[8] V. Shklovsky, *Materialy i stil v romane L. N. Tolstogo 'Vojna i mir'* (Moscow 1928), pp. 232, 237.

The new technique develops at the periphery of the text, until it is capable of occupying the foreground. The foreground – not the entire stage. The first chapters of *Ulysses* – where polyphony has not yet disentangled itself from the stream of consciousness, and the latter is overwhelmingly the dominant technique – are not discarded. Despite the autonomization of the fragment, Tiresias remains at the centre of *The Waste Land*, like the note to line 218 ('What Tiresias *sees*, in fact, is the substance of the poem'), with the naturalization of polyphony that it suggests. Many bridges with the past are severed. But not all. Why?

I think the answer should be: chance. A somewhat stricter Pound would have reserved the same fate for Tiresias as for Gerontion. A somewhat more avant-garde Joyce might even – who knows? – have rewritten the first *Ulysses*, or published it separately, or even burned it. Instead, they gave us these composite works, where extremely disparate technical phases crowd the same space – like the faces and bodies of *Les Demoiselles d'Avignon*, where the laws of perspective coexist with ever more radical spatial distortions nearer the margins of the canvas. It is a sign of volcanic times, piling invention upon invention. The stream of consciousness would suffice to make *Ulysses* one of the great novels of the century. But there are also the experiments of the central part, and polyphony, and then polyphony without motivation . . .

This rhythm of permanent revolution, of course, has its price. *Ulysses*, *The Waste Land*, *Les Demoiselles* – if you look at them with a certain detachment, they are all works that hold together as if by a miracle. *Bricolage*, but serious *bricolage*. Or, to quote once more Stephen Jay Gould's 'Panda principle':

> Odd arrangements and funny solutions – paths that a sensible God [or a sensible Writer, for that matter] would never tread, but that a natural process, constrained by history, follows perforce.[9]

In short, all extremely *imperfect* works: not properly welded together, unstable – unrepeatable. And indeed, in the space of a few years, Picasso moves from the *Demoiselles* to Cubism, and then to collage; Joyce goes far beyond *Ulysses*, with *Finnegans Wake*; and Eliot falls far short of *The Waste Land*. And yet, for all their imperfection, these structures have also

---

[9] S. J. Gould, *The Panda's Thumb*, Penguin, London 1983, p. 20.

for a century been the major canon of Western modernism. In spite of
the *bricolage* that produced them? On the contrary: *because of it.* Because,
if literature is rarely capable of perfection, it is also true that human
societies *almost never need perfection.* Better, far better, to have *bricolage*
than engineering. Because *bricolage* does not dream of unattainable (and
often worse) final solutions, but accepts the heterogeneity inherent in the
modern world-system. A heterogeneity of historical times, first of all:
non-contemporaneity again, which in the years of modernism becomes
a *formal fact*, giving birth to the two or three different novels that make up
Ulysses, and to the two or three poems that are contained within *The
Waste Land.* These works are veritable stylistic deposits, in which techniques from different epochs outcrop from one another like so many
geological strata. In the next section, we shall concern ourselves with the
most recent of these strata.

Liberation of the device

That a technique may get rid of its motivation, like the polyphony of
Ulysses, is a possibility of which the most brilliant critical mind of Joyce's
generation is keenly aware:

> Sterne – writes Viktor Shklovsky – was a radical revolutionary as far as
> form is concerned. It was typical of him to lay bare the device. The
> aesthetic form is presented without any motivation whatsoever.[10]

A revolution of form: in Sterne, and still more in the early twentieth century. But for what reason? Because, in Hegelian fashion, history is pressing,
and new literary materials wish to make their appearance? Not at all. In the
Formalist diagnosis, the decisive factor is a 'negative' force: not the desire
for novelty, but the collapse of an old constraint[11] – of the 'realistic illusion',

---

[10] V. Shklovsky, *Theory of Prose*, Dalkey Archive Press, Elmwood Park 1990, p. 147.

[11] 'Doing a thing not because [the artist] wants to, or because he should, but because
he can' (W.B. Yeats, 'The Twenty-eight Incarnations: Phase Twenty-three', in *A
Vision*, Laurie, London 1925, p. 98). Yeats's *Vision* is not exactly a model of scientific integrity, but the sentence quoted expresses very well the 'possibilist' state
of mind of modernist experiments.

that required 'explanation of a plot-structure in terms of actual mores'.[12] *skikele*
And 'realistic illusion' basically meant one thing to the Formalists: *anthro-pocentrism*. For Tomashevsky, it is the hero: a veritable 'personification of motivation'; a 'guiding thread' allowing the reader to 'find his way amid the mass of motives'.[13] And as for Shklovsky's *Theory of Prose*, narrative devices are all motivated by characters' actions; the imbrication of different stories, by the existence of a group of narrators; the multiplicity of themes, by the hero's journeys; their combination, by kinship relations; the endlessness of the plot, by the need to save one's life; and so on.

Well, in the twentieth century polyphony frees itself because this anthropocentric framework – which simultaneously sustained and limited it – eventually disintegrates. And anthropocentrism disintegrates because the notion of a unitary individual – upon which it was premised – in turn collapses. But the expression 'in the twentieth century', here, may be deceptive. For if it is quite true that the process *is completed* in the twentieth century, it nevertheless begins much earlier. A contemporary – and great admirer – of Sterne:

> He sang thirty tunes on top of each other and all mixed up: Italian, French, tragic, comic, of all sorts and descriptions, sometimes in a bass voice going down to the infernal regions, and sometimes bursting himself in a falsetto voice he would split the heavens asunder [. . .] Here we have a young girl weeping [. . .] there a priest, king, tyrant [. . .] or a slave obeying. He relents, wails, complains, laughs [. . .] a one-man show featuring dancers, male and female, singers of both sexes, a whole orchestra, a complete opera-house, dividing himself into twenty different stage parts [. . .] a woman swooning with grief, a poor wretch abandoned in the depth of his despair, a temple rising into view, birds falling silent at eventide . . .[14]

---

[12] V. Shklovsky, 'Literatura i kinematograf' (1923), quoted in V. Erlich, *Russian Formalism*, Mouton, The Hague and Paris 1969, pp. 177 n. and 194. The expression 'realistic illusion' is used by B. Tomashevsky in his essay 'The Construction of the Plot' (1928): see T. Todorov, ed., *Théorie de la Littérature: textes des formalistes russes*, Seuil, Paris 1966.

[13] Ibid.

[14] D. Diderot, *Rameau's Nephew*, translated by Leonard Tancock, Penguin, Harmondsworth 1981, pp. 102–4.

Rameau: in *Phenomenology of Mind*, the first figure of the modern – who embarks on the great venture of 'self-estrangement', nourishing his own individuality upon the countless forms of modern culture. But that dream of totality is by now unattainable. A passage from Simmel, which we have already seen in the preceding chapter:

> The development of modern culture is characterized by the prepon-
> derance of what one may call the 'objective spirit' over the 'subjective
> spirit' [. . .] If we view the immense culture which for the last hundred
> years has been embodied in things and in knowledge, in institutions
> and in comforts, and if we compare all this with the cultural progress
> of the individual during the same period [. . .] a frightful disproportion
> in growth between the two becomes evident. The individual in his
> intellectual development follows this growth very imperfectly and at an
> ever increasing distance.[15]

The individual follows this growth very imperfectly . . . For all his genius, Rameau's mimicry of objective culture is already the sign of a crisis. It makes him the first divided Self, *'sa tête tout à fait perdue'* – just like Dostoevsky's Underground Man, equally eager to speak the countless languages of modern polyphony. There is little to be done: anthropocentrism and modernity do not really go together. Jürgen Habermas:

> The project of Modernity formulated in the eighteenth century by the
> philosophers of the Enlightenment consisted in their efforts to develop
> objective science, universal morality and law, and autonomous art
> according to their inner logic. At the same time, this project intended
> to release the cognitive potentials of each of these domains from their
> esoteric forms. The Enlightenment philosophers wanted to utilize this
> accumulation of specialized culture for the enrichment of everyday life
> [. . .] The twentieth century has shattered this optimism.[16]

The *twentieth* century? Yes – but here, too, not because it has invented any-

---

[15] G. Simmel, 'The Metropolis and Mental Life', in *The Sociology of Georg Simmel*, translated and edited by Kurt Wolff, Collier-Macmillan, London 1950, p. 421.

[16] J. Habermas, 'Modernity – an Incomplete Project', in H. Foster, ed., *The Anti-Aesthetic*, Bay Press, Washington 1983, p. 9.

thing new. It is just that time has passed, and in a century and a half the rift between objective culture and anthropocentrism – which was already open, and perfectly visible, at the end of the eighteenth century – has grown so much worse, that not even Faust's compact, or Rameau's madness, can hold it together any longer. Man, Ulrich reflects, has become 'ridiculous and anti-economic'. Respect for the 'human and earthly measure', Adrian Leverkühn echoes, is a fetter, an encumbrance: it must be removed, since it hinders that 'development according to the inner logic of art' which is the sole path of intellectual progress. And in his *Theory of Harmony*, in some of the most sober and yet most radical pages of theoretical modernism, Arnold Schönberg dismisses the whole idea of consonance and dissonance, as a mere 'compromise' with 'the imperfection of our senses': a convention lacking any objective foundations, hence simply 'false'.[17] Man is really no longer the measure of all things.

We began with the emancipation of polyphony as a characteristic feature of the modernist moment. Following Shklovsky, we located its cause in the collapse of anthropocentrism, which for its own part is a phenomenon that gets under way in the late eighteenth century. If this sequence holds, then modern*ism* is really just a chapter in the far broader history of Western modern*ity*. And a chapter which – if you read Goethe, and Diderot, and Hegel – *had inevitably to occur*: predestined, inscribed from the outset in the genetic code of European culture. Awaited, or feared, for a century and a half. But if this is so, then instead of the habitual: 'Why modernism?', a new question suggests itself: '*Why so late?*' What on earth blocked its arrival for over a hundred years?

---

[17] 'The more immediate overtones contribute *more*, the more remote contribute *less*. Hence, the distinction between them is only a matter of degree, not of kind. They are no more opposites than two and ten are opposites [. . .] and the expressions "consonance" and "dissonance", which signify an antithesis, are false.' And further on: 'Much of what has been considered aesthetically fundamental, that is, necessary to beauty, is by no means always rooted in the nature of things, so that the imperfection of our senses drives us to those compromises through which we achieve order. For order is not demanded by the object, but by the subject' (A. Schönberg, *Theory of Harmony* (1922), translated by Roy Carter, University of California Press, Berkeley 1978, pp. 21 and 29).

I believe: the novel. A form that Western Europe was lucky enough to find at its disposal, as the first symptoms of the future crisis were manifesting themselves, and that contained a whole complex of great anthropocentric devices. The novel as perhaps not exactly a conservative, but certainly a *moderating*, form: as a symbolic brake upon modernity.

It is a hypothesis that I have attempted to develop elsewhere;[18] here, let me simply add that even the novel ends up yielding to that growing rift signalled by Simmel. In the space of three or four generations, the Forms become too strong for the Soul, and smash the great compromise of the Goethean *Bildungsroman*. At the start of the twentieth century, as though obeying some secret signal, Conrad and Mann, Musil and Rilke, Kafka and Joyce, all set about writing stories of 'formation' [*Bildung*] – in which the *Bildung* does not occur: in which objective culture, congealed in conventions and institutions, no longer helps to construct individual subjects, but wounds and disintegrates them. 'This objective culture', writes Werner Sombart in 1911, 'stands in opposition to what may be termed personal culture, the *Bildung* of the individual.'[19] And Georg Simmel, in an essay written in the same year:

> A work of art is supposed to be perfect in terms of artistic norms. They do not ask for anything else but themselves, and would give or deny value to the work even if there were nothing else in the world but this particular work. The result of research should be truth and absolutely nothing further. Religion exhausts its meaning with the salvation which it brings to the soul. The economic product wishes to be economically perfect, and does not recognize for itself any other than the economic scale of values. All these sequences operate within the confines of purely internal laws. *Whether and to what extent they can be subsumed in the development of subjective souls has nothing to do with their import*, which is measured through purely objective norms which are valid for them alone [. . .]

---

[18] *The Way of the World: the Bildungsroman in European Culture*, Verso, London 1987 (especially the Introduction and Chapter 1), and, more recently, 'Modern European Literature: a Geographical Sketch', in *New Left Review* 207, 1994.

[19] W. Sombart, 'Technology and Culture' (1911), see T. Maldonado, ed., *Tecnica e cultura. Il dibattito tedesco fra Bismarck e Weimar*, Feltrinelli, Milan 1979, p. 143.

The 'fetishism' which Marx assigned to economic commodities – Simmel concludes – represents only a special case of this general fate of contents of culture.[20]

The general fate of contents of culture . . . In the light of these words, the argument developed so far takes on a new aspect. The emancipation of polyphony from anthropocentric motivation is, to be sure, a development of literary technique: but a formal development that *duplicates a general tendency of modern capitalism.* If the languages of Joycean polyphony seem to 'speak of their own accord', no longer relying on concrete subjects, it is because *they have all become institutional languages,* and follow 'the purely objective norms' of Church, School, Journalism, Nation, Advertising . . . Try making a map of *Ulysses,* and comparing it with the one Pierre Bourdieu once made for *Sentimental Education.* One thing leaps to the eye immediately: Flaubert's Paris is made up of private houses, Joyce's Dublin of public places. Collective spaces, or institutional ones. And *spaces that talk.* 'A cultural object comes into existence which as a total unit is *without a producer,*' writes Simmel again.[21] True, and these new objects are precisely the protagonists of the second *Ulysses.*

Joyce/Kafka

That things are changing is immediately obvious, from the first chapter of the second *Ulysses.* We are at the Newspaper: there is a third-person narrator, long exchanges of dialogue, and segments of stream of consciousness. But as we read it, all this is subordinated to the short titles that punctuate the chapter every ten or twenty lines: a special style, which is not produced by any single character, but by the institution where the scene takes place. Language becomes a function of space: it

---

[20] G. Simmel, 'On the Concept and Tragedy of Culture', in *The Conflict in Modern Culture and Other Essays,* translated by K. Peter Etzkorn, Teachers College Press, New York 1968, pp. 36 and 42 (translation modified).

[21] Ibid., p. 41. Here, incidentally, lies the difference between the Joycean polyphony and Proust's *Pastiches.* The latter are always *personalized,* and pushed towards caricature, whereas Joyce is interested in what is impersonal about a style: its abstract, average, even tedious, rhetoric.

derives its contents from it (School, Restaurant, Cemetery, Hospital), or even its style (Church, Newspaper, Library, Pub, Brothel). It is a shift from time to space that occurs outside *Ulysses* as well: in *Berlin Alexanderplatz*, for example, another epic attempt not much later than Joyce's. 'One thousand metres', writes Walter Benjamin, 'no more, is the radius describing the sphere of this existence round the square. Alexanderplatz rules over its *Dasein*. A cruel ruler, you might say.'[22]

Yes, a cruel ruler. And one so self-confident, it is in no hurry at all. The fiercest thing about the novel, indeed, is perhaps the *slowness* with which Biberkopf goes to the slaughter: commonplace sentences, chance encounters, banal pleonasms, worthy of *Ulysses* – but whose lazy accumulation eventually bars the way back. It is enough to be there, in the vicinity of Alexanderplatz, and your fate is sealed. Franz takes a stroll with his next-door neighbour, sees two men fighting, decides to give a helping hand to the one who has come off worse – and finds himself part of the gang that will cost him the amputation of his arm (*Berlin Alexanderplatz*, V, 'Sunday 8 April 1928'). There are two fellows quarrelling, one says boastfully: 'I might be a pimp, then' – and Franz decides to become a pimp, which will lead to the murder of Mieze and his own insanity (VI, 'Another Man Gets Another Head As Well').[23]

One thousand metres, yes. Actually, it is a matter of a thousand in

---

22 W. Benjamin, 'Krisis des Romans: zu Döblins "Berlin Alexanderplatz"', in *Schriften*, III, Suhrkamp, Frankfurt 1972, p. 234.

23 Another work often cited as an example of 'spatial' narrative is André Gide's *The Counterfeiters* (1925) (translated by Dorothy Bussy, Penguin, Harmondsworth 1966). The novel does indeed open with a chapter entitled 'The Luxembourg Gardens', in which a youth confesses: 'What I should like would be to tell the story – no, not of a person, but of a place – well, for instance, of a garden path, like this' (p. 15); and later the novelist Édouard asks why the narrative material should only be sliced 'in time, lengthwise. Why not in breadth? Or in depth?' (p. 168). If read carefully, however, Gide's novel operates in exactly the opposite way. Certainly there is 'breadth', here: a great number of characters, and a constant shifting from one to another. But there is, above all, frantic pursuit of a fast-moving, lurid plot: a mere fifty pages or so, and the variously illicit and disastrous adventures of Bernard, Olivier, Profitendieu père, Vincent, Georges, Édouard, Passavant, Lilian, Laura, are all in full swing . . . And, as they say, that is only the start.

Ulysses too: and Joyce, in the Linati schema, defines 'Wandering Rocks' – in words worthy of *Alexanderplatz* – as 'The Hostile Context'. But as usual the schema is wrong, and the viceroy's parade passes by the characters in 'Wandering Rocks' without deflecting their course in the least. There is no force of gravity, here, no 'cruel ruler'. *Ulysses* is a polycentric urban universe, where objective culture is divided between countless discrete places and discourses, none of which dominates the others or makes them superfluous. It is a world with many ideologies, but without any really strong ideology. Without a myth, or a Law, to confer unity upon it.

A world without a Law. Yes, despite all the public places figuring in *Ulysses*, precisely the Law Court is absent. Kafka's space: or rather, the space that in *The Trial* captures and annihilates every other kind. When the novel begins, there still exist the places of private life, or of work: K.'s room, that of Fräulein Bürstner, the bank. People mention Else's house, a beer-house, a possible boat-trip . . . But then, a terrifying concentration – Titorelli: 'Everything belongs to the Court' – takes possession of apartment blocks and cathedral, boarding-house and bank, outlying attics and the lawyer's chambers. Those few episodes that might have escaped it – the evening with Else, the trip out of the city to visit his mother, the friendship with public prosecutor Hasterer – are all abandoned after a few paragraphs. Truly, everything belongs to – everything *collapses* into – the Court:

> 'Then you are the man I'm looking for', said the priest. 'I am the prison chaplain.'
> 'Oh, are you?' K. said.
> 'I had you summoned here', said the priest, 'to have a talk with you.'
> 'I didn't know that', said K. 'I came here to show an Italian round the cathedral.'
> 'Keep to the point', the priest said
>
> *The Trial*, 9

The Cathedral, art, the bank, the foreign visitor . . . Keep to the point. One sentence, and nothing is left. It is like being in the vicinity of a black hole, where everything vanishes, and nothing comes back. Centripetal the space, centripetal the plot, centripetal the language: one language, always identical, sounding just the same on the lips of a poor usher or a grand lawyer – and upon which Josef K. is constantly entreated to 'concentrate'. It is really the opposite of the expanding universe of *Ulysses*, where new stylistic worlds take shape in every chapter, and new meanings emerge from them. In Kafka there is *only one* meaning of any importance, and that is the one established by the Law. Established?

> He was warned that these investigations would be held regularly, *possibly not* every week, *but* more and more frequently as time went by. *On the one hand* it was to everyone's advantage that the trial should be brought to a swift conclusion, *but on the other hand* the investigations had got to be thorough from every point of view, *and yet* must never last too long on account of the stress they involved [. . .] *It was assumed,* they said, that he would fall in with this [Sunday hearings], *but if he wanted* a different day they would oblige him *if it were possible.* For instance, hearings could even, they said, be held at night, *but* then K. *might* not be fresh enough. *At any rate. . .*
>
> The Trial, 2, my italics

Possibly not . . . but on the other hand . . . The Court's messages are all like this: one limiting clause after another; a hesitant, doubtful, contradictory tone. Is it the mark of an uncertain, weak Law, and perhaps of an experimental discourse, in which '*Where one believed there was the law, there is in fact desire and desire alone*'?[24] I ask you. If anything, it is the style of arbitrary power, whose ambiguity reinforces that power, by exempting it from any control. It incorporates every objection in the act of indictment itself, and so – in exchange for worthless concessions – deprives the accused of speech and every other right. It is a strategy duplicated by the plot of *The Trial*, from the moment when the guard carrying out the arrest affectionately offers K. his help: a textbook double bind ('have faith

---

[24] G. Deleuze and F. Guattari, *Kafka: Towards a Minor Literature*, translated by Dana Polan, University of Minnesota Press, Minneapolis 1986, p. 49. The italics are those of the authors, who must have been attached to the idea. In a hundred-odd pages, the book by Deleuze and Guattari contains a truly impressive amount of nonsense; just the opposite, to be fair, of Derrida's essay on *Ulysses*, which in the same number of pages says absolutely nothing (J. Derrida, 'Ulysses Gramophone: Hear Say Yes in Joyce', in *Acts of Literature*, Routledge, New York 1992).

in your enemy!'), which makes every action by K. illogical, and thus ends up paralysing him. Every episode here 'means' the same thing as every individual sentence: a perfect, implacable system, which encloses *The Trial* within a hermetically sealed world.

If in *Ulysses* . . in *The Trial*, by contrast . . . The argument by antithesis will have reminded the reader of certain pages from the previous chapter – Proust and Joyce, or Joyce and Faulkner. But there is a difference. Then, I wanted to highlight some diachronic facts: the novelty of *Ulysses* vis-à-vis *À la recherche*, for instance; or the stylistic restoration which gets underway with *The Sound and the Fury*. With Joyce and Kafka, however, something different, and far more interesting, is involved: not a discontinuity between the modernist moment and the one that comes before (or after) it, but a polarization *within* modernism itself. And indeed – unlike what usually happens in cultural history – modernism seems precisely to constitute quite a vast field, but one entirely *lacking a centre*: a field that does not have a common language, and does not crystallize into widespread conventions. Perry Anderson:

> The persistence of the 'anciens régimes', and the academicism concomitant with them, provided a critical range of cultural values *against which* insurgent forms of art could measure themselves [. . .] Without the common adversary of an official academicism, the wide span of new aesthetic practices have little or no unity: their tension with the established or consecrated canons in front of them is constitutive of their definition as such.[25]

'Modernism', in short, as a purely reactive reality: like Yeats's twenty-third phase of the moon, disengaging from pre-existing tradition but nothing more. It is the Big Bang of European literature: a sudden liberation of energies giving life to the most disparate forms, and projecting in antithetical directions the two greatest novelists of the twentieth century. But it is a Big Bang that we are still far from knowing adequately, because until now we have been searching for a non-existent unity – 'modernism' – instead of accepting the idea that in

---

[25] P. Anderson, 'Modernity and Revolution', in *New Left Review* 144 (1984), p. 105.

early twentieth-century literature *there exists no common denominator.* A difficult admission, because it forces us to give up belief in the *Zeitgeist,* and to deal with a multiplicity of mutually disconnected phenomena. But the choice of unifying the field – be it called 'modernism', or 'avant garde', or anything else – really does not work: in order to hold together authors as different as Hofmannsthal and Pound, Stein and Pirandello, or indeed Kafka and Joyce, our concepts have become so generic as to be almost empty of cognitive content. Better, then, to accept the total diversity of the phenomena in question – perhaps following the example of the Museum of Modern Art, which has renounced its Picasso-centric modernism, in order to set up rooms with Chagall, Boccioni, and Kandinsky, just a few inches away from each other. It is not clear where this road leads, nor that it is the right one. But at least it is not the wrong one.

Leaving aside the Big Bang metaphor, the Joyce/Kafka polarization brings us back to a question already discussed in Chapter 4: the difference between polyphony and allegory. In the nineteenth century, remember, the two devices were still largely intertwined: the great historical novelty was constituted by polysemy, and its specific modalities (polyphonic, or allegorical) remained relatively in the background. A century later, however, the differences have grown enough to erase all similarity. On the side of polyphony (which is Joyce's), there has been an almost infinite multiplication of *signifiers*; on that of allegory (Kafka), an equally unlimited growth of *signifieds*. In the former case, there is no limit to the number of languages it is possible to generate, or to their freedom: every style is added to the rest, without claims to supremacy or uniqueness. In the case of allegory, however, there is a constraint, and a very powerful one: the Law. An 'unalterable' constraint, the prison chaplain explains to K.: a genuine 'sacred text', which no interpretation will ever be free to set aside – and which indeed makes the interpretive process into a literal matter of life or death. In *The Trial*, then, the semantic trajectory of 'allegory run amok' is reversed: we start off with a polysemous situation, in which the Law is interpreted in various ways by various people, and then, little by little, this semantic freedom is revoked – and from within the Law itself *one particular interpretation* of K.'s case is chosen, which entails his execution. This 'official' interpretation is never explicated, true: but this means only that the Court's decisions are removed from the public sphere – as is only right, after all, with a sacred text.[26] *Auctoritas, non veritas, facit legem.*

Soul and precision

Let us return to our main argument. We have seen the genesis of polyphony from the stream of consciousness. Then, its emancipation from the anthropocentric framework. Lastly, its spatial and institutional rooting. At this point, what Groden described so well, without really explaining it, finally becomes comprehensible. There are two *Ulysses*, fine – but why? Now we can see why. The novel of the stream of consciousness, and that of polyphony: the last anthropocentric attempt, and then its overturn. The last language of the modern individual; the first language of modern *institutions*.

In the course of Joyce's work, as we know, institutional languages have the last word. They win out. And they win out because they are *stronger*, implied the first great Joycean plagiarism, the baroque sermon of *Portrait*: a rhetoric in which centuries of faith and violence are objectified dominates the individual and reduces him to silence. In *Ulysses*, however, things change. Coercion has become hegemony; and abstractly social styles prevail, not because they are stronger, but because they are *more meaningful*. 'Aeolus':

THE IRON FOREMAN
Mr Bloom laid his cutting on Mr Nanetti's desk.
 – Excuse me, councillor, he said. This ad, you see. Keyes, you remember?
 Mr Nanetti considered the cutting awhile and nodded.
 – He wants it in for July, Mr Bloom said.

---

[26] It is by no means certain, of course, that Kafka intended to end *The Trial* with K.'s execution. Brod's edition continues to convince me, nonetheless, because its irreversibility is consistent with Kafka's work as a whole. The single passage of Scripture quoted in *The Trial* – the parable 'Before the Law' – is characterized precisely by an irreversible course, as are 'The Judgement', 'In the Penal Colony', 'The Metamorphosis', and even (in its own way) *The Castle*.

The foreman moved his pencil towards it.

– But wait, Mr Bloom said. He wants it changed. Keyes, you see. He wants two keys at the top.

Hell of a racket they make. He doesn't hear it. Nannan. Iron nerves. Maybe he understands what I.

The foreman turned round to hear patiently and, lifting an elbow, began to scratch slowly in the armpit of his alpaca jacket.

– Like that, Mr Bloom said, crossing his forefingers at the top.

Let him take that in first.

Mr Bloom, glancing sideways up from the cross he had made, saw the foreman's sallow face, think he has a touch of jaundice, and beyond the obedient reels feeding in huge webs of paper. Clank it. Clank it. Miles of it unreeled. What becomes of it after? O, wrap up meat, parcels: various uses, thousand and one things.

Slipping his words deftly into the pauses of the clanking he drew swiftly on the scarred woodwork.

WE CAN DO IT

– Like that, see. Two crossed keys here. A circle. Then here the name. Alexander Keyes, tea, wine and spirit merchant. So on.

Better not teach him his own business.

– You know yourself, councillor, just what he wants. Then round the top in leaded: the house of keys. You see? Do you think that's a good idea?

The foreman moved his scratching hand to his lower ribs and scratched there quietly.

– The idea, Mr Bloom said, is the house of keys. You know, councillor, the Manx parliament. Innuendo of home rule. Tourists, you know, from the isle of Man. Catches the eye, you see. Can you do that?

I could ask him perhaps about how to pronounce that *voglio*. But then if he didn't know only make it awkward for him. Better not.

– We can do that, the foreman said. Have you the design?

– I can get it, Mr Bloom said. It was in a Kilkenny paper. He has a house there too. I'll just run out and ask him. Well, you can do that and just a little par calling attention. You know the usual. Highclass licensed premises. Longfelt want. So on.

The foreman thought for an instant.

– We can do that, he said. Let him give us a three months' renewal.

ORTHOGRAPHICAL

A typesetter brought him a limp galleypage. He began to check it silently. Mr Bloom stood by, hearing the loud throbs of cranks, watching the silent typesetters at their cases.

Want to be sure of his spelling. Proof fever. Martin Cunningham forgot to give us his spellingbee conundrum this morning. It is amusing to view the unpar one ar alleled embarra two ars is it? double ess ment of a harassed pedlar while gauging au the symmetry with a y of a peeled pear under a cemetery wall. Silly, isn't it? Cemetery put in of course on account of the symmetry.

I should have said when he clapped on his topper. Thank you. I ought to have said something about an old hat or something. No. I could have said. Looks as good as new now. See his phiz then.

Ulysses, VII, 120–73

I apologize for the extremely lengthy quotation, but it helps to grasp a number of things. The 'Aeolus' chapter (which is the one, it will be recalled, in which polyphony makes its appearance) is all arranged on two levels: a composite and often confused level, which registers actions, words and the stream of consciousness of the characters; and then, every ten or twenty lines, the polyphonic level, constituted by sixty-odd titles in as many different styles of modern journalism. The first level, of course, takes up far more space than the other, and is much richer in material. But the second is far more important, because it performs a higher structural function. For the titles, breaking the narrative continuum, capture the reader's attention and direct it towards certain parts of the text rather than others. When we read the phrase 'The Iron Foreman', for example, we focus upon Mr Nanetti, and what directly concerns him; all the rest (Bloom, the advertisement, the machines. . .) passes into the background. Thanks to the titles, in short, an amorphous and almost uncontrollable jumble acquires relief and hierarchy. It is exactly the same process of selection which, according to Louis Hjelmslev, governs the formation of meaning in language:

We thus recognize in the linguistic content, in its process, a specific form, the content-form, which is independent of, and stands in arbitrary relation to, the purport [. . .] We may conclude from this fact that in one of the two entities that are functives of the sign function, namely the content, the sign function institutes a form, the content-form, which from the point of view of the purport is arbitrary and which can be explained only by the sign function and is obviously solidary with it.[27]

The content-form. Well, this is how the antithesis between stream of consciousness and polyphony could be rewritten. The stream of consciousness is a catch-all technique, which seeks to register every least stimulus, and which therefore leaves the semantic content in a fairly disorganized state: it is a pool of barely outlined possibilities, closely recalling the 'purport of the content' of Hjelmslev's system. In polyphony, however, meaning crystallizes: the amorphous content coagulates, and acquires a definite form. Definite – but nonetheless still arbitrary, as Hjelmslev reminds us.[28] So arbitrary, in fact, that only a handful of readers will have noticed a little trick with the quotation from *Ulysses* above: the first two titles, 'WE SEE THE CANVASSER AT WORK' and 'HOUSE OF KEY(E)S', were replaced with ones invented by me, 'THE IRON FOREMAN' and 'WE CAN DO IT' (although the third title, 'ORTHOGRAPHICAL', is the right one). A trick with pure intentions, of course, designed to make clear the independence of the polyphonic form from the narrative material, and the fact that the same material could easily be formed in very different ways.[29]

A meaning established through an arbitrary selection. Nevertheless: established. When I said that polyphony prevails over the stream of

---

[27] L. Hjelmslev, *Prolegomena to a Theory of Language*, translated by Francis Whitfield, Waverly Press for Indiana University, Baltimore 1961, pp. 32 and 34.

[28] 'Each language lays down its own boundaries within the amorphous "thought-mass" [. . .] It is like one and the same handful of sand that is formed in quite different patterns, or like the cloud in the heavens that changes shape in Hamlet's view from minute to minute' (ibid., p. 32).

[29] While I was at it, I also shifted the last lines of the 'HOUSE OF KEY(E)S' passage to the beginning of the following section, 'ORTHOGRAPHICAL' (whose final lines I then left out): I wanted to suggest that there existed other, equally plausible, ways of cutting up the textual continuum. For there is no reason internal to the narrative material that requires an interruption every ten or twenty lines: the regularity of the titling, which creates a meaning at preset intervals, is a purely mechanical and arbitrary choice. But, once again, an initially arbitrary convention can easily become a wholly 'natural' habit: the newspapers we read every morning are put together in a very similar way to the pages of 'Aeolus'.

consciousness because it is 'more meaningful', I was thinking precisely of pages like these: where the polyphonic level constrains the overflowing materials of *Ulysses* onto the narrow tracks of meaning. A book by Julia Kristeva, *The Revolution of Poetic Language*, saluted in Joyce the 'semiotic' subversion of the 'symbolic' order: alas, exactly the opposite is true. The second *Ulysses* is a genuine factory of meaning: and polyphony, to extend the metaphor, is a sign of the division of labour that reigns within it, and allows it to function. Chapter after chapter, the average, anthropocentric style of nineteenth-century narrative becomes more and more remote, overwhelmed by a succession of 'special' languages: a whole host of them, self-contained, abstract, above and beyond any individual inflection.

The Man Without Qualities, another work fascinated by the division of labour and of languages, will help us understand what is happening. The first page of the novel:

> There was a depression over the Atlantic. It was travelling eastwards, towards an area of high pressure over Russia, and still showed no tendency to move northwards around it. The isotherms and isotheres were fulfilling their functions. The atmospheric temperature was in proper relation to the average annual temperature, the temperature of the coldest as well as of the hottest month, and the a–periodic monthly variation in temperature. [. . .] In short, to use an expression that describes the facts pretty satisfactorily, even though it is somewhat old-fashioned: it was a fine August day in the year 1913.
>
> *The Man Without Qualities*, I, 1

Isotheres, a–periodic variation – fine August day. One of the numerous challenges faced by Musil consists in his attempt to build a bridge from the former to the latter: from formalized languages reserved for specialists ('at the outside two dozen people in the world': I, 63) to a language for all, interested in the concrete human relief of things. It is the interweaving of 'soul and precision' characteristic of *The Man Without Qualities*, and of its favourite rhetorical figure: the simile.[30] It is Musil's 'essayism', and not his alone:

---

[30] Analytical and rational, the simile establishes a symmetry between two fields (A:B = C:D), while still maintaining the distinction between them (whereas metaphor, more peremptory, superimposes them). From this *limited* efficacy of the

The essay form has not yet, today, travelled the road to independence which its sister, poetry, covered long ago – the road of development from a primitive, undifferentiated unity with science, ethics and art.[31]

Although art and science have separated historically, Adorno comments a half century later:

the opposition between them should not be hypostatized. Aversion to an anachronistic conflation of the two does not render a compartmentalized culture sacrosanct. For all their necessity, those compartments represent institutional confirmation of the renunciation of the whole truth.[32]

To resist the intellectual division of labour: to reunite art and truth, spirit and life.[33] To find Musil's right simile; to transform the story into reflection and advice, like Proust, or Mann, or Broch. 'To utilize this accumulation of specialized culture for the enrichment of everyday life,' as Habermas said of the Enlightenment.[34] And indeed, as Alfonso Berardinelli has written, essayism always refers to 'a concept of "public" and "socialized" humanity', of an enlightenment kind:[35] to that 'rational

---

simile derives the always somewhat melancholy irony accompanying it in *The Man Without Qualities*, which makes it the refined, but doubtful, descendant of the 'cunning duplicate in mind' of *Moby-Dick*. However, the limit does not erase the efficacy of Musil's rhetorical choice. A century after Melville – a century that mathematizes the natural sciences and invents the human 'sciences', with the multiplication of languages that the process entails – the simile still offers a meeting point between human beings: a 'common' language, albeit precarious and certainly far from immediate.

[31] Lukács, 'On the Nature and Form of the Essay', in *Soul and Form*, translated by Anna Bostock, MIT Press, Cambridge Mass. 1974, p. 13.

[32] T.W. Adorno, 'The Essay as Form', in *Notes to Literature*, vol. 1, translated by Shierry Weber Nicholsen, Columbia University Press, New York 1991, p. 7.

[33] 'The irony I mean consists in the critic always speaking about the ultimate problems of life, but in a tone which implies that he is only discussing pictures and books . . .' (Lukács, *Soul and Form*, p. 9).

[34] Habermas, 'Modernity – an Incomplete Project', p. 9.

[35] A. Berardinelli, 'La critica come saggistica', in A. Berardinelli, F. Brioschi and C. Di Girolamo, *La ragione critica*, Einaudi, Turin 1986, p. 47.

public sphere' where different interests and discourses communicate with one another, and which has constituted an incomparable habitat for the European intellectual.

In the twentieth century, however, does such a public sphere still exist? Those very authors whom I have just quoted seem to doubt it. The Verdurins' is the salon transformed into a parody of itself; Broch's Germany, a world of 'sleepwalkers' rather than rational beings; the encyclopaedism of the Collateral Campaign, an amateurish waste of time; the humanism of Serenus Zeitblom, a nineteenth-century remnant disliked by the Third Reich and unknown to its enemies. And so, no, perhaps the public sphere really does no longer function: and yet, these novelists continue to *write* as though it still existed: to use the rich, synthetic style of the European intellectual. Whereas Joyce, who is not an intellectual, gets rid of it without a second thought. In *Ulysses*, where almost everything takes place 'in public', precisely the language of the public sphere is absent. From 'Ithaca':

Did he fall?

By his body's known weight of eleven stone and four pounds in avoirdupois measure, as certified by the graduated machine for periodical selfweighing in the premises of Francis Froedman, pharmaceutical chemist of 19 Frederick street, north, on the last feast of the Ascension, to wit, the twelfth day of May of the bissextile year one thousand nine hundred and four of the christian era (jewish era five thousand six hundred and sixtyfour, mohammadan era one thousand three hundred and twentytwo), golden number 5, epact 13, solar cycle 9, dominical letters C B, Roman indiction 2, Julian period 6617, MCMIV.

Ulysses, XVII, 90–99

It is a passage that presents, in miniature, the stylistic slippage of *Ulysses* as a whole: from a thoroughly normal event (Bloom's fall: just like, on a larger scale, Bloom's day) to a labyrinth of ever more elaborate interpretive settings. It is Musil's opening paragraph, but upside down: it starts off from a concrete human experience, and ends up in a most complicated calculation aimed at establishing – but why on earth? – the date of Easter

1904.[36] And this is the way it is, throughout the chapter: if Bloom turns the faucet, a highly detailed description of Dublin's aqueduct comes out; if his age is mentioned, it is at once followed by an avalanche of equations halting only at the 83,300-year mark. It is the earthly-human that leaves the stage. We are approaching the end of the chapter, and Bloom is thinking about the adultery that has just occurred between Molly and Boylan:

Envy?

Of a bodily and mental male organism specially adapted for the super-incumbent posture of energetic human copulation and energetic piston and cylinder movement necessary for the complete satisfaction of a constant but not acute concupiscence resident in a bodily and mental female organism, passive but not obtuse.

Ulysses, XVII, 2156–61

Here there is no longer anybody: Molly, Boylan, Bloom, envy, any other feeling – all vanished. There remains only a mechanical pedantry, stiffening human actions into equally mechanical movements. It is the earthly-human that disappears – and precisely in the 'Ithaca' chapter. Leopold Bloom may well return home to Number 7 Eccles Street; to feel at home *in language*, however, is a thing of the past.

We have come a long way from the polyphony of *Faust* Part Two. There, metrical or lexical differences never disrupted a unitary, 'Goethean', stylistic field. In the second *Ulysses*, however, there is really nothing that is 'Joycean': merely languages that do not communicate with one another, and that are sometimes as impenetrable as genuinely foreign languages. The epic ambition, according to a Hegelian thesis drawn upon by Lukács in *The Historical Novel*, consists in representing 'the totality of objects'. For Joyce, we should speak of the 'totality of languages'. Or rather, of the totality of languages *as objects*:

---

[36] Don Gifford's *'Ulysses' Annotated* (University of California Press, Berkeley–Los Angeles–London 1988) devotes a whole column of commentary to the last two lines of the passage quoted, and concludes (like Musil, but not like Joyce): 'What it all adds up to is that Easter Sunday occurred on 3 April 1904' (p. 568).

Common to all these manifestations is a spirit that distinguishes them singularly and decisively from the life forms of earlier centuries: a character of specialization and abstraction; of willed inevitability; of purposeful, ordered thought, without surprises or humour; of complex uniformity: a spirit that seems to justify the choice of the word 'mechanization' even from the emotional standpoint.

This is not a literary critic, but the president of the *Allgemeine Elektrizität Gesellschaft*, Walter Rathenau, writing about the 'Mechanization of the World'.[37] And yet, the complexity devoid of inspiration he describes is well known to the reader of *Ulysses*. 'Pound is that curious thing', writes Wyndham Lewis with delicate perfidy, 'a person without a trace of originality of any sort.'[38] It is the charge often directed at Mahler (want of creativity, 'the failing . . . [of] performers'[39]), and which Joyce himself admits, in a letter to George Antheil, albeit without giving it too much weight: 'I am quite content to go down to posterity as a scissors and paste man [a *bricoleur*!] for that seems to me a harsh but not unjust description.'[40]

How to conclude, then? Perhaps, radicalizing the thesis of Curtius's great essay on *Ulysses*:

> A metaphysic nihilism is the basis of Joyce's work [. . .] This entire wealth of philosophical and theological knowledge, this power of psychological and aesthetic analysis, this culture of the mind educated in all the literatures of the world, this ratiocination which is so far above all positivistic commonplaces – all these gifts are deployed only to be dissipated and nullified in a universal conflagration [. . .] What remains? Odour of ashes, horror of death, apostate melancholy, tortures of conscience . . .[41]

[37] Walter Rathenau, 'Die Mechanisierung der Welt' (1912), in *Gesammelten Schriften*, vol. 1, S. Fischer Verlag, Berlin 1918, p. 48.
[38] W. Lewis, *Time and Western Man*, Chatto and Windus, London 1927, p. 85.
[39] P. Boulez, 'Mahler, Our Contemporary', in *Orientations*, translated by Martin Cooper, Faber and Faber, London and Boston 1986, p. 301.
[40] Stuart Gilbert, ed., *Letters of James Joyce*, vol. 1, Faber and Faber, London 1966, p. 297.
[41] E.R. Curtius, 'James Joyce and his *Ulysses*' (1929), see R. H. Deming, ed., *James Joyce: the Critical Heritage*, vol. 2, Routledge and Kegan Paul, London 1970, p. 469 (translation modified).

A universal conflagration of culture? Yes and no. True, *Ulysses* is the sign of a deep change: twenty years ago, the crisis of anthropocentrism would have been called, with justice, the 'death of man'. But the most disturbing feature of Joyce's novel is not Curtius's 'dissipation', but an incomprehensible, unstoppable *productivity*. It is the opposite of essayism: it multiplies discourses, subdivides them, estranges the various viewpoints, until we are given a world *full of culture* – and totally *devoid of wisdom*. It is the new polyphony: the polyphony of the metropolis, and of its division of labour. Here, all the variety and all the intelligence of the various languages remains *imprisoned* within them: a 'melancholy of abstract objectivity', as Jung will say in his 1932 essay on Joyce.[42] Bloom, and with him the reader, 'enters' and 'exits' from one style to another as though they were watertight chambers. Everything changes, here, but nothing remains: the spiritual positions progressively adopted remain immobile, inert. 'A man without qualities is made up of qualities without a man', Musil said. True, and likewise for Bloom, and for *Ulysses* too: a novel without style, which is made up of styles without a novel . . .

One of the last scenes in *The Magic Mountain* comes to mind: Hans Castorp, at night, beside the gramophone, listening to the many voices of modern music. Voices without bodies, 'a music of phantasms' – and in a place of death. In its way, another little 'Walpurgis Night'. But the dehumanizing force of polyphony has been exorcised. For once, Castorp shrugs off his passivity, and makes every passage into a life experience: 'It needed no effort of imagination to enable Hans Castorp to feel with Radames all this intoxication, all this gratitude . . .'; 'Here is the dream Hans Castorp dreamed . . .'; 'The singer, a character warmly sympathetic to our young man's heart, was called in the opera Valentine; but Hans Castorp named him by another and dearly familiar, sadness-evoking name . . .' In short, Castorp 'translates' the musical form into the language of his emotions: and by doing so, of course, he also betrays that 'inner logic' so dear to another, and greater, Thomas Mann hero. But this betrayal is also an act of comprehension. The young dilettante twists

---

42 C.G. Jung, ' "Ulysses". A Monologue', translated by R.F.C. Hull, in *Collected Works*, vol. 15, Routledge and Kegan Paul, London 1971, p. 117.

objective culture towards himself, in order to draw counsel from it. In his own way, he performs an act of wisdom.

And so, culture or wisdom? Culture, answers *Ulysses* – and, for what it is worth, the writer of this book agrees. However, something important has been lost.

CHAPTER

8

Complexity. II

In the first chapter of *The Blind Watchmaker*, Richard Dawkins characterizes the 'complicated things' that biology is concerned with in terms of two criteria: the diversity of the individual components, and the non-trivial interactions that take place between them.[1] As for the first criterion, there is no doubt that *Ulysses* fits it perfectly: a novel made up of two or three distinct levels, numerous different styles, and in which each chapter is a self-contained world. Fine. But what about the other criterion – interaction? Returning to Edgar Morin's distinction, quoted at the end of Part One, what is *Ulysses*? An 'organized whole'? Or rather, like *Faust* before it, 'the sum of its individual parts'?

Criticism, these days, opts decisively for the organized whole, and usually supports its thesis either with the Homeric substratum, or with those self-reflexive chapters ('Wandering Rocks', 'Circe', 'Ithaca') whose subject is *Ulysses* itself. In both cases, the idea is that there exists a place – 'within' *Ulysses*, or 'beneath' it – where those same materials, which at first sight appear highly heterogeneous, in fact reveal a secret affinity. Interaction between the parts is conceived, in short, as coherence: as

---

[1] R. Dawkins, *The Blind Watchmaker*, Penguin, Harmondsworth 1988, pp. 1–15.

homogeneity.[2] Organization and homogeneity, however, are by no means synonyms. Speaking about Mahler's symphonies, which pose problems fairly similar to those of *Ulysses*, Adorno writes:

> Mahler mobilized the constructive forces of the system, however much he may have been perplexed by them. In the productive conflict of the contradictory elements his art flourishes.

And again:

> Through the unqualified primacy of the whole over the parts in Viennese classicism, the figures in that music frequently resembled each other and converged. They shunned extreme contrasts, without which the Mahlerian whole would not be formed. He looks for support not only in declining late Romanticism, but above all in vulgar music. This offers him crude stimulants that the selective taste of higher music has rejected.[3]

A whole that is formed *in* extreme contrasts, rather than in their resolution: this is the opposite of the model of Richards and Brooks. Interaction, here, is *polarization*: a 'productive conflict of the contradictory elements', which dynamizes the many languages of Mahlerian polyphony by radicalizing their latent features. It is the 'love of conflicts' evoked by Bruno Walter: 'his inclination to extremes, to excesses, and to the use even of the grotesque'.[4] It is the sentiment that becomes mawkishness in

---

[2] The idea probably goes back to a book that, in its day, had a considerable influence on English-language criticism: *Modern Poetry and the Tradition*, by Cleanth Brooks. The reflections on the metaphysical poets, which open the book, define a 'principle of complexity' based precisely on the primacy of homogeneity: 'the balance of reconcilement of opposite or discordant qualities' (Coleridge); 'resolving the apparent discords' (I.A. Richards). See C. Brooks, *Modern Poetry and the Tradition*, North Carolina University Press, Chapel Hill 1939, pp. 40–41 and 167 ff. Incidentally, Brooks's book – along with the works of Eliot and Empson – constitutes the main theoretical reference for the first manifesto of R. Venturi, *Complexity and Contradiction in Architecture*, The Museum of Modern Art, New York 1966.

[3] T.W. Adorno, *Mahler*, translated by Edmund Jephcott, University of Chicago Press, Chicago 1992, pp. 65 and 50.

[4] B. Walter, *Gustav Mahler*, translated by James Galston, Kegan Paul–Trench Trübner, London 1937, pp. 16, 90 (translation modified).

the *Adagietto*; certain sudden *fortissimos* intended to hurt the ears; the encyclopaedic vein that degenerates into the unbearable pedantry of 'Ithaca'; the religious parody that becomes the naked, coarse blasphemy of 'Circe'.

A whole as a 'force field', in short.[5] As intensification. And why not? Complexity requires interaction: not homogeneity, and still less the elimination of differences. Just think about the stream of consciousness, and about polyphony: the language of the individual, and those of society, I said earlier. Fine, and now we know what relation binds them: a negative magnetism, a mutual repulsion that is insignificant at first, but then grows to the point where it becomes irreconcilable. As in Adorno's metaphor about the relationship between avant-garde and mass culture, *Ulysses* is made up of two halves – which no longer form a whole. And this, of course, confronts us with a new query: can a symbolic system without a common language be tolerated? Or is it not perhaps uninhabitable – like a world without atmosphere? Could there be *too much complexity*, in Joyce's novel?

Let us look at the matter by starting from the text. A passage from 'Circe':

(*The beagle lifts his snout, showing the grey scorbutic face of Paddy Dignam. He has gnawed all. He exhales a putrid carcasefed breath. He grows to human size and shape. His dachshund coat becomes a brown mortuary habit. His green eye flashes bloodshot. Half of one ear, all the nose and both thumbs are ghouleaten.*)

PADDY DIGNAM

(*in a hollow voice*) It is true. It was my funeral. Doctor Finucane pronounced life extinct when I succumbed to the disease from natural causes.

(*He lifts his mutilated ashen face moonwards and bays lugubriously.*)

BLOOM

(*in triumph*) You hear?

---

[5] 'Mahler's art of instrumentation is a force field, not a style': Adorno, *Mahler*, p. 119.

PADDY DIGNAM

Bloom, I am Paddy Dignam's spirit. List, list, O list!

BLOOM

The voice is the voice of Esau.

SECOND WATCH

(*blesses himself*) How is that possible?

FIRST WATCH

It is not in the penny catechism.

PADDY DIGNAM

By metempsychosis. Spooks.

A VOICE

O rocks.

Ulysses, XV, 1204–29

The citizen's dog (Chapter XII), Dignam (IV–VI), the carcass (III), the cannibalism–religion link (V), Hamlet (I, IX), the catechism (XVII), metempsychosis (IV), the 'rocks' ('wandering' in X; but also in IV and VIII) of the final curse – and who knows how much else. It is quite true: in 'Circe', all the other chapters of *Ulysses* return and interact. But on the basis of what principle do they interact, and with what results?

Let me begin by saying that, in the dizzy slide from allusion to allusion, some linkage is always present: Dignam – dead – will become like a carcass, but might also return in the guise of a ghost like the elder Hamlet; the link between *Hamlet* and Esau was already in one of Stephen's thoughts in the ninth chapter (IX, 981); from the Old Testament to Christianity the step is a short one – and so on to metempsychosis, and then back again to spooks . . . All plausible transitions, easy to justify. And it is the same everywhere. Starting off from *Hamlet*, there is no difficulty in reaching women's bottoms (V, 455), or a slang expression for pay day in the theatre (VII, 237). In 'Circe' alone, *Hamlet* is successively linked to a grotesque seduction of Mrs Breen (467), an imaginary plea in defence of Bloom (952), the death of Dignam (1218), a little speech to keep Zoe at a distance (1965), the quarrel between Bloom and Bella Cohen (3194), Bloom's potato (3522), the reading of Stephen's palm (3655), erotic tittle-tattle about Bloom (3820), an exchange on love, matrimony and widowhood (3853), the attempt on Bloom's part to calm Stephen down (3941), Stephen's drunkenness (4157), a political exchange between Stephen and a soldier (4576–77), and a traditional representation of Ireland (4582).

216

A single source – and a dozen different landings.[6] There is no doubt, *Ulysses* is capable of connecting everything with everything else. Developing an image of Umberto Eco's, the European cultural system operates, here, like a gigantic railway network: each encyclopaedic 'entry' a kind of station – with its changes, its timetables, and rails going off in different directions. It is a mechanism that confers upon 'Circe', and by extension upon *Ulysses*, its peculiar, highly intricate, unity. But it is also – and perhaps above all – a mechanism so easy to set in motion that it almost always ends up being *dominated by chance*: by trivial affinities, for example, or by the accidental similarities that trigger all the passages quoted above.

Is it a defect of *Ulysses*, this unstoppable glissade? Not for me. A cultural system at the mercy of chance – splendid idea.[7] A text, moreover, that rewinds upon itself in such different ways really does open up a new terrain for literary complexity:

> Complexity is the property of a system that can be modelled to show behaviours that are not all predetermined (*necessary*), even if they are potentially foreseeable by an institutional observer of the system (*possible*). This definition suggests a method of conceptual evaluation of the instantaneous complexity of a system (a 'complexity measure'), by matching:
> – the number of possible behaviours of this system (balanced, if need be, by their likelihood of occurrence)
> – to the number of certain (or certainly predeterminable) behaviours of the system.[8]

---

[6] The thing is all the more impressive, considering that the allusions almost all refer to a single scene – the encounter between the ghost and Hamlet – which is among the shortest and most unambiguous in the play.

[7] From the disorder of chance, a certain statistical order does, of course, emerge. From *Hamlet* the most disparate directions *can* be taken: *in fact*, however, we encounter a relatively ordered distribution: one third of the transitions lead to Eros, another third to the father, smaller percentages to politics and art, and about one fifth go wherever they like. *A priori*, there is no way of predicting the direction that the text will take, other than in a purely probabilistic sense.

[8] J.-L. LeMoigne, 'Progettazione della complessità e complessità della progettazione', in G. Bocchi and M. Ceruti, eds, *La sfida della complessità*, Feltrinelli, Milan 1985, p. 93.

Non-predeterminable behaviours. It had been the discovery of Wagner's 'art of transition' – and the semantic stations of *Ulysses* duplicate it in the sphere of verbal language. In Joyce's novel, possible behaviours really are vastly more numerous than determined ones: and not just at the beginning (as happens with every narrative), but above all *at the end*, when the 'Circe', 'Ithaca' and 'Penelope' chapters remix the materials of the novel – here, too, in a way not so different from Wagner's recapitulation – in ever more unpredictable combinations. In this context the style of 'Eumaeus', where every assertion is scrupulously specified, as though to exorcise the crazy proliferations of the brothel[9] – the *univocal* style, in short, that should 'close' the semantic net, by fixing the story in a definitive form – is by now simply ridiculous.

And yet – is it really possible to have so many mechanisms capable of complicating things, but not one that can simplify them? It is the same question as before: is not *Ulysses* perhaps too complex? Does it not contain too many – and too unpredictable – interactions? One last analytical passage, and I shall try to give an answer.

In his essay on chaotic enumeration, Leo Spitzer refers fleetingly at one point to the 'poetry of proper nouns' inaugurated by Walt Whitman. But where does this poetry come from? Or, to begin at the beginning, where does the 'meaning' of proper nouns come from?

Iliad, Book Two: the muster of ships – hundreds upon hundreds of proper nouns. And since, with signs of this type, the risk is much higher than usual that the listener will not grasp the meaning of the message, they are introduced in a quite particular way – like so many 'entries' in an encyclopaedia:

---

[9] 'His (Stephen's) mind was not exactly what you would call wandering, but a bit unsteady and on his expressed desire for some beverage to drink Mr Bloom in view of the hour it was and there being no pump of Vartry water available for their ablutions let alone drinking purposes . . .' (XVI, 4–7). And again: 'They passed the main entrance of the Great Northern railway station, the starting point for Belfast, where of course all traffic was suspended at that late hour and passing the backdoor of the morgue (a not very enticing locality, not to say gruesome to a degree, more especially at night) . . .' (XVI, 45–9).

Men of that island [Euboea], then, the resolute
Abantes, those of Chalcis, Eretria,
and Histiaea, of the laden vines,
Cerinthus by the sea, the crag of Dion,
those of Carystus, those of Styra – all
who had young Elephenor Chalcodontiades,
the chief of the Abantes, for commander.
Quick on their feet, with long scalp locks, those troops
enlisted hungering for body armour
of enemies to pierce with ashen spears;
and Elephenor's black ships numbered forty.

Iliad, II, 536–45

An interweaving of genealogy, history and geography: here is all that we need to attribute to 'Elephenor' its meaning. And broadly speaking, a hundred different listeners will all reach more or less the same conclusion. But then:

> Lord Beaconsfield, Lord Byron, Wat Tyler, Moses of Egypt, Moses Maimonides, Moses Mendelssohn, Henry Irving, Rip van Winkle, Kossuth, Jean Jacques Rousseau, Baron Leopold Rothschild, Robinson Crusoe, Sherlock Holmes, Pasteur . . .

Ulysses, XV, 1845–9

Jerusalem Athens Alexandria
Vienna London

The Waste Land, 374–5

at Bayeux, at Coutances, at Vitré, at Questanbert, at Pontorson, at Balbec, at Lannion, at Lamballe . . .

Remembrance of Things Past,
'Swann's Way. Place-Names: the Name'

Here, everything has changed. And it has changed because – where the ancient epic was able, and almost obliged, to construct its own encyclopaedia – the modern epic is not, because encyclopaedias already exist. Indeed, there are a great many of them, and very different from one another. So every reader 'fills up' Lord Beaconsfield, Vienna, or

Pontorson, with the elements present in (or missing from) their own mental encyclopaedia – which will inevitably be unlike anyone else's. And since the list in Proust and Joyce is a weak context, that does not guide the attribution of meaning in any way, the result is that the proper noun of the twentieth century – unlike Homer's Elephenor – produces a genuine interpretive explosion. Roland Barthes:

> If the Name (as we shall henceforth call the proper noun) is a sign, it is a voluminous sign, a sign always pregnant and crammed full of meanings that no use can reduce or flatten; unlike the common noun, which never allocates more than one of its meanings for each syntagm. The Proustian Name is already, in and of itself, and in all cases, the equivalent of a whole dictionary entry [. . .] It is immune from any kind of selective restriction, and the syntagm in which it is located is a matter of indifference to it. In a certain sense, the Name is thus a semantic monstrosity, for, although provided with all the features of the common noun, it can still exist and function outside any projective rule. Such is the price – the counterpart – of the phenomenon of 'hypersemanticity' that it harbours, and that relates it very closely, of course, to the poetic word.[10]

Or, as Proust himself puts it:

> But if these names thus permanently absorbed the image I had formed of these towns, it was only by transforming that image, by subordinating its reappearance in me to their own special laws; and in consequence of this they made it more beautiful, but at the same time more different from anything that the towns of Normandy or Tuscany could in reality be, and, by increasing the arbitrary delights of my imagination . . .

> *Remembrance of Things Past*,
> 'Place-Names: the Name'

A semantic monstrosity. The arbitrary delights of the imagination. 'Not only must the reader of *The Cantos* know exactly what books Mr Pound

---

[10] R. Barthes, 'Proust et les noms', in *Le degré zéro de l'écriture, suivi de Nouveaux essais critiques*, Seuil, Paris 1972, pp. 125–6.

used,' writes Blackmur, 'but must himself use them in the way Mr Pound used them.'[11] As if to say: in order truly to understand *The Cantos*, you must have the same encyclopaedic competence as the author. Establish the same immediate connections with the thirty-four proper nouns of the fourth Canto; or the forty-seven of the fifth; or the forty-two of the sixth (on average, one every two or three lines). And this is not possible. In the field of semantic associations, Gottlob Frege once wrote, '*si duo idem faciunt, non est idem*'.[12] If two people say the same word, it is not the same. All the more so, if you have Pound's taste for idiosyncratic details that break up the sense of every episode into a tortuous sequence of particulars: the murder of Alessandro de' Medici presented from the point of view of his cousin Lorenzo, predicted in Perugia by the astrologer Del Carmine, recounted by Benedetto Varchi, in bilingual form, Italian and English . . .

'Commonly accepted symbols' have disintegrated, observes Erich Heller in connection with the difficulties of modern poetry: they 'may mean

---

[11] R.P. Blackmur, 'Masks of Ezra Pound' (1934), now in J. Sullivan, ed., *Ezra Pound. A Critical Anthology*, Penguin, Harmondsworth 1970, p. 162.

[12] 'The reference and sense of a sign are to be distinguished from the associated idea. If the reference of the sign is an object perceivable by the senses, my idea of it is an internal image, arising from memories of sense impressions which I have had and acts, both internal and external, which I have performed. Such an idea is often saturated with feeling; the clarity of its separate parts varies and oscillates. The same sense is not always connected, even in the same man, with the same idea [. . .] There result, as a matter of course, a variety of differences in the ideas associated with the same sense. A painter, a horseman, and a zoologist will probably connect different ideas with the name "Bucephalus" [a coincidence, perhaps, but 'Bucephalus' is a proper noun: F.M.]. This constitutes an essential distinction between the idea and the sign's sense, which may be the common property of many, and therefore is not a part of a mode of the individual mind. [. . .] It might perhaps be said: Just as one man connects this idea, and another that idea, with the same word, so also one man can associate this sense, and another that sense. But there still remains a difference in the mode of connection. They are not prevented from grasping the same sense; but they cannot have the same idea. *Si duo idem faciunt, non est idem*' (G. Frege, 'On Sense and Reference' (1892), in P. Geach and M. Black, eds, *Translations from the Philosophical Writings of Gottlob Frege*, Basil Blackwell, Oxford 1952, pp. 59–60).

this or that or nothing at all'.[13] And the 'Dedication' to *Faust*: 'They are far from me now who were so close,/And their first answering echo has so long/Been silent. Now my voice is heard, who knows/By whom?' Well, with Joyce's and Pound's use of the proper noun, the disappearance of the narrow circle is no longer felt as a loss, but as *a liberation of sense*. The 'first answering echo', faithful to the true meaning of the work, would *stifle* the semantic potential of *Ulysses* or *The Cantos*, which is realized fully only amid the countless idiosyncratic interpretations – this or that or nothing at all – of who knows whom. If two people read the same word, in other words, it is not the same – *and that is a good thing*. For these are books whose ideal reader is no longer the individual, *but an entire society*. It is the epic ambition again, re-emphasizing the growing rift between individual and species that we have often encountered. World texts – and texts written *for* the world.

However, the *real* reader of *Ulysses* and *The Cantos* is still a single individual: and how on earth will she manage to tackle them? How will she *defend herself against them*?

Countermodernism

A semantic network, proper nouns in a list, stylistic polarization: disparate techniques, but which all work together to make *Ulysses* a highly complex structure. *Too complex*, I have suggested on more than one occasion. 'Man is an overcomplicated mechanism,' writes Pound. 'If he is doomed to extinction he will die out for want of simplicity.'[14] And Wolfgang Iser:

---

[13] E. Heller, *The Disinherited Mind*, Bowes and Bowes, London 1975, pp. 282 and 268. Let us be clear, it is not that words once had an 'objective' meaning, and we then lost it with the Reformation (which is the moment at which Heller situates the break), or at the end of the last century. In every sign there is *always* an oscillation between a fairly well defined semantic core, and a vague, jagged periphery. The relationship between *the latter and the former*, however, changes a great deal from culture to culture, and in the modern West a complex of factors – religious tolerance, personal freedom, growth of specialisms, political pluralism – have strengthened the semantic periphery at the expense of the core, thus accentuating the 'openness' of the sign.

[14] E. Pound, *Guide to Kulchur*, New Directions, New York 1938, p. 135.

In *Ulysses* [. . .] the overprecision of the system presents more conceivable material than the reader is capable of processing as he reads. And so it is not the style of the novel but the overtaxed reader himself that reduces the amount of observable material to manageable proportions.[15]

That reduces . . . Short, indeed, the season in which complexity grows. *Ulysses* is barely out, and the tide is already starting to turn. Punctuated equilibria: the 'short moment of terror' once over, the 'long period of boredom' resumes. And it resumes with a work – *The Waste Land* – which usually passes for a kind of *Ulysses* in verse, but which in fact embodies the opposite tendency.

In the poetry of the twentieth century, the experience of complexity had been interwoven, in a particularly significant manner, with the technique of free verse. As Tynyanov wrote in 1923, free verse replaces the regular recurrence (*versus*) of metric units by 'the principle of irresolution, which prohibits dynamic preparation'.[16] Ir-resolution: provoking expectations, then leaving them unfulfilled. It is the delight in dissatisfaction of Adorno's Wagner: the increase of possible behaviours as against necessary ones. And the parallel can be pushed even further. Tynyanov again:

This tendency to single out unified rhythmical groups revealed the specific essence of verse, expressed in the subordination of the unifying principle of one type to the unifying principle of another. Here verse is revealed as a system *of complex interaction and not of combination*. Metaphorically speaking, verse is revealed as a struggle of factors, rather than as a collaboration of factors.[17]

Not combination, but complex interaction: a struggle between different factors. Just as, in its day, between libretto and score of the *Ring*.

---

[15] W. Iser, *The Implied Reader*, Johns Hopkins University Press, Baltimore and London 1974, p. 204.

[16] J. Tynyanov, *The Problem of Verse Language*, translated by Michael Sosa and Brent Harvey, Ardis, Ann Arbor 1981, p. 50.

[17] Ibid., p. 40. Osip Brik's 1927 essay 'Ritm i sintaksis', *Novy Lef* 3–6 (included in T. Todorov, ed., *Théorie de la littérature: textes des formalistes russes*, Seuil, Paris 1966) moves in the same direction; in it, poetry is several times defined as a 'verbal complex'.

Furthermore, free verse incorporates 'prose elements', thereby dynamizing the 'constructive principle' of the poetic series, forced to contend with a 'foreign object'.[18] And, finally, once the rigid segmentation of the Whitmanian list (one line = one syntactical unit) has been overcome, asymmetry of rhythm and syntax generates further interactions *between* line and line, as well as within each individual line.[19]

At each new move the complexity increases. And the question posed for *Ulysses* is thus posed anew for poetry: how to master complexity? In Iser's words, how to reduce 'the amount of observable material to manageable proportions'? First of all – it is Eliot's reply – with *brevity*. The five hundred lines of *The Waste Land*, against the fifteen thousand of *The Cantos*. The half hour it takes to read the poem, instead of the fifty hours needed for Pound or for Joyce. Vulgar materialism? Perhaps so. But useful, because the dimensions of a work are not just a quantitative matter, but a formal one: in the sense that a much shortened *Ulysses* is not the same structure, shorter, but *a different structure*. A concentrated system like *The Waste Land* – which keeps shrinking from draft to draft, unlike *Ulysses* and *The Cantos*, which never stop expanding – such a system possesses so strong a centripetal force, that its thematic material achieves a solidity that would be unthinkable in *Ulysses* or *The Cantos*. It is the story of polyphony in Eliot. Let us see.

Perhaps the most polyphonic chapter in *Ulysses*, 'Oxen of the Sun' is made up of around thirty different styles. On average, each of them continues for fifty-odd lines, and thus has plenty of time to crystallize its own lexico-grammatical peculiarities, and to highlight them. Our attention shifts from the story narrated to the way (or rather, the *ways*) of presenting it: we forget the 'what' and concentrate upon the 'how'. In Frege's terms, we bracket off the 'meaning', in the singular, which is always more or less the same, and we lose ourselves in the polyphony of (always different) 'associated ideas', provoked by the page of Milton, or Defoe, or Thomas Huxley. Each style appears to us, in short, as a historical complex complete in itself: as a concrete and meaningful way of interpreting experience.

---

[18] Tynyanov, *Problem of Verse Language*, p. 60.

[19] Ibid., pp. 49 ff; see also Brik, 'Ritm i sintaksis', in Todorov, ed., *Théorie de la littérature*.

Then we open *The Waste Land* – and everything changes. The manuscript originally contained three long passages *à la* Joyce (I, 1–54; III, 1–70; IV, 1–82): all gone, cut out. Far from fifty lines, each style here is allowed about five words: fleeting allusions, fragments. The accent falls on what is enigmatic about them: hence, on the indecipherability of the polyphony that fragments embody. If we wish to understand them, we must mentally bracket off the historical specificity of the various styles, and think instead about the mythical substratum uniting them all: drop the different 'hows', and stick to the 'what'. Forget 'associated ideas', in short, and concentrate on the single meaning underlying them.

I shall try to explain what I mean. In lines 47–50, the voices of Madame Sosostris, Shakespeare and Walter Pater ring out, one after another. 'Oxen of the Sun' would have amplified their differences, to create three symbolic worlds with nothing in common. In *The Waste Land*, however, the stylistic diversity is not given time to put down roots; it thus becomes, so to speak, transparent. The differences between the symbolic worlds of a charlatan, an Elizabethan playwright and a *fin de siècle* aesthete recede into the background: the essential thing is that all three express the same mythical opposition between fertility and barrenness, and indeed 'demonstrate' its permanence through the ages. And the same goes for Baudelaire, Dante, and the narrator of the passage on the 'Unreal City': three variants of the City as Hell. Or further on, in the third section, for John Day, the Eliot of '20, an obscene Australian ballad, and Verlaine: so many forms of the Impossible Purification.

This crushing of the fragment upon an immutable substratum is not the only 'mythical' technique of *The Waste Land*. For example, there is the truly unusual insistence – pointed out, in his day, by Hamilton[20] – with which Eliot employs the definite article: a device suggesting an ancient familiarity with the object, and inviting the reader to 'recognize' it:

> I do not find
> *The* hanged man
>
> *The* nymphs are departed.
> And their friends, *the* loitering heirs . . .

---

[20] G.R. Hamilton, *The Tell-Tale Article*, Oxford University Press, Oxford 1950.

Mr Eugenides, *the* Smyrna merchant

Phloebas *the* Phoenician, a fortnight dead

Who is *the* third who walks always beside you?
The Waste Land,
54–55, 179–80, 209, 312, 359

The hanged man, *the* Smyrna merchant: not 'a' merchant among others, but the one we all know. The definite article encourages what we might call the 'sinking' of the personages into a common archetype: something to which Eliot alludes in the most important note to the poem,[21] and which very closely recalls the rituals described by Mircea Eliade:

> An object or an act becomes real only insofar as it imitates or repeats an archetype [. . .] everything which lacks an exemplary model is 'meaningless', i.e. it lacks reality. Men would thus have a tendency to become archetypal and paradigmatic.[22]

So: definite articles; archetypal figures; and fragments. Each technical choice flows into the others, and sustains them. And from each of them, the same message reaches us: the enigma of *The Waste Land* can be solved only if we are willing to peer through its heterogeneous surface, and halt at its mythical substratum. To 'understand' *The Waste Land*, in short, means to bracket off everything that is historical: languages, styles, ideologies, personages. See them – and then forget them. As the famous formulation goes:

---

[21] I mean the note to line 218: 'Tiresias [...] is yet the most important personage in the poem, uniting all the rest. Just as the one-eyed merchant, seller of currants, melts into the Phoenician Sailor, and the latter is not wholly distinct from Ferdinand Prince of Naples, so all the women are one woman, and the two sexes meet in Tiresias.'

[22] M. Eliade, *The Myth of the Eternal Return*, Pantheon, New York 1954, p. 34. One of Pound's favourite techniques – the 'anecdote' – works in exactly the opposite direction: its protagonists, although often invested with an 'archetypal' role (political or religious leader, artist, beloved . . .), detach themselves from their own roles, and express idiosyncratically their own irreducible uniqueness.

[The mythical method] is simply a way of controlling, of ordering, of giving a shape and a significance to the immense panorama of futility and anarchy that is contemporary history.[23]

Eliot's remark to Woolf, quoted at the beginning of Chapter 7, resurfaces here: *Ulysses* 'would be a landmark, because [. . .] it showed up the futility of all the English styles'. But polyphonic futility – which Eliot, in the conversation with Woolf, seemed basically to like – has now become anarchy: a danger, to be kept under control. *And this is precisely the purpose served by myth: to tame polyphony.* To give it a form and a meaning. One. As I said earlier, *The Waste Land* is not a shorter *Ulysses* – it is a monologic *Ulysses*.[24]

Compromise

The 'cruel rule' of Alexanderplatz. The single language of *The Trial*. The iron 'sense of order' of Adrian Leverkühn. The archetype of *The Waste Land*. The 'pre-history' with which Adorno's Stravinsky 'disciplines' music.[25] We are in Europe, in the twenties and thirties, and the abrupt *reduction of complexity* effected by these choices cannot fail to evoke political reaction. And indeed, with the exception of *Ulysses*, the totalitarian temptation – present from the start in the modern epic (the aged Faust, Ahab's dictatorship, Julian the Apostate, the ring of omnipotence) – is really almost never absent in the world texts of modernism. The sudden increase of complexity encouraged an equally abrupt, and at times

---

[23] '*Ulysses*, Order and Myth', in *The Dial*, November 1923.

[24] 'Futility', it must be admitted, is a really well chosen term. The Latin root indicates something 'easily poured', hence destined to disperse in the void. As Albert Hirschmann writes, '[The Futility Thesis] says [. . .] that the attempt at change is abortive, that in one way or another any alleged change is, was, or will be largely surface, facade, cosmetic, hence illusory, as the "deep" structures of society remain wholly untouched' (*The Rhetoric of Reaction*, Harvard University Press, Cambridge Mass. 1991, p. 43). Hirschmann's thesis is fully corroborated by the semantic structure of *The Waste Land*: variety of its linguistic *surface* – immutability of its *underlying* themes.

[25] T.W. Adorno, *The Philosophy of Modern Music*, translated by Anne Mitchell and Wesley Blomster, Seabury Press, New York 1973, pp. 165 ff.

brutal, reduction: 'primitive', as it is often called in the early years of the century. But it is a wholly Western primitivism, generated as an internal counterforce of development, and which has far more to do with Paris and Berlin than with Oceania and the Congo.

So, yes: the totalitarian temptation is almost always present in the modernist world text, as a reaction to a complexity that has grown beyond every expectation. But it is just a temptation – which never becomes the dominant presence. And, let us be clear, it is not that literature cannot be fascist. It can very well be fascist, and indeed has been. But it is harder for that to happen *in the case of world texts*. Culturally impure, transnational, with no longer any sense of the 'enemy', hypereducated, indulgent towards consumption, enamoured of eccentricities and experiments: hard to make reactionary works, with such ingredients. Hard, above all, to do so with *fragments*. From an essay by Gottfried Benn, published in 1934 in the collection *Kunst und Macht* [Art and Power]:

> Form [as] immense human power, sheer power, victory over naked circumstance, civilizing factors; and as the Western, the commanding view, the real spirit with its own categories, the reconcilement and composure of fragments.[26]

Composure of fragments: thus speaks totalitarian poetics – with in mind, who knows, Siegfried forging the sword. But the modernist epic cannot sacrifice the fragment: for it would lose the most immediate, the most telling, of its world effects. A Fascist fascist like Ezra Pound may well sing the praises of Mussolini ('the Boss'), and insert here and there bits of unadulterated ideology: but I would not really call the *overall structure* of *The Cantos* fascist. The man was weak, but the form was strong.

Reaction as a powerful temptation, in short; but one which could not be yielded to entirely, without the epic dimension itself disappearing. So a compromise formation eventually imposes itself – of which *The Waste Land* is the best example – in which the polyphonic complexity of modernism is not abolished, but precisely 'controlled and ordered'. On the surface – clearly visible – fragments: dissonant, opaque, polyphonic, intertextual. But underneath this mosaic, as its secret filigree, a collection of *colossal commonplaces*: 'the metropolis as hell', 'the destructiveness of

---

[26] G. Benn, 'Dorische Welt' (1934), in *Sämtliche Werke*, Band 4 (Prosa II), p. 151.

romantic love', 'the sterility of the modern world'. . . It is not easy to dis-inter these commonplaces from beneath the poem's dazzling erudition: but the difficulty makes them still more precious. It re-consecrates them: because, in the last resort, *it is only thanks to them that 'The Waste Land' acquires a meaning.* It is a method perfectly described by T.E. Hulme: 'Literature: a method of sudden arrangement of commonplaces. The *suddenness* makes us forget the commonplace.'[27]

The suddenness makes us forget the commonplace . . . Extraordinary tightrope walking in *The Waste Land*. Its twofold structure heralds Gellner's dualistic world: standardization, and anomie. Standardization in the *common-*places; and in myth, which draws every image towards a tendentially unique meaning. But anomie on the surface: with its broken, unpredictable tex-ture, and with the fragments triggering the most idiosyncratic associations. Unfreedom – and anarchy. It is the same mixture – or, more precisely, the same presence of unreconciled extremes – that we encountered in *The Nibelung's Ring*: tightening the net of the world text, but without losing its boundlessness. Wagner's plot, and Eliot's myth, to ensure solidity; the music, and the fragments, to suggest expansion.

As in *bricolage* – and, indeed, as in the collages of Eliot's day, which are *bricolage* stretched almost to breaking point – old bits and pieces are grouped together here, to suggest a unitary figure. And – just as with cer-tain bottles in Bracque and Picasso, or certain guitars that do not emerge fully from the wallpaper and newspaper – the undertaking is always only partly successful. The original consistency of the materials comes into conflict with their re-use: the line from Baudelaire, or the Shakespearian Rag, draw attention to themselves (too), by causing the archetype at times to be forgotten. Between materials and plan, in short, a discrepancy subsists: a tension. But this is not a *limit* of collage and of *The Waste Land*: rather, it is the specific form of their effectiveness. It is the allegory of a heterogeneous – but forcibly unified – reality. The most abstract form of 'totality' imaginable in the capitalist world-system. And, perhaps, the most truthful.

---

[27] T.E. Hulme, 'Notes on Language and Style', in *The Criterion*, July 1925, p. 489.

One Hundred Years
of
Solitude

9

Let us move to a new horizon. After so much discussion of Western literature, magical realism transports us to the one continent not mentioned at all in *The Waste Land*: to Cuba and Haiti, Guatemala, Colombia, Mexico, Brazil, Argentina . . . For the first time in modern history, the centre of gravity of formal creation leaves Europe, and a truly worldwide literary system – the *Weltliteratur* dreamed of by the aged Goethe – replaces the narrower European circuit.

Away from Europe, then. And yet, no postwar work has been greeted by the Old World with more enthusiasm than *One Hundred Years of Solitude*. Does this mean that García Márquez's novel really belongs, like it or not, to the Western tradition? Not exactly. Or rather, it half belongs to it (just like *Midnight's Children*, which I shall often mention too): sufficiently at home there to make itself understood – but also sufficiently alien to say different things. And to succeed, moreover, in solving symbolic problems that European literature was no longer able to work through. But let us begin at the beginning.

Magical realism

The expression 'magical realism' appears for the first time in a book by Alejo Carpentier, *The Kingdom of This World*. 'At the end of 1943,' we read in the prologue to the novel, 'I had the good fortune to visit the kingdom of Henri Christophe . . .' And during his stay in Haiti, Carpentier reflects critically upon the experience of the European avant garde:

> [The] exhausting attempt to invoke the marvellous which has charac-
> terized certain European literatures of the last thirty years. The
> marvellous pursued in old prints [. . .] The marvellous, pathetically
> evoked in the skills and deformities of fairground characters [. . .] The
> marvellous, produced by means of conjuring tricks, bringing together
> objects which would never normally meet . . .

In the long run, Carpentier concludes, this wish achieves the opposite effect: 'the miracle workers turn into bureaucrats'. Whereas, in Haiti:

> I found myself in daily contact with something which might be called
> *marvellous reality*. I was treading on land where thousands of men anx-
> ious for freedom had believed in the lycanthropic powers of Macandal,
> to the point where this collective faith produced a miracle on the day
> of his execution [. . .] I had breathed the atmosphere created by Henri
> Christophe, a monarch of incredible exploits, far more astonishing
> than all the cruel kings invented by the surrealists [. . .] At every step I
> encountered this *marvellous reality* . . .
>
>   *The Kingdom of This World*, 'Prologue'

Lo real maravilloso. Not magical *realism*, as it has unfortunately been translated (and as it will inevitably continue to be called), but marvellous
reality. Not a poetics – a state of affairs. In Haiti, Carpentier writes, sur-
realism is in the things themselves. It is an everyday, collective fact, which
restores reality to modernist techniques: which takes the avant garde,
and sets its feet back on the ground. Does *Ulysses* separate polyphony
from any concretely recognizable 'voice' whatsoever? Well, in *Midnight's
Children* the opposite happens, and polyphony is re-motivated: there are
many languages in the novel, because India is divided into many cultures,
and Saleem, with his extraordinary hearing, manages to hear them all. The
technical complexity remains, but it is *naturalized* (and also, if the truth be
told, somewhat attenuated). In *The Death of Artemio Cruz*, to take another
example, the stream of consciousness is motivated: its confusion is attributed to Cruz's dying (and is clarified, moreover, by copious narrative
accounts). In *Three Trapped Tigers*, it is the turn of puns, and intertextu-
ality: presented as the nocturnal pastime – halfway between Hollywood
and *Finnegans Wake* – of three young Cuban intellectuals. Cortázar's

Hopscotch naturalizes the category of possibility, presenting it as the sign of a bohemian lifestyle; *Conversation in the Cathedral* naturalizes montage, motivating it with a long, disjointed chat in a bar.

Other examples could be added. But the tendency is clear. Magical realism restores the link that Joyce's generation had severed: technique – and anthropocentrism. I am thinking of Artemio Cruz, or Saleem Sinai, whose life gradually replicates the modernization of an entire country. And I am thinking, of course, of Aureliano Buendia:

> Colonel Aureliano Buendia organized thirty-two armed uprisings and he lost them all. He had seventeen male children by seventeen different women and they were exterminated one after the other on a single night before the oldest one had reached the age of thirty-five. He survived fourteen attempts on his life, seventy-three ambushes, and a firing squad. He lived through a dose of strychnine in his coffee . . .[1]

Nothing abstract here. No 'objective' reason for wars. Everything springs from a concrete, flesh-and-blood, subject, unalterably repeated at the beginning of nine consecutive long sentences. Is it a mythical way of explaining events, as Karl Popper so often said of Homer's gods? Yes, certainly. But it is an explanation. And after half a century of enigmas, there is always a great need for explanations.

Set modernism's feet back on the ground. And then, heal 'the great divide' (Adorno) between modernism and mass culture. It is the 'return of narrative', as people would say in the sixties of *One Hundred Years of Solitude*: an avant-garde work, but with a gripping story. It is the product of a literary evolution different from that of Europe. For many reasons, of course, but perhaps above all because, more than three centuries ago, the Inquisition decided to forbid the sale of European novels in Latin America. An act of censorship with very clear intentions – and very strange consequences. Because, once the novel was eliminated, the result (other things being equal) was a literary system that, far from being poorer, was *much richer than its European counterpart*. An absurd result, at first sight: a subtraction producing an increase. But a bit less absurd if you

---

[1] G. García Márquez, *One Hundred Years of Solitude*, translated by Gregory Rabassa, Avon, New York 1970, p. 104.

think of literature as a kind of ecosystem, and of the novel, for its part, as the most fearsome predator of the last half millennium. In such a scenario, a world without novels certainly loses one narrative form: unlike Europe, however, it preserves *all the other forms* that the novel would otherwise have swept away.[2] In particular, pre-realistic narrative forms survive (myths, legends, romances of chivalry); and hybrid forms, such as the *cronica*, where the boundary between invention and historical fact is unclear. Latin America is a world without novels, writes Mario Vargas Llosa:

> A world without novels, yes, but a world into which fiction had spread and contaminated practically everything: history, religion, poetry, science, art, speeches, journalism, and the daily habits of people.[3]

A world, in short, in which the extraordinary, the monstrous, the miracle – in a word: *adventure* – still occupies the centre of the picture. It was not this – not this at all – that those zealous priests intended. But infinite are the ways of the Lord, and those of evolution still more so.

From Lübeck to Macondo

Thinking of the genre to which *One Hundred Years of Solitude* belongs, 'family saga' is perhaps the best choice. The form of *Buddenbrooks*, *The Viceroys*, *The Forsyte Saga*, *The Radetzky March*, the Snopes trilogy. It is a hybrid genre, with strong epic components, whose absence may have already surprised more than one reader. Why *Bouvard and Pécuchet*, but not *Buddenbrooks*?

Retrospectively, I think it can be explained as follows. A study of the

---

[2] The image of the predator is no exaggeration. When we have historical atlases of literature at our disposal, it will be seen how the spread of the novel erased all sorts of pre-existing forms from the map of Europe. Between the eighteenth and nineteenth centuries, for example, when oral narratives began to be collected, their areas of maximum diffusion (Balkans, Baltic, northern Scandinavia) coincided with those that remained outside the development of the novel. England, the Île de France, or northern Italy, present the opposite correlation: a high incidence of novels, and scant presence of other narrative forms.

[3] M. Vargas Llosa, 'Latin America: Fiction and Reality', in J. King, ed., *Modern Latin American Fiction: a Survey*, Faber and Faber, London and Boston 1987, p. 5.

modern epic has two paths from which to choose: it can focus on either temporal, or spatial, extent. Initially, to be honest, I was thinking mainly of the former. But then, as I was working on *Faust*, it struck me that the historical aspect of Goethe's poem did not make much sense *as such*, and should rather be interpreted as a grand rhetorical figure: as metaphor for a geographical breadth. And from this first hypothesis (though I did not know it at the time, of course), many others have flowed. Polyphony, for instance, became interwoven in turn with the geography of the world-system. The epic dimension became identified with synchronic breadth, rather than with diachrony. Digression became interesting, and the plot secondary. And the category 'modern epic' was gradually filled with texts that were exactly the opposite of *Buddenbrooks*.

Was it right, that initial decision? Let us hope so. Whether it is shared or not, however, there is another point upon which it is perhaps easier to agree: namely, that in *Faust* both space and time have a prominent place. Stress may be laid on the one (and *Faust* becomes a world text), or on the other (and it becomes a kind of national saga). But it is clear that the two aspects both exist, and are woven together. A hundred years later, however, things have changed. *Buddenbrooks* is an entirely temporal construction, and *Ulysses* a spatial one. In the twenty-four hours of the world text, the search for spatial totality has reduced the temporal flow practically to zero. In the hundred years of the family saga, the opposite has happened: history has become longer, and space narrower. Because *Buddenbrooks* is not, as is often said, a novel on 'Germany', but on Lübeck – and perhaps not even that, but on the house of Buddenbrook. It is a spatial contraction that returns in *The Viceroys*, and then in *The Leopard*, where the temporal survival of houses and palaces is one of the main narrative themes. Houses again, and a narrow region, are the sites of the Faulkner cycle. And as for *The Forsyte Saga* (which is similarly a novel about London, rather than about Great Britain, and still less the Empire), my Penguin edition diligently includes the various houses in the genealogical tree – as if they were so many human beings.[4]

---

[4] In this, *The Radetzky March* – which shifts from one end to the other of a multinational empire – is different from the other family sagas. In Roth too, however, there is an absolutely Austrian nucleus – the March, the language, the portrait of Franz Joseph: the house of Habsburg – which accompanies the Trottas wherever they go.

It is like a zoom shot: from the world to the nation state to the city to the house. Spaces ever more tightly defined, ever smaller and more homogeneous. And in *One Hundred Years of Solitude* too, of course, there is a house: the house of Buendia, which like that of Buddenbrook lasts for an entire century, and never moves from Macondo. And yet Macondo is, as it were, larger than Lübeck: because more open to the world. It is a reality that surfaces from the very first words of the novel, with ice and wars – and it continues with gypsies' inventions and Arab traders, Italian dandies and French whores, the wise Catalonian, the wandering Jew, the Flemish airman . . .

Macondo as a *m[ac]ondo* [world], in short. The story of *Buddenbrooks* – in the context of the world-system. No wonder Europe went crazy over *One Hundred Years of Solitude*.[5]

Towards the middle of the novel, one of Aureliano's seventeen children is looking for a house so that he can send for his mother and sister tò join him in Macondo. He stumbles across a 'run-down big house', and with a heave of his shoulder he knocks down the front door:

> Aureliano Triste stood on the threshold waiting for the dust to clear and then he saw in the center of the room the squalid woman, still dressed in clothing of the past century, with a few yellow threads on her bald head, and with two large eyes, still beautiful, in which the last stars of hope had gone out, and the skin of her face was wrinkled by the aridity of solitude. Shaken by that vision from another world,

---

[5] 'The great transformation that took place between 1945 and 1970 in Latin America can also be defined succinctly as the transition from a situation of equilibrium between city and countryside to another situation characterized not just by urban primacy, but more precisely by hegemony of the great metropolises': so wrote M. Carmagnani and G. Casetta, in *America latina: la grande trasformazione*, Einaudi, Turin 1989, pp. 16–17. The urban setting is perhaps the main difference between *One Hundred Years of Solitude* and the great novels of the preceding generation, such as *Men of Maize*, or *The Lost Steps*. Although Macondo is isolated, and a very long way from any other centre of population, *One Hundred Years of Solitude* makes practically no mention of agricultural activities; and even the banana company, which brings with it a typically urban type of technology, separates Macondo yet more hermetically from its rural hinterland.

Aureliano Triste barely noticed that the woman was aiming an anti-
quated pistol at him.

One Hundred Years of Solitude, 223–4

It is Rebeca, widow of Josè Arcadio: ' "Holy God!", exclaimed Ursula,
"She's still alive!" ' With her, non-contemporaneity returns – for which
the family saga is, in any case, structurally predisposed. But while in
Europe the overlap is usually limited to just two generations – Johann and
Jean, Jean and Thomas, Thomas and Hanno; the hero of Solferino and
the District Commissioner, the District Commissioner and Karl Joseph:
fathers and sons – in Macondo, the situation is quite different. The
Buddenbrooks live spiritually in the epoch of the reigning paterfamilias:
but the Buendias, who are an extended family and absurdly longlived to
boot, always inhabit a hybrid, ill-defined epoch:

> Amaranta Ursula [fifth generation] and little Aureliano [sixth] would
> remember the rains as a happy time. In spite of [fourth-generation]
> Fernanda's strictness, they would splash in the puddles in the courtyard,
> catch lizards and dissect them, and pretend that they were poisoning
> the soup with dust from butterfly wings when Santa Sofia de la Piedad
> [third] was not looking. Ursula [first] was their most amusing plaything.
>
> One Hundred Years of Solitude, 333

Fifty words – and five out of six generations appear in them (the second,
which no longer has any survivors, is evoked immediately afterwards,
when Ursula thinks little Aureliano 'was her son the colonel during the
time he was taken to see ice'). And it is not just a question of biological
coexistence: through individuals, whole cultures overlap. When
Remedios the Beauty flies up into the sky, there succeed one another
within half a page: gossip typical of a patriarchal society, Christian faith
in miracles, the government's political calculation, Mr Brown's American
technology, and Aureliano's weary opposition. Non-contemporaneity
here closely recalls Bloch's original idea: a bundle of thrusts and counterthrusts, where old and new combine in the strangest ways, always
keeping Macondo's fate in suspense. It does not so much bring to mind
Buddenbrooks, with its declining (*Buddenbrooks. The Decline of a Family*)
but still orderly trajectory, as De Roberto's *The Viceroys*: another
extended (and somewhat crazy) family from a region only recently
annexed to a modern nation state. In short, another story of accelerated

modernization, and of combined development – where the compiler of heraldic manuals sits at the same table as the unscrupulous young politician. But before turning to this, one last look at the structure of the family saga.

The history of every family, inevitably, is a history of shadows. Two or three generations, and the dead outnumber the living. The story unfolds in reverse: towards memory, or nostalgia. 'The past grew daily more vivid', reflects Saleem Sinai, 'while the present seemed colourless, confused, a thing of no consequence' (*Midnight's Children*, 'Abracadabra'). But there is past and past. In *Buddenbrooks* or *The Radetzky March*, for example, the past is lamented because of its order. It is a world to be kept alive for its homogeneity: because it is made up of a single class, and speaks a single language.[6] It is the world of habit:

> These open-air concerts would all take place beneath the Chief District Commissioner's balcony, and they would all begin with the Radetzky March. Although the march was so familiar to the members of the band that any one of them could have played it in his sleep without a conductor, their bandmaster nevertheless considered it essential to follow every note of the score. Each Sunday, with a burst of musical and military zeal, as though he were trying it out for the first time, he would raise his head, his eye, his baton [. . .] The bluff drums would roll, the sweet flutes pipe, and the bright cymbals crash. Pleased and pensive smiles would spread over the faces of his audience, and the blood would tingle in their legs. Though they were standing still, they felt they were marching.
>
> *The Radetzky March*, 2 (translation modified)

---

[6] The bitterest moment in *The Radetzky March* occurs when the news of Sarajevo reaches the garrison on the Empire's eastern frontier, and there is a sudden eruption of incomprehensible insults in Hungarian. To defend the language of the Habsburgs ('We must ask you gentlemen to continue your conversation in German', *The Radetzky March*, 19), there remains only a Slovene captain, whose own half-grown sons talk of South Slav independence, read pamphlets which 'might have been written in hostile Belgrade', and seem to him as 'incomprehensible as great-grandchildren'.

One Hundred Years of Solitude

Roth's civilization is one of repetition: a world that strips events of their irreversibility: that tones down, attenuates, protects. The dominant tense is the imperfect, as befits any self-respecting bureaucratic account – and as turns out to be the case, rather to our surprise, also in *One Hundred Years of Solitude*:

> It seemed as if some penetrating lucidity permitted her to see the reality of things beyond any formalism. That at least was the point of view of Colonel Aureliano Buendia, for whom Remedios the Beauty was in no way mentally retarded, as was generally believed, but quite the opposite. 'It's as if she's come back from twenty years of war', he would say. Ursula, for her part, thanked God for having rewarded the family with a creature of exceptional purity, but at the same time she was disturbed by her beauty, for it seemed a contradictory virtue to her . . .
>
> *One Hundred Years of Solitude*, 202–3

Continuity in Roth, continuity in García Márquez. But the repetition evoked by verbal forms possesses a completely different reality in the two novels. In *The Radetzky March*, it is a sign of modesty: it indicates obedience, meticulousness. In *One Hundred Years of Solitude*, by contrast, repetition has been transformed into a haunted, hyperbolic obsession: goldfish, reading the cards, inventions, cockfights, invisible doctors, Sanskrit parchments . . . 'A madhouse', in Ursula's words: a world where the imperfect tense signals not order, but confusion. And, indeed, this is exactly the point. Unlike *The Radetzky March*, no regret is expressed in *One Hundred Years of Solitude* for the certitude of unchanging concerts: if there is any nostalgia, it is *nostalgia for disorder*. The world was beautiful when it was full of gypsies and military revolts, foreign traders and midnight's children. When it was formless, composite, unstable:

> A thousand and one children were born; there were a thousand and one possibilities which had never been present in one place at one time before; and there were a thousand and one dead ends.
>
> *Midnight's Children*, 'My tenth birthday'

A thousand and one possibilities – a thousand and one dead ends. 'We would have no meaning' – adds Rushdie in 'Alpha and Omega' – 'until we were destroyed'. They are 'the days of the end of possibility', like the petrified present of *The Death of Artemio Cruz*, which in the chapters on the revolution might instead have taken very different paths. 'All the doors open', reflects Santiago Zavala in *Conversation in the Cathedral*, '– at what moment did they begin to close, and why?'

Non-contemporaneity. II

In his fine analysis of *One Hundred Years of Solitude*, Vargas Llosa describes the basic narrative cell of the novel as follows:

> 1. At the start of an episode, the main fact in the narrative unit is mentioned: it is usually the last, in chronological terms. In other words, the episode begins with a leap towards the future [. . .] 'Many years later, as he faced the firing squad . . .' [. . .]
> 2. The narrative then jumps to the remotest past of the fact mentioned, whence it follows a linear chronological account of events, until it reaches the future fact that has been displaced and reported at the start of the episode: in this way the circle is closed, and *the episode ends where it began, just as it had begun where it would end.*[7]

Future, past, future. It is an interplay of prolepsis and flashback that endows the novel with its peculiarly unforgettable quality: announcing a fact long before it takes place, and then recalling it long afterwards – like the *Leitmotiv* in the *Ring*, or in *Ulysses* – endows it with a truly epic grandeur. But there is more. Cesare Segre:

> These wide or narrow turns of the wheel of time have the primary function of pointing, at the start of a cycle of life, to its conclusion, so that the present is also already perceived in the past perspective that will give it its future.[8]

A present pursued by the future, which drives it towards the past . . . A 'strange' present: unstable, overdetermined. It is yet another version of non-contemporaneity – with a tremendous novelty, as compared with *Faust* and *Ulysses*. For, in magical realism, the heterogeneity of historical

---

[7] M. Vargas Llosa, *García Márquez: historia de un deicidio*, Barral Editores, Barcelona 1971, p. 549.

[8] C. Segre, *I segni e la critica*, Einaudi, Turin 1969, p. 253.

time is also, for the first time, *narratively interesting*: it produces plot, suspense. It is not just the sign of a complex, stratified history: it is also the symptom of *a history in progress*. At the precise moment when Nehru proclaims the independence of India, and solemnly announces an irreversible break with the past – 'A moment comes [. . .] when we step out from the old to the new; when an age ends . . .' (*Midnight's Children*, 'Tick, tock') – at that precise moment the demon of non-contemporaneity, to complicate an excessively linear path, gives birth to a thousand and one babies endowed with magical powers. And who will eventually prevail: the modern state, or the children of magic? And the same in Macondo. A small, peaceful town: but the gypsies arrive, with inventions that seem to drop from the future, and history begins to run.

But the gypsies arrive . . . As always, the interweaving of different times is actually an interweaving of different *spaces*: Dutch telescopes, Asian parchments, British sextants, ice from somewhere or other . . . Read in this light, *One Hundred Years of Solitude* – like *Faust* – tells the story of an 'incorporation': of an isolated community that is caught up in the modern world-system, which subjects it to an unexpected, extremely violent acceleration. It is the novel of uneven and combined development: the *marvellous reality*, indeed, in which a prophecy in Sanskrit coexists with photography, and South American phantasms with Italian mechanical pianolas.

A circle that goes from the future to the past to the future, Vargas Llosa wrote of *One Hundred Years of Solitude*. True: and a circle, we can now add, often triggered *by an external geographical reality*. The twofold prolepsis that opens the novel is due to the gypsies' trading, and to the army of a distant capital. And so on: the history of Macondo is continually intersected and deflected by other histories: by processes that begin in Europe and in Asia, in 'Colombia', Latin America, the United States. A far cry from Mann's Lübeck, or De Roberto's Catania. This, again, is the geography of the world text: broad, heterogeneous, complex. With respect to *Faust*, however, *the perspective has been reversed*. We no longer see things from the core of the world-system – but from the periphery. And from this new viewpoint, epic digressions become something else. *Interferences*: weighty events, with long-lasting consequences. In *The Forty-Second Parallel*, the story of United Fruit is a brief parenthesis abroad; in *One Hundred Years of Solitude*, it is the turning-point

243

from which Macondo will never manage to recover. A single fact, and two different outcomes. A single world-system – and two different histories.

One Hundred Years of Solitude as the story of an incorporation, then. And in this overall process, three phases, and three quite distinct geographies. The first half of the novel is the moment of simple trading relations: in an irregular, creative medley, objects and people flow into Macondo from every part of the world. It is the moment of combined development, in the most striking sense of the term: the telescope, and Melquiades' dead language; Father Nicanor's levitations, and the ebullient French whores. Great confusion, of course – the semi-madness of the first of the Buendias, in which the old and the new clash most dramatically – but nothing worse. The encounter with the world-system produces freaks, but no irreversible consequence. In this first phase, indeed, interference enriches the life of Macondo: it makes it more varied, more open. It is the moment in which the key word of modernism – *possibility* – pervades every page of the story. It is the hour, as it were, of *white magic.*

This first section also encloses the second: the phase (to simplify somewhat) of Aureliano's wars. Here, the space of the story changes completely. Aureliano leaves Macondo; the network of international exchanges unravels. The very small and the very large recede into the background, while the foreground is occupied by a third geographical entity, of intermediate dimensions, which has wedged itself between the small isolated town and the world-system: the nation state. A centralized reality, and one that demands the monopoly of violence.

The state wins, the war ends, and Macondo comes back into contact with the outside world. With the *world*? Not any more. With only part of it: the United States. And, at this point, what was at stake in the civil war suddenly becomes clear: Macondo's role in the international division of labour. A relatively independent development – or a banana republic. On the one hand, the productive imbalance of the semi-periphery: the sense of possibility, and sometimes of real prosperity, that accompanies the early stages of development. On the other (just as in *Men of Maize*, by Miguel Angel Asturias), enslavement to monoculture: a peripheral, other-directed role. Not even Aureliano had understood it. And by the time the reader does so, it is too late.

244

All the doors open, said the character in Vargas Llosa: at what moment did they begin to close, and why? When the pressure of the world-system, answers *One Hundred Years of Solitude*, forces your country into a more complete – and hence more rigid – integration. A thousand and one possibilities then really do become a thousand and one dead ends: the multiplicity of possible developments, a set route. It is the hour of black magic: an 'incredible' that is no longer bound to a whirlpool of bizarre combinations, but to the enormity of the crimes committed. It is the train loaded with corpses, which vanishes from the collective memory as though it had never been. And in *Midnight's Children*:

> Shaheed and I saw many things which were not true, which were not possible, because our boys would not could not have behaved so badly; we saw men in spectacles with heads like eggs being shot in side-streets, we saw the intelligentsia of the city being massacred by the hundred, but it was not true because it could not have been true . . .
>
> *Midnight's Children*, 'Sam and the Tiger'

Rhetoric of innocence. II

'Colonel Aureliano Buendia organized thirty-two armed uprisings and he lost them all.' Subject, verb, predicate, conjunction, subject, verb, predicate . . . It is a sentence that would be impossible in the twenties, when the plane of enunciation is a terrain of radical experiments. But *One Hundred Years of Solitude* is not bothered about that: it is to the story, and its internal ramifications, that it seeks to bind us. 'When' must be by far the most common word in the novel – which begins, indeed, with the phrase: 'Many years later . . .'. And then, in a real bombardment of time markers: At that time, As soon as, Even then, But one day, Shortly before, The next night, During the time, Until the day, From that moment, Years later, There was at that time, While waiting, This time, Later, As long as . . .

A really strange place, Macondo. A city of madmen, where nobody has anything in common with anybody else. But where *language is the same for everybody*. While you are reading, you pay no attention to it – it is all so lovely. But if you reopen the novel with a little detachment, you find that the narrator's impersonal voice covers more or less *ninety-five per cent* of the textual space. In direct speech, one or two sentences per page: and so short that no voice ever stands out from the rest.[9] And here, we really are at the antipodes to modernism. Think of *Ulysses*: a non-story, told in innumerable styles. With all its problems, a real triumph of polyphony. And now, *One Hundred Years of Solitude*: endless stories, told in a non-style. For all its beauty, a real triumph of monologism.

From polyphony to monologism. It occurred in the nineteenth century, from Goethe to Flaubert; and again in the twentieth, from Joyce to García Márquez. The history of techniques follows its undulating curve, made up of short creative explosions and long countertrends. But there is something more: the fact that the style of *One Hundred Years of Solitude* – this writing without polyphony, and without irony; this writing as *transparent* as a fine summer morning, to which the novel owes so much of its success – had long ago become impossible for European literature, which had discovered the omnipresence of ideologies, hence the impossibility of an 'objective' viewpoint. Well, it is as though a flash of genius had revealed to García Márquez the secret wish of the educated European reader: to have faith once more in the story. To read a strange and complicated story, yes: but 'objective'. In short, to read a novel *without ideology*.

Can this be true? Of *One Hundred Years of Solitude*, the novel of '68?

---

[9] Apart from rare exceptions, moreover, direct speech here has just one function: to describe a state of affairs. It is a retrospective and basically superfluous act (hence Aureliano's dumbness), which fixes the event in a few words. As an example, here are the novel's first sentences in direct speech: 'Things have a life of their own; it's simply a matter of waking up their souls'; 'It won't work for that'; 'Very soon we'll have gold enough and more to pave the floors of the house'; 'Science has eliminated distance; in a short time man will be able to see what is happening in any place in the world without leaving his own house'; 'The earth is round like an orange'; 'If you have to go crazy, please go crazy all by yourself; but don't try to put your gypsy ideas into the heads of the children'; 'It's the smell of the devil'; 'Not at all; it has been proven that the devil has sulphuric properties and this is just a little corrosive sublimate'; 'Incredible things are happening in the world; right there across the river there are all kinds of magical instruments while we keep on living like donkeys'; 'It's all right; the main thing is not to lose our bearings'; 'God damn it! Macondo is surrounded by water on all sides'. With the exception of one (half) performative sentence, they are all observations.

Let us start with a preliminary question: the political meaning of magical realism. It is a widening of horizons, Carpentier maintains in *The Kingdom of This World*, that carries with it new possibilities of political emancipation. It is a dangerous trick, retorts Naipaul in *The Bend in the River*, where the Big Man, the dictator, wants to be 'the greatest magician' his country has ever seen. 'Is it important to keep the myths alive?', an interviewer asks Carlos Fuentes, who replies: 'Yes, why should we become impoverished?'[10] Because, Franz Fanon would perhaps have answered, the 'richness' of myth can have a paralysing effect.[11] And so on. It is not surprising that *Midnight's Children*, which is the latest and most self-reflective text of magical realism, should continually oscillate from one position to the other:

> Midnight's children can be made to represent many things, according to your point of view; they can be seen as the last throw of everything antiquated and retrogressive in our myth-ridden nation, whose defeat was entirely desirable in the context of a modernizing, twentieth-century economy; or as the true hope of freedom, which is now forever extinguished.
>
> *Midnight's Children*, 'My tenth birthday'

A backward-looking myth, or the one hope of freedom. For now, let us leave the matter in suspense. What is certain is that myth (understood in its broadest sense) is the sign and instrument of a *symbolic resistance* to

---

[10] See 'Carlos Fuentes: An Interview with John King', in John King, ed., *Modern Latin American Fiction*, Faber and Faber, London 1987, p. 146.

[11] 'The zombies are more terrifying than the settlers [. . .] We no longer really need to fight against [the settlers] since what counts is the frightening enemy created by myths [. . .] During the struggle for freedom, a marked alienation from these practices is observed [. . .] After centuries of unreality, after having wallowed in the most outlandish phantoms, at long last the native, gun in hand, stands face to face with the only forces which contend for his life – the forces of colonialism. And the youth of a colonized country, growing up in an atmosphere of shot and fire, may well make a mock of, and does not hesitate to pour scorn upon the zombies of his ancestors, the horses with two heads, the dead who rise again, and the djinns who rush into your body while you yawn. The native discovers reality . . .' (F. Fanon, *The Damned*, translated by Constance Farrington, Présence Africaine, Paris 1963, pp. 44–6).

Western penetration. *Men of Maize*, which in so many ways is the proto-type of magical realism, tells precisely the story of how mythical thought is reinvigorated by forced modernization, which it seeks to oppose by every means. And to oppose it, of course, not (just) by taking up explicit positions, but by means of its particular narrative technique. By taking the various aspects of social transformation, *and rewriting them as something else*: as so many magical phenomena, or the return of ancient archetypes. The devastation remains, of course, as does occupation: but they become, if nothing else, (mythically) comprehensible, and even familiar. 'All societies are in history and change', writes Claude Lévi-Strauss:

> But societies react to this common condition in very different ways. Some accept it, with good or bad grace, and its consequences [. . .] assume immense proportions through their attention to it. Others (which for this reason we call primitive) want to deny it, and try, with a dexterity that we underestimate, to make the states of their develop-ment they consider 'prior' as permanent as possible.[12]

Dexterity: just the right word, for the world of Asturias – and, in general, for the resistance to the 'disenchantment' that modernization tends to carry with it. For rewriting an event in mythical form is tantamount to making it *meaningful*: freeing it from the profane world of causes and effects, and projecting into it the symbolic richness of the archetype. Vargas Llosa:

> In Latin America [. . .] we still have great difficulty in differentiating between fiction and reality. We are traditionally accustomed to mix them in such a way that this is, probably, one of the reasons why we are so impractical and inept in political matters for instance. But some good also came from this novelization of our whole life. Books like *One Hundred Years of Solitude*, Cortázar's short stories and Roa Bastos's novels wouldn't have been possible otherwise.[13]

Inept in political matters – but great novelists. We are back to Rushdie's hesitation over the historical meaning of myth. I shall not resolve the uncertainty: I do not know enough about Latin America, or India, to

---

[12] C. Lévi-Strauss, *The Savage Mind*, London 1962, pp. 232–4.
[13] M. Vargas Llosa, in King, ed., *Modern Latin American Fiction*, p. 5.

do so in a responsible way. On the role of magical realism *in the West*, however, I do feel able to advance a couple of hypotheses. The first is a development of Gellner's diagnosis: the desire of contemporary societies for 'meaning', imagination, *re-enchantment*. A wish that, in Europe, comes up against centuries of Weberian coldness, and is therefore hard to fulfil; but which can quite well find an outlet in stories belonging *to another culture*. Especially if that culture is a perfect compromise formation: sufficiently European ('Latin') to be comprehensible – and sufficiently exotic ('American') to elude critical control. We are ready to believe almost anything about what is far away from us: it was true for the *cronicas* of the Conquista, and has been true again for magical realism.

A complicity between magic and empire, in short. And it is only logical, after all. Ever since modern science launched its attack on the omnipotence of thought, European culture has kept shifting its location: to art, said Freud; to consumption, added Gellner; finally, to other continents. These are, so to speak, the reserves of magic of the modern world-system: places of prophecies and archetypes; of apparitions, and pacts with the Devil.

And here, one final distinction. In Asturias and Carpentier, in Rushdie and Guimarães Rosa, magic is a thing of the past, and of the periphery. In García Márquez, however, it belongs *to the future*: to the West, to the core of the world-system. Compared with the compass or the mechanical pianola – not to speak of ice – flying carpets and spooks are irrelevancies:

> It was as if God had decided to put to the test every capacity for surprise and was keeping the inhabitants of Macondo in a permanent alternation between excitement and disappointment, doubt and revelation, to such an extreme that no one knew for certain where the limits of reality lay. It was an intricate stew of truths and mirages that convulsed the ghost of Josè Arcadio Buendia under the chestnut tree with impatience, and made him wander all through the house even in broad daylight.
>
> *One Hundred Years of Solitude*, 230–31

A stew of truths and mirages . . . Reading these lines, you would not say: but García Márquez is talking about the cinema and the telephone. Because the true magic of this novel is not magic: it is technology. The

Weberian side of our existence – which the flash of genius of Macondo has succeeded in re-enchanting. And re-enchanting it in a *substantially benign* form. Nothing frightening, in the products of Western technology. They seem a game. A fantastic present sent from Europe to that faraway village: truly, a *marvellous reality*. Afterwards, to be sure, the banana company comes along too. But, adding it all up, the forced modernization of *One Hundred Years of Solitude* is a story of extraordinary delight. Anybody would have liked to live in Macondo.

A rhetoric of innocence, we said of *Faust*. A rhetoric of dubious efficacy, if absolution is granted by the defendant himself. But if absolution comes from the victim . . .

The sixties. With the withdrawal from Africa, the phase of open colonial conquest comes to an end: the phase of gunboats, and military violence. And a novel reaches Europe which recounts those hundred years of history as an adventure filled with wonder. Is this perhaps the secret of *One Hundred Years of Solitude*?

INDEX

Adorno, Theodor Wiesengrund 58n,
  90n, 107 and n, 110 and n, 113 and n,
  157 and n, 158 and n, 207 and n, 214
  and n, 215 and n, 223, 227 and n, 235
Ager, Derek 75n
Aiken, Conrad Potter 171n, 178
Ainsworth, William Harrison 58n
Alighieri, Dante 77, 225
Althusser, Louis 148
Ambrosino, Guido 24n
Anderson, Perry 2, 200 and n
Antheil, George 107n, 210
Aragon, Louis 141n, 153
Arnheim, Rudolf 59 and n, 60 and n,
  141 and n, 148n
Asch, Shalom 178
Asturias, Miguel Angel 244, 248, 249
Atget, Eugène 131
Attridge, Derek 148n, 188

Babel, Isaac 42n
Bagnara, Sebastiano 138n
Bakhtin, Mikhail 39 and n, 40, 56 and
  n, 58, 74, 182
Balzac, Honoré de 147
Barbie, Klaus 24n
Barthes, Roland 59, 70, 71n, 152 and n,

155, 220 and n
Baudelaire, Charles 78, 112n, 225, 229
Bauer-Lechner, Natalie 58n
Beach, Joseph Warren 170, 171n, 177
Bell, F.A. 96n
Bely, Andrei, pseudonym of Boris
  Nikolaevich Bugaev 145
Benjamin, Walter 78, 83 and n, 124, 197
  and n
Benn, Gottfried 228 and n
Bentham, Jeremy 6
Berardinelli, Alfonso 207 and n
Bercovitch, Sacvan 32n
Bhabha, Homi K. 67n
Black, Max 221n
Blackmore, Richard 46 and n
Blackmur, Richard Palmer 221 and n
Blanchot, Maurice 14 and n, 33 and n
Bloch, Ernst 41, 42 and n, 49, 50 and n,
  51, 88, 140, 239
Bloch, Jean-Richard 175n
Bloomfield, Morton W. 47, 48 and n, 49
Blumenberg, Hans 35, 36 and n, 37, 40,
  83 and n, 84 and n
Bocchi, Gianluca 95n, 217n
Boccioni, Umberto 201
Boucicaut, Aristide 126n

251

Boulez, Pierre   115 and n, 117 and n,
   118n, 142 and n, 143, 210n
Bourdieu, Pierre   178 and n, 196
Bourget, Paul   112n
Bowlby, Rachel   126n
Bradley, Andrew C.   12 and n
Brage, Dominique   171n, 175n, 178
Braque, Georges   229
Braudel, Fernand   2
Breton, André   108, 153
Brik, Osip   223n, 224n
Brioschi, Franco   207n
Broch, Hermann   42n, 145, 171, 177
   and n, 178, 179, 207, 208
Brod, Max   202n
Brooks, Cleanth   214 and n
Brunngraber, Rudolf   70n
Burke, Peter   52, 53n
Butler, Eliza M.   15n, 52n
Byron, George Gordon, Lord   11n, 43

Carmagnani, Marcello   238n
Carpentier, Alejo   233, 234, 247, 249
Casetta, Giovanni   238n
Castelnuovo, Emma   7
Céline, Louis-Ferdinand, pseudonym of
   Louis-Ferdinand Destouches 71
Ceruti, M.   95n, 217n
Chagall, Marc   201
Champollion, Jean-François   83 and n
Chase, Richard   95 and n
Chaunu, Pierre   45n
Chop, Max   158
Christophe, Henri   234
Cixous, Hélène   148n
Clair, Jean   134n
Cohen, Ralph   75n, 180n
Cohn, Dorrit   177n
Coleridge, Samuel Taylor   214n
Colli, Giorgio   106n
Conrad, Joseph, pseudonym of Teodor
   Józef Konrad Korzeniowski   28, 54,
   195
Cortázar, Julio   234, 248
Cotten, Joseph   123

Culler, Jonathan   78, 161 and n
Curran, Stuart   37n
Curtius, Ernst Robert   182, 210 and n,
   211

Dahlhaus, Carl   118
D'Annunzio, Gabriele   145
Dante: see Alighieri
Darwin, Charles Robert   5, 6, 20, 177,
   184
Dawkins, Richard   213 and n
Day, John   225
Debenedetti, Giacomo   149, 153n
Decoin, Henri   171n, 175n, 178
Defoe, Daniel   224
Deleuze, Gilles   199n
Della Volpe, Galvano   31n
De Man, Paul   78
Deming, Robert H.   210n
De Roberto, Federico   239, 243
Derrida, Jacques   199n
Descharmes, René   68, 69n
Dickens, Charles   66
Diderot, Denis   192n, 194
Di Girolamo, Costanzo   207n
Döblin, Alfred   58, 71, 125n, 184
Dos Passos, John   4, 152, 172n, 178,
   179, 184
Dostoevsky, Fyodor   50n, 193
Dubuisson, Paul   128 and n, 129 and n,
   131 and n
Dujardin, Édouard   174 and n, 175 and
   n, 176, 177, 179 and n, 184
Duncan, Ronald   60n

Eckermann, Johann Peter   45, 46, 47,
   48, 59, 60, 77, 80, 97n
Eco, Umberto   185 and n, 187 and n, 217
Eldredge, Niles   22n, 75
Eliade, Mircea   226 and n
Eliot, Thomas Stearns   1, 3, 54, 73n, 108,
   109, 111, 112n, 113, 119n, 182, 186 and
   n, 187, 190, 214n, 224, 225, 227, 229
Ellmann, Richard   13n
Empson, William   214n

Erlich, Victor 192n
Eulenberg, Herbert 64

Fanon, Frantz 247 and n
Faulkner, William 171, 173, 176, 177, 178, 179, 182, 200, 237
Fénelon, François de Salignac de la Mothe 68
Ferrer, Daniel 148n, 188n
Feuerbach, Ludwig Andreas 109, 115
Fiedler, Leslie 33 and n
Flaubert, Gustave 58, 60, 67–8, 69, 70n, 71, 72, 73, 74n, 97, 142, 147, 152, 162, 180, 196, 246
Foster, Hal 193n
Frank, Joseph 149
Frank, Waldo 178
Franz Joseph I, Emperor 237n
Frege, Friedrich Ludwig Gottlob 221 and n
Freud, Sigmund 23n, 140n, 146 and n, 164 and n, 165 and n, 166 and n, 173, 249
Friedman, Melvin 176n
Frye, Northrop 4n, 38 and n, 96 and n
Fuentes, Carlos 172n, 247 and n

Gabler, Hans Walter 155
Gadamer, Hans Georg 82 and n, 83, 87
García Márquez, Gabriel 233, 235n, 241, 246, 249
Gates, Henry Louis Jr 29n
Geach, Peter 221n
Gehlen, Arnold 162 and n
Gellner, Ernest 91, 133 and n, 134, 229, 249
George, Stefan 2
Gide, André 145, 197n
Giehlow, Karl 83n
Gifford, Don 209n
Gilbert, Stuart 174n, 210n
Girdner, John H. 124 and n
Goebbels, Paul Joseph 117
Goethe, Johann Wolfgang 4, 14–18, 19 and n, 21, 23, 25, 27, 29, 32–4, 35 and

n, 38–41, 44, 45 and n, 46–8, 50, 52, 53, 55, 57–61, 73, 77–80, 84, 85, 88, 91, 93, 96, 97 and n, 104, 107, 108 and n, 110, 142, 143, 152, 173, 188, 194, 195, 209, 233, 237, 246
Goffman, Erving 156 and n
Gogol, Nikolai 50n
Goldman, Albert 106n, 109n, 114n, 116n
Gopnik, Adam 133n, 134n, 158n
Göschel, Carl Friedrich 16n
Gottschall, Rudolf von 58n
Gould, Stephen Jay 20n, 22n, 75, 190 and n
Griffiths, Frederick T. 50n
Grisebach, A. 127n
Groden, Michael 184n, 202
Grossman, Allen 64 and n, 65, 67
Guattari, Félix 199n
Guimarães Rosa, João 249

Habermas, Jürgen 193 and n, 207 and n
Habsburg dynasty 237n
Hacking, Ian M. 68n
Hamilton, George R. 225 and n
Hamsun, Knut 145
Hango, Hermann 52n
Hartung, Johann Adam 24n
Hawthorne, Nathaniel 83n, 85, 87
Hayford, Harrison 58n
Hederich, Benjamin 84
Hegel, Georg Wilhelm Friedrich 11 and n, 12, 13, 14 and n, 16, 29, 46, 59, 79, 90n, 142, 150, 191, 194, 209
Heidegger, Martin 70n, 73n
Heine, Heinrich 15
Heller, Erich 153n, 221, 222n
Hesiod 37, 38
Hirschmann, Albert 227n
Hjelmslev, Louis 204, 205 and n
Hofmannsthal, Hugo von 3, 201
Home, Henry, Lord Kames 46, 47 and n
Homer 16, 46, 102, 158, 213, 220, 235
Hulme, Thomas Ernest 229 and n
Huxley, Thomas 224
Huyssen, Andreas 90n

Ibsen, Henrik   13, 142
Ingenhoff, Annette   110n, 111
Irwin, John T.   83n
Iser, Wolfgang   148 and n, 149 and n, 222, 223n

Jacob, François   22n, 37 and n, 38
Jacob, Max   175n
James, William   135 and n, 136 and n
Jameson, Fredric   2, 3 and n, 90n, 127 and n, 131n
Jauss, Hans Robert   178 and n
Jehlen, Myra   32n
Jolles, André   72 and n, 73n
Joyce, James   4, 14n, 19n, 38n, 50, 58, 107, 108, 110, 119 and n, 132, 133, 137, 141–3, 145, 147 and n, 148n, 149, 150, 151 and n, 152–4, 155n, 157, 162, 163 and n, 164–6, 169, 173–4, 175 and n, 176–83, 184 and n, 188, 190, 191, 195, 196 and n, 197, 198, 200–202, 206, 208, 209 and n, 210 and n, 211, 215, 218, 220, 222, 224, 225, 235, 246
Julian, Emperor ('the Apostate')   13, 227
Jung, Carl Gustav   211 and n

Kafka, Franz   2, 3, 89, 195, 198, 199 and n, 200, 201, 202n
Kamen, Henry   90n
Kandinsky, Wassily   201
Kern, Stephen   136n
King, John   236n, 247n, 248n
Klee, Paul   183
Klinger, Friedrich Maximilian   15n
Koselleck, Reinhardt   51 and n
Kraus, Karl   58, 59, 71 and n, 152
Kristeva, Julia   148n, 206
Kruse, Jens   42 and n, 78, 85 and n

Lacassagne, Jean Alexandre Eugène   130n
Lamarck, Jean-Baptiste de   6
Larbaud, Valéry   175n, 179, 184n
Lawrence, David Herbert   2

LeMoigne, J-L   217n
Lenau, Nikolaus   23n
Lessing, Gotthold Ephraim   25n
Lévi-Strauss, Claude   19, 148, 248 and n
Lewis, Wyndham   132, 133n, 145, 210 and n
Liszt, Franz   118 and n
Litz, Walton   185 and n
Loesch, Johann Christoph Ernst   24n
Loewe, Johann Carl Gottfried   38n, 84 and n, 92
Lukács, György   26, 97 and n, 173, 182, 207n, 209

Madach, Imre   4, 51
Madelénat, Daniel   96 and n
Mahler, Gustav   58 and n, 142, 157, 210, 214
Maldonado, Tomás   195n
Mallarmé, Stéphane   3, 179 and n
Mann, Thomas   15 and n, 102 and n, 107 and n, 172, 174, 176, 182, 195, 207, 211, 243
Mannheim, Karl   89 and n, 90
Marlowe, Christopher   16, 17, 18, 43, 44
Marx, Karl   78, 79, 80, 90n, 91 and n, 134, 196
Mason, Ellsworth   13n
Matthiessen, Francis Otto   67
Mayakovsky, Vladimir   2
Medawar, Peter   2
Melville, Herman   26, 32, 33, 45n, 50, 58, 60, 61, 62, 63, 73, 74n, 83n, 85, 86, 87, 89, 95, 96, 142, 207n
Mendelson, Edward   4 and n
Meyrink, Gustav   145
Michaels, Walter B.   64n
Mies van der Rohe, Ludwig   3
Mill, John Stuart   90n
Miller, Michael B.   128n
Milton, John   224
Möller, Otto   134
Montinari, Mazzino   106n
Moretti, Franco   20n, 50n, 75n, 180n, 195n

Index

Morin, Edgar   95 and n, 97 and n, 118, 213

Mozart, Wolfgang Amadeus   80, 159

Musil, Robert   70n, 97, 147, 148n, 149, 152, 182, 195, 206, 207 and n, 208, 209n, 211

Mussolini, Benito   228

Naipaul, Vidadhur Surajprasad   71, 247

Nehru, Shri Jawaharlal   243

Nietzsche, Friedrich Wilhelm   42n, 53 and n, 106 and n, 107 and n, 108, 112n

Orlando, Francesco   52, 53n, 104 and n, 117, 118n, 166 and n

Orwell, George, pseudonym of Eric Blair   66

Packard, Vance   130 and n

Pagnini, Marcello   87 and n

Paige, Douglass D.   60n

Panofsky, Erwin   22n, 66

Parker, Hershel   58n

Parrinder, Patrick   60n

Pasternak, Boris   38, 50n

Pater, Walter   225

Pavel, Thomas   104n

Pease, Donald E.   64n

Picasso, Pablo   190, 201, 229

Pilnyak, Boris   42n

Pirandello, Luigi   145, 201

Polanyi, Karl   66

Popper, Karl   235

Portelli, Alessandro   49 and n, 67n, 87 and n

Pound, Ezra   1, 38, 54, 58, 60n, 73 and n, 96, 107 and n, 108, 119 and n, 120, 147 and n, 152, 186, 187, 188, 190, 201, 210, 220, 221, 222 and n, 224, 226n, 228

Pratt, Mary Louise   29n

Prigogine, Ilya   69n

Proust, Marcel   2, 149, 150, 151, 153 and n, 154 and n, 156, 157, 163n, 172, 196n, 200, 207, 220

Pushkin, Aleksandr   50n

Quételet, Adolphe   68 and n

Quint, David   47 and n, 48, 49

Rabinowitz, Stanley J.   50n

Racine, Jean   70

Rathenau, Walter   210 and n

Raveau, P.   158n

Read, Forrest   119n, 147n

Richards, Ivor Armstrong   38, 214

Rilke, Rainer Maria   153n, 195

Roa Bastos, Augusto   248

Roth, Joseph   237n, 241

Royster, Paul   32n

Rushdie, Salman   248, 249

Sachs, Curt   158

Said, Edward   160 and n

Sallet, Friedrich von   24n, 85n

Sartre, Jean-Paul   26, 70n

Schiller, Friedrich von   25, 45, 47

Schinkel, Carl Friedrich   127 and n

Schlaffer, Heinz   40 and n, 41 and n, 78, 79, 80

Schlumberger, Jean   171, 178

Schmitt, Carl   149 and n

Schneidau, Herbert   96n

Schnetger, Alexander   85n

Schnitzler, Arthur   170, 175, 176, 177, 178, 182

Schönberg, Arnold   20, 21n, 108, 114 and n, 115, 185, 194 and n

Schönheich, Christoph   140 and n

Schopenhauer, Arthur   115

Schwerte, Hans, pseudonym of Hans Ernst Schneider   16n, 23, 24n, 58n

Sedlmayr, Hans   127n

Segre, Cesare   242 and n

Senn, Fritz   135n

Shakespeare, William   225, 229

Shaw, George Bernard   52, 101 and n, 102

Shklovsky, Viktor   20 and n, 22n, 188, 189 and n, 191 and n, 192 and n, 194

Simmel, Georg   123, 124 and n, 131 and n, 132 and n, 133, 136 and n, 137 and n, 155, 168, 193 and n, 195, 196 and n

Simpson, David   67n

Sitney, P. Adams   3

Soden von Sassenfart, Count Friedrich Julius Heinrich von   15n

Sombart, Werner   31 and n, 195 and n

Spengler, Oswald   94 and n, 95 and n, 108, 132n

Spinoza, Baruch   92n, 186

Spitzer, Leo   64, 65n, 133 and n, 134 and n, 150 and n, 151 and n, 218

Sprinchorn, Ewert   106n, 109n, 114n, 116n

Staiger, Emil   25 and n, 39 and n, 95, 96 and n, 102 and n, 158 and n

Stanley, Henry Morton   29n

Stein, Gertrude   201

Steinberg, Erwin R.   135n

Stengers, Isabelle   69n

Sterne, Laurence   96, 97, 191, 192

Strachey, James   166n

Stravinsky, Igor   227

Strindberg, August   42n

Sullivan, J.   221n

Swedenberg, Hugh T. Jr   46

Talmeyr, Maurice   144n

Tocqueville, Charles-Alexis Clérel de 66n

Todorov, Tzvetan   192n, 223n, 224n

Tolstoy, Leo   50n, 169 and n, 170, 173, 174, 177

Tomashevsky, Boris   192 and n

Topia, André   188 and n

Torgovnick, Mariana   29n

Twain, Mark, pseudonym of Samuel Rosenstock   161

Tynyanov, Yuri   223 and n, 224n

Tzara, Tristan   2

Vargas Llosa, Mario   236 and n, 242 and n, 243, 245, 248 and n

Varnedoe, Kirk   133n, 134n, 158n

Venturi, Robert   214n

Verlaine, Paul   225

Verne, Jules   28, 161 and n

Virgil: Publius Vergilius Maro   46

Vischer, Friedrich Theodor   15

Vossler, Karl   151n

Vrba, Elisabeth   20n

Wagner, Richard   3, 13, 33, 50, 101–4, 105 and n, 106 and n, 107 and n, 108 and n, 109 and n, 110 and n, 111, 112 and n, 113 and n, 114 and n, 115, 116 and n, 117, 118 and n, 119 and n, 133n, 142, 157, 158 and n, 159, 218, 223, 229

Wallerstein, Immanuel   2, 44 and n, 45n

Walter, Bruno   214 and n

Weber, Max   133, 249, 250

Weinrich, Harald   151n

Weisse, Christian Hermann   24n, 85n

Wells, Herbert George   133n

Wenders, Wim   164

Wesendock, Mathilde von   113

Whitman, Walt   3, 63, 64, 66, 67 and n, 73, 218, 224

Wieland, Renate   40n, 41 and n

Wilhelm II, Kaiser   43

Williams, Rosalind H.   40n, 130 and n

Wilson, Edmund   149

Wind, Edgar   90 and n

Wolff, Kurt   124n, 193n

Woolf, Virginia   153n, 171, 176, 179, 182 and n, 227

Wright ('of Derby'), Joseph   31

Yeats, William Butler   108, 109, 191n

Zamyatin, Yevgeny   66

Zola, Émile   31, 125, 126n, 127, 129n, 131n, 149